Legal Polycentricity and International Law

Legal Polycentricity and International Law

Surya Prakash Sinha

Professor of Law, Pace University School of Law
Associate, Columbia University Seminar on Peace

Carolina Academic Press
Durham, North Carolina

Printed in the United States of America

ISBN 0-89089-929-0
LCCN 95-68004

Carolina Academic Press
700 Kent Street
Durham, North Carolina 27701
Telephone (919) 489-7486
Fax (919) 493-5668

To
Jessica, Sonya and Paul

and to
John Hazard,
to whom I owe my career

Contents

Legal Polycentricity and International Law

Chapter 1

The Focus of Legal Polycentricity upon International Law

Legal Polycentricity is the name given to a project in legal thought inaugurated in 1992 at the Conference on Legal Polycentricity, convened by the Institute of Legal Science of the University of Copenhagen.[1] This Conference was inspired by the writings of certain anthropologists, sociologists, social scientists, social psychologists, and jurists, including, according to the organizers, my own humble contribution during the past two decades. The purpose of this book is to apply legal polycentricity to international law.

In this chapter, we shall first present the central themes of legal polycentricity and then notice that, when applied to international law, it points to the civilizational pluralism of states whom this law governs.

Legal Polycentricity

Legal polycentricity consists in a critique of the single-value approach to law, a denial of radical relativism, and an acceptance of moral pluralism.

1. Critique of Single-value Approach

Legal polycentricity rejects the model of the single-value approach to matters of morals and law.[2] Under the single-value approach, all true val-

1. Under the direction of Professor Hanne Petersen, Professor Kirsten Ketscher, and Professor Henrik Zahle. Professor Zahle is credited with inventing the term.

2. *Cf.* my criticism of the single-value approach of the International Bill of Human Rights. S.P. Sinha, "The Axiology of the International Bill of Human Rights," 1 *Pace Yearbook of International Law* 21 (1989); S.P. Sinha, "The Missing First Step in the Human Rights Movement," in American Branch, International Law Association, *Proceedings and Committee Reports*, 71 (1985–86); S.P. Sinha, "Human Rights: A Non-Western Viewpoint," 67 *Archiv*

ues are compatible, so that there is one ultimate right answer to moral questions and, consequently, the moral task rests in coming up with a single set of principles to resolve moral conflicts.

Moral philosophy abounds with attempts to seek a unitary, absolute, monistic system of values. Thus, for example, in Plato's Dialogues, Socrates presents virtue as a single whole knowledge.[3] Aristotle propounds his paradigmatic[4] construct of the good man to provide this unitariness.[5] Kant's categorical imperative is single and unconditional.[6] The Kantians seek duty in the deontic element that one ought to do something because one is bound to do it, regardless of results, and they posit universalized principles to test the validity of particular intuitions about how to act. Bentham and other Utilitarians seek the value unitariness in terms of consequences, as distinguished from deontologists. A certain type of consequences, such as producing greatest happiness for the greatest number, determines what is good and, therefore, moral.[7] Marx's philosophy searches for unity beyond all antagonisms.[8] Rawls' version of the contractarian theory seeks this unitariness in the practices of rational persons negotiating in an original position in ignorance of their contingencies of ability, wealth, etc.[9] And so on.

Such an approach has great attractions. Its attractiveness lies in its promise to comfort us with the right answer.[10]

---

für Rechts- und Sozialphilosophie 76 (1981); S.P. Sinha, "Freeing Human Rights from Natural Rights," 70 *Archiv für Rechts- und Sozialphilosophie* 342 (1984); S.P. Sinha, "Human Rights Philosophically," 18 *Indian Journal of International Law* 139 (1978); S.P. Sinha, "The Anthropocentric Theory of International Law as a Basis for Human Rights," 10 *Case Western Reserve Journal of International Law, Human Rights Issue* 469 (1978). See also, S.P. Sinha, "Why Has It Not Been Possible to Define Law," 75 *Archiv für Rechts- und Sozialphilosophie* 1 (1989); S.P. Sinha, *What Is Law?* (1989); S.P. Sinha, *Jurisprudence: Legal Philosophy in a Nutshell* (1993).

3. Hamilton and Cairns, eds., *The Collected Dialogues of Plato*, 309, 351 (1963).

4. Sometimes, paradigms are used to cap open textures. Moore, "The Semantics of Judging," 54 *Southern California Law Review* 151, 204–207 (1981); Moore, "Moral Reality," 1982 *Wisconsin Law Review* 1061, 1144–46.

5. Aristotle, Nichomachean Ethics, 1113a, 1114a, in R. Mckeon, ed., *Basic Works of Aristotle*, 970–971, 1035 (1941). However, it is possible to find pluralism in the Aristotelian tradition. See D. Wiggins, "Deliberation and Practical Reason," in A. Rorty, ed., *Essays on Aristotle's Ethics*, 221, 239 (1980).

6. Findlay, *Kant and Transcendental Object*, 296 (1981).

7. Sinha, *What is Law?*, 130–133, 136–138.

8. Tucker, *The Marxian Revolutionary Idea*, 53 (1969).

9. J. Rawls, *A Theory of Justice*, 136–142 (1971). However, Rawls' more recent writings indicate a shift toward a pluralistic view. J. Rawls, "The Idea of Overlapping Consensus," 7 *Oxford Journal of Legal Studies* 4, 5, 13 (1987); W.A. Galston, "Pluralism and Social Unity," 99 *Ethics* 711, 715–716 (1989),

10. Levi, *Philosophy and the Modern World*, 5 (1977).

However, legal polycentricity considers this approach to moral questions both misleading and dangerous.

It is misleading for two reasons.

Firstly, it is misleading because it obscures the fact that human values are many and that they are not all harmonious,[11] or else we would not have the problem of making a moral choice. We face conflicting values both in personal and community life. It is an inaccurate representation of common life experience to suggest that these conflicting values are reconcilable under one truth, rather than poised for bargaining and give-and-take, that they are resolved into one absolute, rather than subject to multiple evaluations and multiple judgments in context of their contingent factors, that the neat tidiness of the single-value solution speaks for its truth, rather than the truth being the checkered and messy struggles of moral life.

Secondly, the single-value approach is misleading because it takes the conception of man that he is self-created, so that he should be able to accept that single value by his act of volition. All he has to do is to accept the right answer. However, this conception ignores the reality that his aims and allegiances are not all of his choosing, that he belongs to his history and to his circumstances which, indeed, constitute his identity. In wrenching him away from his history and circumstances, this approach diminishes that identity.

In addition to being misleading, the single-value approach is dangerous as well. It is dangerous for three reasons.

In the first place, it breeds pessimism because of its inherently deterministic nature. It presents reality not as a mess of individual experiences in which we participate through our active moral choices but as a unified totality which possesses its own single truth in which our action cannot make a difference. Moral action is, in it, determined by the necessity dictated by the single truth, rather than liberated to the possibility of a variety of action.[12]

Secondly, it gives us a false notion of comprehensiveness, that all solutions are contained within it, that all conflicts are reconciled within it, that all moral problems are referable to it. Thereby, it forces us to distort reality. Its procedure calls for fitting diverse moral dilemmas into one pattern, which can be done only by sacrificing aspects that do not fit.

Finally, it provides a convenient justification for tyranny. Since there is only one ultimate right answer because all true values are compatible, the

---

11. I. Berlin, *Concepts and Categories*, 81, 96–102 (1979); I. Berlin, *Against the Current*, 130, 158 (1979); I. Berlin, *Four Essays on Liberty*, 118, 169 (1969).

12. W. James, *The Will to Believe and Other Essays in Popular Philosophy*, 32–62, 145–183 (1956); W. James, "Hegel and His Method and Monistic Idealism," in J. McDermett, ed., *The Writings of William James: A Comprehensive Edition*, 497–529 (1977).

task becomes that of discovering that answer and then implementing it. That is a sure prescription for tyranny.

Therefore, the single-value approach is both misleading and dangerous.

2. *Denial of Radical Relativism*

While legal polycentricity rejects the absolutism of the single-value approach, that does not mean, for it, an acceptance of a radical relativism that precludes moral criticism and ends up maintaining that anything goes. The ethical pluralism of legal polycentricity does not preclude moral criticism of other people on the ground that no definite answers are available or achievable,[13] or that contradictory ethical views may be asserted without either of them being mistaken,[14] or that all are equally valid patterns of life.[15] Studies in anthropology, psychology, and sociology have shown that while there are differences among people, there are similarities as well. These similarities assist us in constructing ethical standards without either relapsing into the absolutist dogma or conceding that anything goes.

Thus, anthropologists have debated whether the variety in ethical codes is basic or superficial. They have considered whether the variations relate to means or ends. They have examined such questions as whether there are principles that cut across cultures. They have looked into these issues conceptually as well as empirically.[16] They have investigated cultural similarities through environmental, technological, and economic constituents thereof.[17] They have put forth a variety of propositions. For example, they have suggested that the same dynamic forces as those thousands of years ago have shaped social life,[18] or that there are biopsychological frames that are produced by cultural constraints of family, religion, war, communication, etc., which frames are variably filled with cultural content,[19] or that the diversity of cultural patterns is characterized by an underlying uniformity,[20] or that there are primary conceptual likenesses whereunder varia-

13. A. Edel, *Ethical Judgment*, 30 (1955).

14. R. Brandt, *Hopi Ethics*, 11 (1954).

15. R. Benedict, *Patterns of Culture*, 278 (1934).

16. G. Murdock, "The Common Denominators of Cultures," in R. Linton, ed., *The Science of Man in the World Crisis* (1945); C. Kluckhohn, "Universal Categories of Culture," in *Anthropology Today* (1953).

17. I. White, "Energy and the Evolution of Culture," 45 *American Anthropologist* 335 (1943); J. Steward, "Cultural Causality and Law," 51 *American Anthropologist* 1 (1949); G. Childe, *Social Evolution* (1951).

18. I. Boss, *The Mind of Primitive Man*, 195 (rev. ed., 1938).

19. C. Wissler, *Man and Culture* (1923).

20. A.I. Kroeber, "The Concept of Culture in Science," 35 *Journal of General Education* 188 (1949).

tions occur as to details of such matters as prescribed behavior, instrumentalities, and sanction.[21] These propositions suggest the possibility of developing standards to judge moral choices, rather than accepting that anything goes.

Psychologists, too, have offered propositions that make standards possible. For example, they have shown that it is possible to make evaluations of good and bad, right and wrong, desirable and undesirable, on the basis of reliable knowledge of what man can be under certain conditions that we call good and upon the supposition that he is at peace with himself when engaged in realizing his potential.[22] They have shown that individuals and cultures do not differ widely with respect to what they consider the ultimate ethical goals.[23] They have shown that cultural differences are compatible with identity in values, since the value of an act may be right if it fits one set of conditions and wrong if it violates them.[24]

Sociologists have presented the possibility of certain identical basic structures of functions in the psychic systems of the world, since the basic field conditions for the emergence of the human psyche have been society, culture, symbolic interaction, and the potentialities of biological organisms that interact in the basic process of socialization.[25] They have demonstrated that pluralistic values are not limitless, since moral standards are interdependent with other factors that determine action.[26] They have explained this non-limitlessness by pointing out that human infants are invariably dependent, that they confront the problems of sibling competition, and that they possess similar neurological defense mechanisms.[27]

Our purpose in pointing out the above examples of theories in anthropology, psychology, and sociology is not to uncritically endorse them but to make our point that in rejecting the absolutism of values, legal polycentricity is not doomed to embracing radical relativism that claims that anything goes and that moral standards are impossible. Anthropology, psychology, and sociology assist us in developing these standards.[28]

---

21. R. Linton, "Universal Ethical Principles: An Anthropological View," in R. Anshen, ed., *Moral Principles of Action*, 646 (1952); R. Linton, "The Problem of Universal Values," in R.F. Spencer, ed., *Method and Perspective in Anthropology*, 150 (1954).

22. A. Maslow, "Psychological Progress in Understanding Human Nature and a Scientific Ethics," 10 *Main Currents* 75 (1954).

23. Frenkel-Brunswik, "Social Research and the Problem of Values: A Reply," 49 *Journal of Abnormal and Social Psychology* 466 (1954).

24. S. Asch, *Social Psychology*, 375–378 (1952).

25. Kolb, "A Social-Psychological Conception of Human Freedom," 63 *Ethics* 180 (1953).

26. T. Parsons and E. Shils, *Toward a General Theory of Action*, 171 (1951).

27. G. Roheim, *Psychoanalysis and Anthropology*, 435 (1950).

28. Sinha, *What Is Law?*, 82–85.

3. *Acceptance of Moral Pluralism*

Legal polycentricity accepts the pluralism of moral values. It, therefore, conceives the problem of legal relationships in terms of relations among various normative orders within a legal system and seeks their recognition within that legal system.[29]

The emergence of the concept of legal pluralism is owed to those social scientists from the West who began studying the social order of the societies in Asia, Africa, and the Pacific which the Europeans Powers had colonized. Thus, anthropologists explored how these societies maintained social order without the law from Europe.[30] They called this order indigenous law.[31] When European law was imposed upon this indigenous law, they examined the effect of the colonial law upon the native ways[32] and they perceived in it a plurality of legal orders.[33] The indigenous law was subjugated to the European law by such devices as the repugnancy principle which limited the application of local custom within the bounds of what the European rulers called natural justice, equity, and good conscience, or the inconsistency principle which disallowed local custom if it conflicted with the enacted law.[34] While the European chauvinists called this imposition of

29. *Cf.* J. Griffiths, "What is Legal Pluralism?" 24 *Journal of Legal Pluralism* 1, 2 (1986); S.F. Moore, *Social Facts and Fabrications: Customary Law on Kilimanjaro, 1880–1980* (1986); L. Pospisil, *The Anthropology of Law: A Comparative Theory of Law*, 107 (1971); S.E. Merry, "Legal Pluralism," 22 *Law and Society Review* 869, 870 (1988); M. Minow, "Pluralisms," 21 *Connecticut Law Review* 965, 966 (1989).

30. For example, B. Malinowski, *Crime and Custom in a Savage Society* (1926).

31. As to the concept of legal pluralism, see L. Nader, ed., *Law in Culture and Society* (1969); J. Gillisen, *La pluralisme juridique* (1972); International Legal Center, *Law and Development: The Future of Development Research* (1974); A.N. Allott and G.R. Woodman, eds., *People's Law and State Law: The Bellagio Papers* (1985); P.G. Sack and E. Minchin, eds., *Legal Pluralism: Proceedings of the Canberra Law Workshop VII* (1986); J. Griffiths, *supra* note 29; M. Chiba, *Legal Pluralism: Toward a General Theory through Japanese Legal Culture* (1989).

32. For example, M. Chanock, *Law, Custom, and Social Order: The Colonial Experience in Malawi and Zambia* (1985); T. Ranger, "The Invention of Tradition in Colonial Africa," in E. Hobsbawm and T. Ranger, eds., *The Invention of Tradition* (1983); M. Chiba, ed., *Asian Indigenous Law—In Interaction with Received Law* (1986);

33. C. Geertz, *Local Knowledge: Further Essays in Interpretive Anthropology*, 226 (1983); J. Griffiths, *supra* note 29, at 5, 7, 8; M.B. Hooker, *Legal Pluralism: An Introduction to Colonial and Neo-Colonial Laws*, 1 (1975).

34. H.W.O. Okoth-Ogendo, "The Imposition of Property Law in Kenya," in S.B. Burman and B.E. Harrell-Bond, eds., *The Imposition of Law*, 147, 160 (1979); O. Adewoye, "Legal Practice in Abadan, 1904–1960," 24 *Journal of Legal Pluralism* 57 (1986); K. Bentsi-Enchill, "The Colonial Heritage of Legal Pluralism," 1 *Zambia Law Journal* 1 (1969); R.L. Kidder, "Formal Litigation and Professional Insecurity: Legal Entrepreneurship in South India," 9 *Law and Society Review* 11 (1974); R.L. Kidder, "Toward an Integrated Theory

European law Europe's greatest gift to colonized peoples, more critical observers saw in it the promotion of European self-interests.[35]

In the last twenty years or so, sociologists have extended the concept of legal pluralism to noncolonized societies, such as United States,[36] United Kingdom,[37] or the Netherlands.[38] Thereby, they have invested this concept with the connotation of relations between dominant groups and subordinate groups within a society. These groupings exist on a variety of bases,[39] such as religion, ethnicity, gender, sexual preferences, culture, immigration, and social networks or institutions.

No longer, therefore, does the concept of legal pluralism signify a type of society but, rather, it indicates a condition that exists in most societies.[40]

Legal polycentricity accepts this pluralism. It conceptualizes a complex relationship of interaction between the plural forms of ordering that par-

---

of Imposed Law," in Burman and Harrell-Bond, *Imposition*, 289.

35. Chanock, *Colonial Experience*; J. Comaroff, *Body of Power, Spirit of Resistance: Culture*and History of a South African People (1985); J. Comaroff and J.L. Comaroff, "Christianity and Colonialism in South Africa," 13 *American Ethnologist* 1 (1986); Moore, *Social Facts and Fabrications.*

36. S.F. Moore, "Law and Social Change: The Semi-Autonomous Social Field as an Appropriate Subject of Study," 7 *Law and Society Review* 719 (1973); N. Forer, "The Imposed Wardship of American Indian Tribes: A Case Study of the Prairie Band Potawatomi," in Burman and Harrell-Bond, *Imposition*, 89; S.E. Merry, "Going to Court: Strategies of Dispute Management in an American Urban Neighborhood," 13 *Law and Society Review* 891 (1979); D.M. Engel, "Legal Pluralism in an American Community: Perspectives on a Civil Trial Court," 3 *American Bar Foundation Research Journal* 425 (1980); D.M. Engel, "The Oven Bird's Song: Insiders, Outsiders, and Personal Injuries in an American Community," 18 *Law and Society Review* 549 (1984); D.M. Engel, "Law, Time, and Community," 21 *Law and Society Review* 605 (1987); L. Nader, ed., *No Access to Law* (1980); C. Greenhouse, "Nature is to Culture as Praying is to Suing: Legal Pluralism in an American Suburb," 20 *Journal of Legal Pluralism* 17 (1982); L. Buckle and S.R. Thomas-Buckle, "Doing Unto Others: Dispute and Dispute-Processing in an Urban American Neighborhood," in R. Tomasic and M. Feeley, eds., *Neighborhood Justice* (1982); S. Macaulay, "Private Government," in L. Lipson and S. Wheeler, eds., *Law and Social Sciences* (1986).

37. S. Henry, *Private Justice* (1983); S. Henry, "Community Justice, Capitalist Society, and Human Agency: The Dialectics of Collective Law in the Cooperative," 19 *Law and Society Review* 303 (1985).

38. F. Strijbosch, "The Concept of Pela and Its Social Significance in the Community of Moluccan Immigrants in the Netherlands," 23 *Journal of Legal Pluralism* 177 (1985).

39. G.R. Woodman, "What Is the Commission About?" 14 *Newsletter of the Commission on Folk Law and Legal Pluralism* 3 (1987–88); S. Macaulay, *supra* note 36; S.F. Moore, "Legal Systems of the World: An Introductory Guide to Classification, Typological Interpretations, and Bibliographical Resources," in Lipson and Wheeler, *Law and Social Sciences*.

40. M. Galanter, "Justice in Many Rooms: Courts, Private Ordering, and Indigenous Law," 19 *Journal of Legal Pluralism and Unofficial Law* 1 (1981); J. Griffiths, *supra* note 29.

ticipate in the same social field. It analyzes this interaction and seeks legal forms of coexistence of these relationships. It rejects the ideology of legal centralism that insists that the state is the only form of ordering. It investigates the relationship between the state and non-state forms of normative ordering with a view to inventing legal forms therefor. It, therefore, is interested in such questions as how state law influences the shaping of other normative orders,[41] how state law, in turn, is shaped by other normative orders,[42] what are the forms of resistance to this interaction between the two, how viewing law as constitutive of social life leads to an inquiry as to how state law constitutes the normative orders within the state and, in turn, is itself constituted by them.[43] It is interested in the question of how plural normative orders persist, how they change, and how they are transformed by historical processes.[44] It is interested in investigating the ideological nature of the various normative orders. It is interested in discovering modes of allocation of decision-making authority that would maximize the coexistence of these normative orders.[45] This allocation of authority occurs among public authorities and private actors, on the one hand, and among different levels of government, on the other.

---

41. J.S. Auerback, *Justice Without Law?* (1983); H.W. Arthurs, *Without the Law: Administrative Justice and Legal Pluralism in Mid 19th-Century England* (1985); L. Nader, "The Recurrent Dialectic Between Legality and Its Alternatives," 132 *University of Pennsylvania Law Review* 621 (1984); C. Harrington, *Shadow Justice: The Ideology and Institutionalization of Alternatives to Court* (1985); J. Brigham, "Right, Rage, and Remedy: Forms of Law in Political Discourse," in *Studies in American Political Development* (1987); S.A. Scheingold, *The Politics of Rights: Lawyers, Public Policy, and Political Change* (1974); S.E. Merry, "Everyday Understandings of the Law in Working-class America," 13 *American Ethnologist* 253 (1986); S. Macaulay, "Images of Law in Everyday Life: The Lessons of School, Entertainment, and Spectator Sports," 21 *Law and Society Review* 185 (1987).

42. R.L. Abel, *The Politics of Informal Justice*, 2 vols. (1982); C. Harrington and S.E. Merry, "Ideological Production: The Making of Community Mediation," 22 *Law and Society Review* 709 (1988).

43. P. Fitzpatrick, "Law and Societies," 22 *Osgoode Hall Law Journal* 115 (1984); Henry, *Private Justice*; S. Henry, *supra* note 37; S. Henry, "The Construction and Deconstruction of Social Control: Thoughts on the Discursive Production of State Law and Private Justice," in J. Lowman, R. Menzies, and T. Palys, eds., *Transcarceration* (1987); D. Nelken, "Review Essay: Beyond the Study of 'Law and Society'? Henry's *Private Justice* and O'Hagen's *The End of the Law?*" 1986 *American Bar Foundation Research Journal* 323; S.S. Silbey and E. Bittner, "The Availability of Law," 4 *Law and Policy* 399 (1982); B. Yngvesson, "Private Nuisance of Public Crime: The Clerk, The Court, and the Constructive Order in a New England Town," 22 *Law and Society Review* 409 (1988); A. Sarat and W. Felstiner, "Law and Strategy in the Divorce Lawyer's Office," 20 *Law and Society Review* 93 (1986).

44. S Starr and J.F. Collier, "Historical Studies of Legal Change," 28 *Current Anthropology* 367 (1987); J. Starr and J.F. Collier, *History and Power in the Study of Law: New Directions in Legal Anthropology* (1989).

45. M. Minow, *supra* note 29, 967 ff.

Therefore, it is possible to conceive of the program of legal polycentricity in either of two ways: descriptive or active.

As a description of the legal order, it would express the normative interrelationships among various normative orders and develop a cognitive postulate for legal reality that comprehends this pluralism. The consequence of this approach would be that the concept of law is expanded to recognize the validity of normative claims not only of state law but of other normative orders as well.[46] Or, it might reconceptualize the relationship of law and society.[47] For example, it might describe how people generate their own rule system in their everyday interaction and, in doing so, how they are influenced by plural rules and institutional elements.[48]

However, the program of legal polycentricity is not merely to extend the concept of law to comprise state law as well as other normative orders in order to describe the nature of law more accurately, but to reform state law so as to give an adequate recognition of this pluralism within the system of state law. It is this active, reform-generating conception of legal polycentricity that distinguishes it from the anthropologists's or the sociologist's description of pluralism.

The persuasion of legal polycentricity lies in several advantages in adopting its approach, namely, (i) maximization of the legitimacy of legal order, (ii) promotion of tolerance, (iii) promotion of non-coercive methodology, (iv) promotion of stability, (v) providing a framework for understanding domination and resistance, (vi) avoidance of the Marxist contradiction, and (vii) avoidance of the pluralist fallacy claimed by the single-value approach.

(i) Maximization of the legitimacy of legal order The legitimacy of legal order depends upon how well that order accommodates demands of liberty, community, and social justice.[49] By securing these demands, the legal order provides the individual a reason for submitting to it, rather than help-

46. L. Nader, "Introduction," in L. Nader, ed., *Law in Culture and Society*, 4 (1969); K. von Benda-Beckmann, "Anthropology and Comparative Law," in K. von Benda-Beckmann and F. Strijbosch, eds., *Anthropology of Law in the Netherlands* (1986).

47. A. Giddens, *Central Problems in Social Theory: Action, Structure, and Contradiction in Social Analysis* (1979); K. von Benda-Beckmann, "Why Law Does Not Behave: Critical and Constructive Reflections on the Social Scientific Perception of the Social Significance of Law," in H. Finkler, ed., *Proceedings of the Symposium of Folk Law and Legal Pluralism* (1983); S. Henry, *supra* note 45; D. Nelken, "Legislation and Its Constraints: A Case Study of the 1965 British Rent Act," in A. Podgorecki, C.J. Whelan, and D. Khosla, eds., *Legal Systems and Social Systems* (1985).

48. S.F. Moore, "Law and Social Change: The Semiautonomous as an Appropriate Field of Study," 7 *Law and Society Review* 719 (1973).

49. Honoré, "The Right to Rebel," 8 *Oxford Journal of Legal Studies* 34, 54 (1988).

lessly succumbing to the state's police power. Tolerance and respect for differences contribute to this legitimacy.[50] The pluralism of legal polycentricity opens up a search for ways to maximize this legitimacy. For example, one way may be the institutionalization of power through discursive communities so as to promote the process of give and take.[51] Other ways can be invented.

(ii) Promotion of tolerance As noted above, legal polycentricity insists that best values are many, that they are conflicting, and that they are incapable of being harmonized into one unitary vision. Acceptance of this view makes it possible to tolerate this variety, whereas the logic of the single-approach, pointed out above, leads to tyranny of one viewpoint forcing itself upon the rest.[52]

(iii) Promotion of con-coercive methodology Since the pluralist approach expands the freedom to choose one's own preferred value, it reduces the need for coercion and it promotes, instead, the methodology of non-coercive give-and-take.[53]

(iv) Promotion of stability The pluralist approach of legal polycentricity provides individuals and associations their own morally preferred space. Thereby, it promotes stability in society. When people are left out, as in the single-value approach, they thereby acquire reason to resist, or even rebel.[54]

(v) Providing a framework for understanding domination and resistance The pluralist approach recognizes the dialectical relationship that exists among various normative orders, in that it seeks to accommodate these

---

50. *Cf.* Macedo, "The Politics of Justification," 18 *Political Theory* 280 (1990); Waldron, "Theoretical Foundations of Liberalism," 37 *Philosophical Quarterly* 127, 149 (1987).

51. R.K Sherwin, "Rhetorical Pluralism and the Discourse Ideal: Countering *Division of Employment v. Smith*, A Parable of Pagans, Politics, and Majoritarian Rule," 85 *Northwestern University Law Review* 388, 397, 407, 409 (1991). See also B. Ackerman, "Why Dialogue?" 86 *Journal of Philosophy* 5, 20–21 (1989).

52. Berlin, *Against the Current*, 78; Kronman, "Practical Wisdom and Professional Character," 4 *Social Philosophy and Policy* 203, 230 (1986); M. Schwarzschild, "Value Pluralism and the Constitution: In Defense of the State Action Doctrine," 5 *The Supreme Court Review* 129, 131–132 (1988).

53. *Cf.* J. Rawls, *supra* note 9, at 5.

54. M. Sandel, "The Procedural Republic and the Unencumbered Self," 12 *Political Theory* 90 (1984); W.A. Galston, "Pluralism and Social Unity," 99 *Ethics* 711, 719–120 (1989). *Cf.* the defense of the primacy of freedom of citizens and of associations over the state. F.W. Maitland, Introduction to Otto von Gierke, in *Political Theory of the Middle Age* (1900); J.N. Figgis, *Churches in the Modern State* (1913); D. Nicholls, *The Pluralistic State* (1975); A. Black, *Guilds and Civil Society in European Political Thought from the Twelfth Century to the Present* (1984).

orders within one legal system. This provides a framework whereby we can understand how dominant groups and subordinate groups relate to each other, how they interact, how law is used to dominate and to put limits on domination, and what are the dynamics of the imposition of law and the resistance to it.[55]

(vi) Avoidance of the Marxist contradiction The Marxist theory suffers from a contradiction of political action. While it aims at a freer society based upon the self-action of the people, its theory of class struggle and dictatorship of the proletariat justifies concentration of state power to crush class enemies.[56] Pluralism avoids this contradiction. It does so because its program for a just society is based upon the recognition, not elimination, of diversity in values, aims, and ideals.

(vii) Avoidance of the pluralist fallacy claimed by the single-value approach Sometimes an argument is made that pluralism suffers from a fallacy, which goes like this. It is argued that pluralism does not possess one privileged perspective that can be used to assess the claims of opposing positions and, yet, the question has to be faced: from which perspective does one analyze the claims of those who differ from him? The only possible answer can be, the argument goes, that he analyzes them from his own perspective. The result is that the claims of others would always be wrong, since they are not his. It is then pointed out under this argument that this result is incongruous with pluralism, which then means, it is argued, that the right place for the pluralist is "every place and therefore no place at all."[57] However, my contention here is that it is the single-value approach which puts one in that unitary trap of having to choose one right value. The pluralist approach of legal polycentricity denies the very necessity of having a privileged, i.e., unitary or single-value, perspective, and, therefore, it avoids this alleged fallacy altogether.

The above advantages make a persuasive case for legal polycentricity. However, it is important to watch out for a neglect of intra-field struggles and for dominance of interest groups. By creating polycentric social fields and focussing upon interaction among them, this approach might tend to neglect the ideological and political forces that are active within a particular social field. By concentrating upon the systemic relationship among these fields, it might lose sight of normative struggles that occur within these

---

55. S.E. Merry, *supra* 29, at 890.

56. C. Erjin, *China, Crossroads to Socialism* (1984).

57. S. Fish, "Interpretation and the Pluralist Vision," 60 *Texas Law Review* 495, 505 (1982). See also, J. White, "Law as Language: Reading Law and Reading Literature," 60 *Texas Law Review* 415 (1982).

fields.[58] Also, legal polycentricity creates a political market where diverse interest groups compete with each other. It is quite likely, and indeed the present political scene well illustrates this, that some interest groups can accumulate enough power to dominate the others, thereby defeating the aims of the polycentric approach.[59] Legal polycentricity must be on the look-out for ways to avoid or, at least, minimize these dangers.

How is legal polycentricity to be realized?

This constitutes probably the most engrossing area of further research in legal polycentricity. One might suggest a variety of modes of such realization. It is, for example, possible to conceive at least four such modes: (i) doctrines of law, (ii) facilitative law, (iii) polycentric categories of individuals and associations, and (iv) institutional structure of the legal system.

(i) Doctrines of law Polycentric aims may be achieved through certain doctrines of law. For example, in common law there is a doctrine of reasonableness that pervades through contract law, tort law, criminal law, and many other areas of law. It is manifested in such concepts as reasonable reliance, reasonable care, reasonable mistake, reasonable time, reasonable delay, reasonable person of ordinary prudence, reasonable provocation, reasonable force, reasonable risk, and so on.[60] The most important quality of this doctrine of reasonableness is that it can neither be reduced to a finite set of rules, nor can it be specified in terms of custom or practices. Therefore, its open-endedness lends itself to pluralistic use. Or, the state action doctrine of American constitutional law provides another example of a pluralism-friendly doctrine. The Fourteenth Amendment to the Constitution of the United States provides that the state shall not deprive any person of life, liberty, or property without due process of law or deny any person the equal protection of law.[61] The provisions of the Bill of Rights are deemed to have been incorporated in this Amendment.[62] The U.S. Supreme Court has generally held that this mandate is binding only upon the institutions of government and not upon private citizens. Thus, this constitutional obligation is limited only to state action. Since the state action doctrine makes the Fourteenth Amendment and the Bill of Rights binding only upon the government, it leaves private persons free to act according to

58. S.E. Merry, *supra* note 29, at 891.

59. R.A. Dahl, *After Revolution* (1970); C.E. Lindblom, *Politics and Markets* (1977); M. Olson, *The Rise and Decline of Nations* (1982).

60. Fletcher has counted over 100 different words in the American Uniform Commercial Code, the Model Penal Code, and the various Restatements that bear the adjective reasonable or the adverb reasonably. G.P. Fletcher, "The Right and the Reasonable," 98 *Harvard Law Review* 949, n. 1 (1985).

61. *E.g.*, Civil Rights Cases, 109 U.S. 3, 11 (1883); Bolling v. Sharpe, 347 U.S. 497 (1954).

62. Fiske v. Kansas, 274 U.S. 380 (1927); Duncan v. Louisiana, 391 U.S. 145 (1968),

their pluralistic values, enabling diverse persons to pursue their diverse values.[63] One might explore other pluralism-friendly doctrines of law.

(ii) Facilitative law The pluralistic aims of legal polycentricity may be achieved through the facilitative law. Facilitative law is that part of law which provides facilities to persons for realizing their particular objectives. It does so by conferring legal powers upon them. Examples of such law are found in the laws of marriage, contracts, wills, trusts, and so on.[64] To the extent this law accommodates the autonomy of the individual or the association, it promotes the pluralistic objective.

(iii) Polycentric categories of individuals and associations Categories may be developed of individuals or associations on the basis of value sectors, such as, gender or race in municipal law. Examples of this approach are seen in the present-day feminist jurisprudence[65] or the critical race theory.[66]

---

63. Burke and Reber, "State Action, Congressional Power, and Creditors' Rights: An Essay on the Fourteenth Amendment," 46 *Southern California Law Review* 1003 (1973); Marshall, "Diluting Constitutional Rights: Rethinking 'Rethinking State Action'," 80 *Northwestern University Law Review* 558 (1985); M. Schwarzschild, *supra* note 54.

64. D. Sugarman, "Law, Economy, and the State in England, 1750–1914: Some Major Issues," in D. Sugarman, ed., *Legality, Ideology, and the State*, 213 (1983).

65. See, S.P. Sinha, *Jurisprudence: Legal Philosophy in a Nutshell*, Ch. 13 (1993). See also K.T. Bartlett, "Feminist Legal Methods," 103 *Harvard Law Review* 829 (1990); A.P. Harris, "Race and Essentialism in Feminist Legal Theory," 42 *Stanford Law Review* 581 (1990); N. Duclos, "Lesson of Difference: Feminist Theory on Cultural Diversity," 38 *Buffalo Law Review* 325 (1990); L. Bender, "Feminist (Re)torts: Thoughts on the Liability Crisis, Mass Torts, Power, and Responsibilities," 1990 *Duke Law Journal* 848 (1990); L. Bender, "From Gender Difference to Feminist Solidarity: Using Carol Gilligan and an Ethic of Care in Law," 15 *Vermont Law Review* 1 (1990); C. McKinnon, *Toward a Feminist Theory of the State* (1989); C. McKinnon, "Feminism, Marxism, Method, and the State: Toward Feminist Jurisprudence," 8 *Signs* 635 (1985); R. West, "Jurisprudence and Gender," 55 *University of Chicago Law Review* 1 (1988); Littleton, "Reconstructing Sexual Equality," 75 *California Law Review* 1279 (1987); M. Minow, "The Supreme Court, 1986 Term—Foreword: Justice Engendered," 101 *Harvard Law Review* 10 (1987); Scales, "The Emergence of Feminist Jurisprudence: An Essay," 95 *Yale Law Journal* 1273 (1986); Schneider, "The Dialectic of Rights and Politics: Perspectives from the Women's Movement," 61 *New York University Law Review* 589 (1986); Kay, "Models of Equality," 1985 *University of Illinois Law Review* 39; Law, "Rethinking Sex and Constitution," 132 *University of Pennsylvania Law Review* 955 (1984); Olsen, "Statutory Rape: A Feminist Critique of Rights," 63 *Texas Law Review* 387 (1984); Freedman, "Sex, Equality, Sex Differences, and the Supreme Court," 92 *Yale Law Journal* 913 (1983); Taub and Schneider, "Perspectives on Women's Subordination and the Role of Law," in D. Kairys, ed., *The Politics of Law: A Progressive Critique*, 117 (1982); H. Petersen, *Informel Ret*, in Danish, summary in English (1991).

66. Sinha, *Jurisprudence*, Ch. 13. See also, G. Torres, "Critical Race Theory: The Decline of the Universalist Ideal and the Hope of Plural Justice—Some Observations and Questions of an Emerging Phenomenon," 75 *Minnesota Law Review* 993 (1991); G. Torres and Milun,

(iv) Institutional structure of the legal system Legal polycentricity may be realized through designing institutional structures of administration of law which would respond to the demands of the pluralistic values. To some extent, the jury system of common law performs this function. In this system, certain randomly selected members of the local community decide the specific issues of rightness or wrongness of a conflict under general guidelines given by the presiding judge. Another example comes from the subsidiarity principle of institutional structure, which has been used in the ecclesiastical law for decentralizing the apostolic powers[67] and is currently being explored in the institutional development of the European Community. In the European Community, it raises such questions as what matters should be governed by the Community and what matters should be left to the private sphere of the individual, the family, firms, trade unions, associations, or cooperatives, what is the appropriate level of government authority for a certain regulatory action, and so on.[68]

The challenge of legal polycentricity, therefore, is, firstly, to identify the pluralistic values within a legal system, and, secondly, to devise modes for their realization.

"Translating Yonnondio by Precedent and Evidence: The Mastpee Indian Case," 1990 *Duke Law Journal* 625; G. Torres, "Local Knowledge, Local Color: Critical Legal Studies and the Law of Race Relations," 25 *San Diego Law Review* 1043 (1988); G. Peller, "Race Consciousness," 1990 *Duke Law Journal* 758; K. Crenshaw, "A Black Feminist Critique of Antidiscrimination Law and Politics," in D. Kairys, ed., *The Politics of Law*, 195 (2d ed., 1990); K. Crenshaw, "Race, Reform, and Retrenchment: Transformation and Legitimation in Antidiscrimination Law," 101 *Harvard Law Review* 1331 (1988); Cook, "Beyond Critical Legal Studies: The Reconstruction Theology of Dr. Martin Luther King, Jr.," 103 *Harvard Law Review* 985 (1990); R. Delgado, "The Imperial Scholar: Reflections on a Review of Civil Rights Literature," 132 *University of Pennsylvania Law Review* 561 (1984); M. Matsuda, "Affirmative Action and Legal Knowledge: Planting Seeds in Plowed-up Ground," 11 *Harvard Women's Law Journal* 1 (1988).

67. J.E. Linna, "Subsidiarity, Collegiality, Catholic Diversity, and Their Relevance to Apostolic Visitations," 49 *The Jurist* 399 (1989); T.J. Green, "Subsidiarity During the Code Revision Process: Some Initial Reflections," 48 *The Jurist* 771 (1988); J.A. Komonchak, "Subsidiarity in the Church: The State of the Question (The Nature and Future of Episcopal Conferences)," 48 *The Jurist* 298 (1988); F. Kaufman, "The Principle of Subsidiarity Viewed by the Sociology of Organizations (The Nature and Future of Episcopal Conferences), 48 *The Jurist* 275 1988).

68. Editorial, "The Subsidiarity Principle," 27 Common Market Law Review 181 (1990).

Legal Polycentricity Applied to International Law

Applied to the society of states and their international law, legal polycentricity focusses upon the civilizational pluralism and civilizational diversity of the members of this society and it examines the consequences of that focus upon the principles of international law.

In our world of today, international law applies to all societies constituted as states and not only to the states of Europe that originally constituted the society of states. Today, in 1994, there are 184 members of the United Nations whereas, at the time of the founding of the United Nations in 1945, this number was 51, of which only 11 were Asian-African states. A little over a hundred years ago, 14 states participated in 1885 at the Congo Conference of Berlin, of which none was Asian-African.[69] More significant than the numeric proliferation of these entities called states has been the fact that today they represent all major civilizations of the world, in contrast with their past of merely the European civilization.

Yet, it is in the particular historical circumstances of Europe of the fifteenth-sixteenth centuries that the particular definition of the entity called the state emerged, as did the particular law governing the relations of these entities, namely, international law. The constitutive characteristic of these entities was, and remains, sovereignty, which is a composite of political independence and juridical equality. The law governing relations of these sovereign states was, and remains, international law, created through the ingenuity of the sovereignty-compatible technique of consent. This consent of states to a principle was, and is, discerned in the conjunction of general and concordant practice of states (*usus diuturnus*) regarding a certain way of doing things with their conviction that they are bound by law to follow that practice (*opinio juris sive necessitatis*). This process is abbreviated under the rubric of custom and has produced a whole body of principles of international law, including the highly potent law of treaties.

It is, then, the genius of international law that in spite of its parochial origin and growth in Europe, it has become universal and it governs states of all civilizations, European and non-European. More importantly, it has done so without abandoning, or even varying, its basic constitutive principles mentioned above. Those principles have enabled it to embrace all differences in military, economic, and political power, all differences in cultures, ways of life, and value preferences, and all differences in ideologies, political systems, and social organizations. It has grown, changed, and developed in accordance with these principles. It continues to provide definitions,

69. S.P. Sinha, *New Nations and the Law of Nations*, 25 (1967).

characterizations, and attitude-formulations for a whole range of human conduct performed through the agency of the state, whether that conduct be noble, such as improving human condition on this planet, or ignoble, such as killing off of human beings.

The inclusion of non-European states into the society of states has not diminished the validity of the system of this law. In fact, nearly three decades ago, in studying the attitudes of newly independent states of Asia and Africa toward this law, I found that "the interest of the new states in international law is threefold. First, they are interested in preserving those rules of international law which help them exist as a member of the society of states and are not inconsistent with their own interests. Second, they are interested in the removal from the existing body of international law those rules which impair or prevent the realization of their interests. Third, they are interested in the creation of new rules which would reap them maximum benefits from the international system."[70] Since then, nothing has happened to change those findings.

But the purpose of this book is not to beat the dead horse of questioning the validity of international law owing to the inclusion of non-European states in today's society of states. Instead, this book is intended to bear the focus of legal polycentricity upon international law. It, therefore, attempts certain clarifications that seem necessary when one locates international law in the context of civilizational pluralism of its subject states of today. More specifically, it examines three aspects of the civilizational question.

One, sometimes there is a tendency to claim more universality for the origin itself of international law than its European context. In Chapter 2, we shall attempt to clarify this issue. We shall see that international law is very much European in its origin.

Two, when we talk about diverse civilizations what is it that we are talking about? First, we shall observe, in Chapter 3, history's tenacity to civilizational pluralism. Next, in Chapter 4, we shall attempt to identify the most basic principles of life and social organization in the Western, the Chinese, the Indian, and the African civilizations and show how they came to be so as a result of their particular history. We shall notice the non-universality of these principles and deny the claim of law (*nomos*) to be universal.[71]

Three, we shall attempt, in Chapter 5, to sort out the consequences of civilizational diversity upon international law. We shall see how most of its principles remain unaffected by this diversity while in certain areas, specifically, in human rights, this diversity is of great importance. While the present international approach to human rights is not exclusively European

70. Sinha, *New Nations*, 145.

71. S.P. Sinha, *What Is Law?*, Ch. 1 (1989); S.P. Sinha, *Jurisprudence: Legal Philosophy in a Nutshell*, Ch. 2 (1993).

in values, its single-catalog approach[72] has prevented it from being sufficiently responsive to the needs of this diversity. This, for us, is not an argument for scrapping the international human rights program, but for improving it. Nor is this an argument for reducing human-rights responsibilities of states, as is sometimes argued, for example, at the 1993 Vienna Conference on Human Rights.

We hope that these clarifications will keep us from either obscuring the genius of international law despite its European origins, or ignoring the need for making it more effective by adopting the pluralistic approach of legal polycentricity.

72. See *supra* note 2.

Chapter 2

The European Imprint of International Law

It is sometimes argued[1] that international law is "a phenomenon which has always emerged and developed among a group of distinct and sovereign political entities whenever sustained and organized relations have come to exist between them."[2] It is, of course, possible to conceive of a concept such as this. However, international law denotes a particular system that was developed in Europe and not a generic, universal phenomenon as claimed above. It was invented to govern relations of those peculiar entities called states, whose essential characteristics were juridical equality[3] and political independence[4] and which emerged in Europe during the sixteenth century

1. For example, R. Ago, "The First International Communities in the Mediterranean World," 53 *British Yearbook of International Law* 213 (1982); R. Ago, "Pluralism and Origins of the International Community," 3 *Italian Yearbook of International Law* 3 (1977). *Cf.* C.H. Alexandrowicz, "The Afro-Asian World and the Law of Nations (Historical Aspects)," *Recueil des Cours* (1968), Vol. I.

2. R. Ago, *supra* note 1 (*BYIL*), 213.

3. Samuel Pufendorf (1632–1694) insisted upon the 'natural' equality of states for the purposes of international law. S. Pufendorf, *De jure naturae et gentium libri octo* (translated in *Classics of International Law*), VIII, 4, Secs. 18, 22 (Equality). *Cf.* Thomas Hobbes (1588–1679), for whom equality was a feature of those living in the state of nature. T. Hobbes, *De Cive* (1642) and *Leviathan* (1651), Latin and English texts by van Vollenhoven, 6 *Bibliotheca Visseriana* 67 *(De Cive)*, 74 (*De corporo politico* and *Leviathan*) (1926).

4. Jean Bodin (1530–1596), prompted by his nationalist desire to strengthen the newly unified kingdom of France, developed his famous theory of sovereignty, namely, the absolute and perpetual power of the monarch over the people without any restraint of human law. J. Bodin, *Six livres de la république* (1576). He, however, maintained the supremacy of God and of the law of nature over sovereigns, which have been regarded as the inherent limitations of his concept of sovereignty. A. Gardot, "Jean Bodin, sa place parmi les fondateurs du droit international," 50 *Recueil des Cours* 549 (1934). Of course, the idea of sovereignty existed much before it was formulated into a theory. The English Statute of Westminster I of 1275 states that the king can do justice to all, even in Wales where the king's writ does not run. About the same time, Beaumanoir wrote in France (*Coutumes de Beauvaisis*, para. 1043) that the king can make laws (*éstablissemens*) for the common good and everyone is subject to his justice. G. Post, *Studies in Medieval Legal Thought,* 280–289, 301–309,

in a process which began in 1499 with the Peace of Basel[5] that separated Switzerland from the Holy Roman Empire and culminated in 1648 with the Peace of Westphalia[6] that established, once and for all, the European state system at the end of the Thirty Years' War (1618–1648).[7]

We shall develop the universalist argument by showing (1) the antecedents of principles and institutions which are part of this international law, (2) the other systems of law which deal with matters that concern this law, (3) the existence of international communities prior to the international community of this law, and (4) the cultural pluralism that existed at the inception of this community. And, yet, we shall show that in spite of these facts, international law is a very particular system invented to govern conduct of the European state system.

1. The Antecedents

Treaties, extradition, protection of alien settlements, warfare, peace, treatment of envoys, protection of aliens, arbitration, reprisals, capture of foreign ships, differentiation between an international agreement and its ratification, and other principles and institutions used by international law can be found in prior times.

Thus, about 3100 B.C. in Mesopotamia, a treaty, inscribed in stone, was entered into between the victorious ruler Eannatum of the city-state of Lagash and the men of the state of Umma that provided for the inviolabil-

445–453, 463–478 (1964); E.H. Kantorowicz, *The King's Two Bodies*, 236–258 (1957).

5. W. Oechsli, *History of Switzerland, 1499–1914*, 1, 14 (1922); A. Nussbaum, *A Concise History of the Law of Nations*, 61 (rev. ed., 1954).

6. A. Rapisardi-Mirabelli, "Le Congrès de Westphalie entre les puissances de l'Europe, etc.," 8 *Bibliotheca Visseriana* 5 (1929); L. Gross, "The Peace of Westphalia," 42 *American Journal of International Law* 20 (1948).

7. This war is regarded by historians as the most devastating conflict in Europe since the barbarian invasion. It was ended after more than three years of negotiations, held simultaneously in Munster and Osnabruck, in which most European powers were represented. The disagreement between France and Sweden on the question of procedure was resolved by according the first place to France in Catholic Munster and to Sweden in Protestant Osnabruck. Hence the two places for simultaneous negotiations. All the leading powers of Europe were represented at these negotiations, except England, Poland, Muscovy, and Turkey. Represented, thus, were the Papacy, the German Empire, France, Spain, Sweden, Venice, Denmark, Portugal, and the States General of Holland. The various German states and the Dukes of Tuscany, Savoy, and Mantua sent delegates. The Swiss cantons were represented through France. The independence of Holland was recognized. England and Poland were included in the Treaty of Osnabruck as allies both of the Emperor and Sweden. M. Bernard, "The Congress of Westphalia," in M. Bernard, *Lectures on Diplomacy*, Vol. II, Ch. 7 (1868). The origins of the modern state, of course, go back to the Medieval times. See J.R. Strayer, *On the Medieval Origins of the Modern State* (1970).

ity of the boundary ditch and the border stone.[8] In the second millennium B.C., several treaties were concluded between the Egyptian, the Hittite, the Babylonian, and the Assyrian rulers that provided for peace, alliances, boundary lines, and extradition.[9] Protection to the alien Greek settlement (*Naucratis*) was accorded by the Egyptian King Amasis (569–527 B.C.).[10] Envoys were taken hostages in Egypt, spared their lives in India, and accorded a special treatment in Greece.[11] Restraints in warfare atrocities were practiced by the ancient Hindus,[12] Israelites,[13] and Greeks.[14] Peace treaties for

8. M. Rostovtseff, "International Relations in the Ancient World," in E. Walsh, ed., *History and Nature of International Relations*, 31, 40 (1922).

9. *Id.*, 41; F. Rey, "Rélations internationales de l'Egypt ancienne du 15em siècle avant Jesus-Christ," 48 *Revue générale de droit international public* 35 (1941–1945).

10. D. Mallet, "Les premiers etablissements des Grecs en Egypte," 12 *Memoires public par les membres de la Missions archéologique française au Caire* 58 (1897), cited in Nussbaum, *Concise History*, 3.

11. Nussbaum, *Concise History*, 4–5. In India, the person of the envoy was inviolable. A king who slew an envoy would be reborn in hell. A.L. Basham, *The Wonder That Was India*, 127 (1954).

12. A chariot warrior could not strike a foot soldier. An enemy who was in flight, or had lost his weapon, or was wounded, or was seeking shelter could not be slain. Poisoned weapons were forbidden. And so on. Basham, *Wonder*, 126. P. Bandhopadhyay, *International Law and Custom in Ancient India* (1920); W.S. Armour, "Customs of Warfare in Ancient India," 8 *Transactions of the Grotius Society* 71 (1923). The Code of Manu (200 B.C.–100 B.C.) provided that one who surrendered, or was without arms, or was asleep, or was naked, or was with hair untied, or was only a spectator must not be killed. It prohibited slaying of the enemy by concealed weapons, or by barbed and poisoned weapons, or by fire-lit arrows. One mounted could not slay one on the ground, or a eunuch, or a suppliant one, or one who says I am the prisoner. *The Ordinances of Manu*, trans. by Burnell and Hopkins, Lect. VII, Nos. 90–93. See also N. Singh, "The Distinguishable Characteristics of the Concept of Law as It Developed in Ancient India," in M. Bos and I. Brownlie, eds., *Liber Amicorum for the R. Hon. Lord Wilberforce*, 91, 93 (1987); W.S. Armour, *supra* this note, 71.

13. The Hebrews surpassed their own Egyptian oppressors in cruelty, as when they waged their war of extermination against the Palestinians, invariably slaughtering male adults and frequently massacring women and children. Letourneau, *La guerre dans les diverses races humains*, Ch. 13 (1895), cited in A.S. Hershey, *The Essentials of International Public Law*, 32 (1921). The Book of Joshua is full of accounts of Hebrew barbarities and the Book of Samuel records the horrible atrocities of Saul and David. Even their God Jehovah is supposed to command Saul, through Samuel, to strike Amalek and "utterly destroy all that they have and spare them not; but slay both men and women, infant and suckling, ox and sheep, camel, and ass," and Samuel was angry when Saul spared Agag. (1 Samuel XV). Or, David put the people of Rabbah "under saws and under harrows of iron, and under axes of iron, and made them pass through the brick kiln." (2 Samuel VIII, 2, and XII, 31). However, the Mosaic Code, especially the laws of Deuteronomy, provided more humane rules of warfare. *Deuteronomy*, XX, 10–20. See also, N Bentwich, *The Religious Foundations of Internationalism*, 5 (1933).

14. Plato limited the concept of war to conflicts with the barbarians, not to be applied to

a definite duration were concluded among the Greeks up to the fourth century B.C. Permanently resident non-Greeks (the *metoikoi*) were given juridical protection, though not political and property rights. Prominent citizens appointed by a foreign state (the *proxenoi*) performed various diplomatic functions. Arbitration was practiced for inter-Greek disputes in such matters as boundary or use of streams and springs, although it was rarely used until the battle of Chaeronea in 338 B.C. that brought Greece under the Macedonian domination.[15] Reprisals were practiced that allowed an individual to use force against the foreign wrongdoer, his country, and his fellow citizens. Under the practice of androlepsia, a foreigner could be seized and abducted. During the era of the kings in Rome, that ended in 509 B.C., a special group of priests called *fetiales* certified to the existence of a just cause for war which made the ensuing war just and pious (*bellum justum et pium*).[16] Treaties concluded by the Romans included vassalage treaties, treaties of surrender (*deditio*), treaties of unequal alliances (*foedera iniqua*), treaties establishing spheres of interest, and commercial agreements. The Romans practiced the distinction between an agreement and its ratification, and the Roman negotiator who was denied the Senate's ratification was extradited to the other party.[17]

2. *Other Systems of Law*

Other systems of law have existed dealing with matters that pertain to international law.

---

conflicts among the Greeks. He suggested moderation in inter-Greek fights. Beyond that, and beyond occasional practice of restraint and clemency, no rules of warfare are found in ancient Greece. Nussbaum, *Concise History*, 9. Great cruelty characterized Greek warfare. For example, the Athenians slew the entire male population of Melos and sold its women and children into slavery in the Peloponnesian War. The Athenian Ecclesia decreed death to all adult male Mytilenaeans and slavery to their women and children. The decree was later rescinded and only revolutionaries were executed. However, the Greeks of the fourth century were more humane than those of the previous century. See, J.B. Bury, *History of Greece*, 98 (1975); J.P. Mahaffy, *Social Life of the Greeks*, 269–271 (1883).

15. de Taube, "Les Origines de l'arbitrage international: Antiquité et Moyen age," 42 *Recueil des Cours* 5 (1932); J.B. Moore, *History of Arbitration*, Vol. 5, Appendix III (1898); M.N. Tod, *International Arbitration Among the Greeks* (1913); A. Raeder, *L'arbitrage international chez les Hellènes* (1912); J. Ralston, *International Arbitration from Athens to Locarno* (1929).

16. Four causes were recognized for a just war: (1) invasion or violation of Roman territory, (2) violation of the rights of ambassadors, (3) violation of treaties and alliances, and (4) military support given to an enemy or attack upon an ally.

17. Nussbaum, *Concise History*, 5–12; C. Phillipson, *The International Law and Custom of Ancient Greece and Rome* (2 vols., 1911).

Thus, traditions of ancient India prescribed humane modes of warfare, as noted above.[18] Combatants were distinguished from non-combatants. Weapons of mass destruction were prohibited. Occupied territories were treated in accordance with certain particular principles.[19] Envoys were accredited to foreign rulers and received from them.[20] *Pacta sunt servanda* (good faith observation of treaty obligations) rules were observed.[21] Principles of equality were practiced among the tribal principalities in the Vedic Age (4000 B.C.–1000 B.C.).[22] Although the concept of territorial sovereignty emerged only after the 6th century B.C.,[23] several grades of rulers existed from a mere king to the suzerain emperor.[24] Laws of war were formulated among them during the Period of the Epic War (1900 B.C.–1000 B.C.), which were later refined and codified by Manu (about 200 B.C.). With the establishment of Greek kingdoms following Alexander's invasion (326 B.C.), envoy practices developed, with concomitant rules for their treatment. The most important envoy was Megasthenes, sent by Seleucus to reside at the Mauryan court at Pataliputra.[25] Treaty rules were developed for conclusion and enforcement of treaties. Rules were developed for conducting warfare with an enemy belonging to a different civilization. Emperor Ashok (274 B.C.–237 B.C.), influenced by the teachings of Buddha (563 B.C.–483 B.C.), enunciated the principle of renunciation of war in international relations, which was inscribed in the 13th Rock Edict of the Emperor after the devastating battle of Kalinga.[26] Rules for the protection of diplomatic missions were further strengthened during subsequent periods and amends were made for their violations.[27]

---

18. *Supra* note 12.

19. Manu lays down that the conquering king shall make the prince of the defeated country the king of that country. He shall not destroy the royal race of his enemy unless it be of ignoble birth. He shall respect the gods and the customs of the defeated country and grant it a temporary exemption from taxation. Cited in, N. Singh, *supra* note 12 at 93. See also, 1 *Cambridge History of India* 290. A celebrated example of such practice is found in a treaty of 305 B.C. between Chandragupta Maurya and Seleukos Nicator. V. Smith, *Early History of India, Including Alexander's Campaigns*, 125 (1924).

20. Smith, *Early History*, 124–125.

21. N. Singh, *supra* note 12, at 98.

22. *Id.*, at 101.

23. B. Prasad, *The State in Ancient India*, 23 (1904).

24. E.B. Havell, *A Short History of India* (1924); P.V. Kane, *History of Dharmasastra*, Vol. III, 65 (1930).

25. Basham, *Wonder*, 51.

26. J. Bloch, *Les Inscriptions d'Asoka*, 125 (1950); V. Smith, *Ashoka, the Buddhist Emperor of India*, 24 (1920).

27. Some of these instances are narrated in N. Singh, *supra* note 12, at 105–106. See also, P. Bandhopadhyaya, *International Law and Custom in Ancient India* (1920); S.V. Viswanatha, *International Law in Ancient India* (1925); B. Pramanathan, *International Law and Cus-*

The Romans developed rules for governing relations with foreigners, the *jus gentium*. While *jus fetiales* (certification of just war by priests) faded with the Roman expansion, a need arose to accommodate non-Romans in Roman territory to whom *jus civile* did not apply. Consequently, the office of the *praetor peregrinus* was established in 242 B.C. for settling disputes among non-Romans and between Romans and non-Romans. The body of *jus gentium* accrued from the edicts of the *praetor peregrinus* and the provincial governors who assisted him. It grew into a law that applied to Romans and foreigners alike, so much so that by the middle of the 1st century B.C., one can find a remarkable similarity between the edicts of the *praetor peregrinus* for foreigners and the *praetor urbanus* for the citizens.[28]

In Islamic law, the concept of *siyar* governs relations of Muslims with non-Muslims. Peace and order is to be achieved in accordance with the *sharia* (the sacred law) for not only the community of believers (*Umma*) but also for the whole world, in order to bring it within the pale of the *Umma*. The reality of the existence of non-Muslim communities is addressed by a distinction between the territory-of-Islam (*dar al-Islam*) and the territory-of-war (*dar al-harb*). The former included the *Umma* as well as the People of the Book, or the *Dhimmis* (Christians, Jews, and others possessing the Scriptures), who held to their religion upon payment of a tax (*jizya*), and who enjoyed internal security, protection from foreign attacks, recognition of their personal law, and access to Islamic courts if they wished to avail of the Islamic justice, although they did not possess all rights of the Muslims. The territory-of-war lacked status to enter into equal and reciprocal relations with the Islamic state. Arrangements with them were regarded only temporary, lacking recognition under the Islamic law. Some jurists, such as Shafi'i, propounded a third category of the territory-of-peaceful-arrangement (*dar al sulh*) or the territory-of-covenant (*dar al-ahd*) and granted it some recognition upon certain conditions, such as payment of an annu-

---

tom in Ancient India (1920). See also, C.H. Alexandrowicz, *An Introduction to the History of the Law of Nations in the East Indies (16th, 17th, and 18th Centuries)* (1967); R.P. Anand, ed., *Asian States and the Development of Universal International Law* (1972); H.S. Bhatia, ed., *International Law and Practice in Ancient India* (1977); N. Singh, *India and International Law* (1973).

28. H.F. Jolowicz, *Historical Introduction to the Study of Roman Law* (2d ed., 1952); F. Schultz, *History of Roman Legal Science* (1946). This historical *jus gentium* must be distinguished from the subsequent philosophical *jus gentium* of the jurist Gaius of the second century A.D., who viewed it as a concept to comprise laws and institutions found among all men by natural reason and, therefore, observed by all peoples or nations (*gentes*). Nussbaum, *Concise History*, 14; A. Watson, *International Law in Archaic Rome: War and Religion* (1993).

al tribute, but the majority of jurists, including the Hanafi School, denied this category.

The territory-of-Islam was in a state of war with the territory-of-war. Nevertheless, the Islamic law obliged the Muslims to respect the rights of its combatants and civilians during hostilities and to respect the rights of its authorities during peace. Thus, while a Muslim is obliged to observe his own law upon entering the territory-of-war as a merchant or under a safe-conduct *(aman)*, except for those rules that did not apply in the enemy territory, he is obliged to respect the authority of that territory and to observe its laws. The state of war did not mean actual hostilities. It meant denial of the equality of status to the states of that territory in diplomatic relations. *Jihad*, a term broader than the war of religion, was the instrument for bringing the territory-of-war into the territory-of-Islam, obliging both the individual and the community to establish God's sovereignty over the world. This duty could be discharged by heart, tongue, hands, or sword. War was permitted only for religious purpose. The Imam (head of state) could start or stop the war of *jihad*. Brief periods of peace might be offered to the inhabitants of the territory-of-war by a treaty. For example, a treaty, not to exceed ten years in duration, would protect that territory from a Muslim attack and would permit its inhabitants to enter the Islamic territory and be protected. In absence of such a treaty, a non-Muslim visitor could enjoy this protection by obtaining an *aman* (safe-conduct). By virtue of certain covenants (*ahd*), permanently resident non-Muslims enjoyed protection of life, property, and religious practices. Since all non-Islamic communities were in the state of war, none possessed the status of neutrality, although a special status of immunity from *jihad* was granted to Ethiopia for certain historical and doctrinal reasons. Other states could obtain temporary protection from *jihad* by peace treaties.[29]

3. Prior International Communities

The community of states of the Peace of Westphalia is not the first instance of the existence of an international community. In the middle of the third millennium B.C., city-states existed in Sumeria that carried on peace, war,

29. M. Khadduri, trans., *The Islamic Law of Nations*, Translator's Introduction, (1966); M. Khadduri, *War and Peace in the Law of Islam* (1962); A. Abel, "'Dar al-Harb' and 'Dar al-Islam'," 2 *Encyclopedia of Islam* 155–157, 170–171 (2d ed., 1960); D.B. Macdonald and A. Abel, "Dar al-Sulh," *id.*, 131; M. Khadduri, "Islam and the Modern Law of Nations," 50 *American Journal of International Law* 358 (1956); A. AbuSulayman, *The Islamic Theory of International Relations* (1987); M. Hamidullah, *Muslim Conduct of State* (5th ed., 1968).

and treaty relationships among themselves.[30] From fifteenth to the end of thirteenth century B.C., monarchies existed in the Mesopotamian region and its neighborhood. In Egypt, they were absorbed by the Middle Empire and, subsequently, by the New Empire. In the Tigris-Euphrates basin, they were first absorbed by the Sumero-Akkadian monarchy and later by the Babylonian monarchy. After this absorption, the principal powers constituted an international community and carried on hegemonies, alliances, vassalages, protectorate relationships, diplomatic relations, delimitation of frontiers, treaty relations, loans, trade, war, settlement of disputes by diplomacy and mediation, and so on.[31] Similar patterns were followed by the maritime monarchies of Crete, Mycenae, and Cyprus, although the system was disrupted by the upheavals of twelfth and eleventh centuries B.C. in the eastern Mediterranean, Hither Asia, and the Nile Delta. In India, tribal kingdoms existed in the Vedic Age (4000 B.C.–1000 B.C.), whose kings conducted warfare and other transactions with each other on behalf of their tribes. The concept of Chakravartin was developed during the Period of the Epic War (1900 B.C. –1000 B.C.), where vassals owed allegiance to Chakravartin emperors.[32] Sixteen republics and many monarchies are reported in the sixth century B.C.[33] In China, Confucius (551 B.C.–479 B.C.) planned the Grand Union of Chinese States.[34]

In the Mediterranean world, the new states of the Hebrews, the Phoenicians, and the Aramaeans revived international transactions in the late eleventh, tenth, and ninth centuries B.C. In the eighth and seventh centuries B.C., this system was replaced by the Assyrian imperial system that stretched from the Mediterranean to the Persian Gulf and from Cappadocia to Upper Egypt. A new balance of power appeared with the collapse of the Assyrian Empire in the sixth century B.C. until, by the end of that century, the Persian Empire became paramount. It, in turn, was replaced by Alexander's Greek Empire in the fourth century B.C. An international community emerged in the Western Mediterranean as the Phoenician colonies were established during the course of two centuries along the coasts of Sicily, Sardinia, the Balearic Islands, Southern Spain, Tripolitania, and Numidia in northern Africa. Carthage was founded in 813 B.C. In the tenth century

30. J. Pirènne, "L'Organisation de la paix dans le Proche-Orient aux 3e et 2e millénaires," 14 *Recueil de la Société Jean Bodin* 200 (1962); J. Pirènne, *Les Grands Courants de l'histoire universelle*, Vol. I, 28 (1959).

31. F. Rey, "Rélations internationales de l'Egypte ancienne du XVe au XIIIe siècle avant Jesus Christ," 48 *Revue générale de droit international public* 35 (1941–1945).

32. B. Prasad, *State in Ancient India*, 28 (1904); E.B. Havell, *Short History of India*, 11 (1924); P.V. Kane, *History of Dharmasastra*, Vol. III, 65 (1930).

33. R. Davids, *Buddhist India*, 23 (1911).

34. Nussbaum, *Concise History*, 4.

B.C., the Ionians migrated from Attica and Euboa to the Cretan and Mycenean centers of the Asiatic coast and founded their own cities. These cities formed a federation in the century following. They imposed a thalassocracy over the Aegean Sea and proceeded to colonize the northeast and the west, completing the process by the end of the sixth century B.C. The Greek world was structured on the basis of city-states (*poleis*), which sometimes formed leagues, such as the Pan-Hellenic League in the fifth century to counter Persian aggressiveness after Persia forged an alliance with Carthage. These city-states concluded treaties of peace, friendship, alliance, territorial boundaries, monetary aid, judicial assistance, control of pirates, arbitration, etc., and practiced customs relating to envoys, hostages, aliens, asylum, passage through another state's land or coastal waters, warships in foreign ports, conduct of war, and so on. Treaties were concluded with non-Greek states as well, such as the Peace of Callias of 449 B.C. between Athens and Persia, giving Athens an exclusive domain in the Aegean Sea and keeping it out of Asia and Egypt, or the treaty of 339 B.C. between Syracuse and Carthage for establishing peaceful relations. The autonomy of the Greek city-states in international matters ended when the Macedonian King Phillip II overpowered them and put them within the Corinthian League. His son, Alexander, expanded the Empire which, after his death, was divided into three powers: the Kingdom of Macedonia, the Kingdom of Egypt, and the Seleucid Kingdom of Asia.

Relations between these three powers remained highly unstable. As a result, several minor states emerged in Asia and a few Greek city-states continued in the Propontis and on the southern coast of the Black Sea. In the middle of the fourth century B.C., Rome emerged powerfully to join this Mediterranean international community and established relations with non-Italic powers as well, such as Carthage. After the First Punic War, it gained pre-eminence in all Italy.

By the end of the third century B.C., five major powers existed in the Mediterranean basin: the Republic of Carthage, the three Hellenistic monarchies that succeeded to the Alexander's empire (the Ptolemies of Egypt, the Seleucids of Asia Minor, and the Antigonids of Macedonia), and the Republic of Rome. Included, further, in this community were the Kingdoms of Pergamum, Bithynia, Pontus, Cappadocia, and Armenia, the Aetolian and Achean Leagues, and a few Greek city-states. This old pan-Mediterranean international community met its end with the emergence of an all-powerful Rome after the deadly struggle between Carthage, Macedonia, and Seleucid Asia on the one hand and Egypt, Rome, the Leagues, and the Greek city-states on the other.

4. *Cultural Pluralism*

As we shall see below, the pattern of political units upon whose basis the modern state came into being emerged in Western Europe from A.D. 1100 to 1600. The pattern eventually hypostatized into the international community whose law our international law is. It has been argued,[35] and correctly, that this international community was culturally pluralistic at its inception in the Middle Ages. At the beginning of the ninth century it included nearly all of Western Europe, much of central Europe, a great deal of southwest Europe, a good part of southwest Asia, and all of northern Africa. There were three segments of this community: one, the three great powers, namely, the Frankish-Longobard Empire of Charlemagne, the Arab dominions of Barcelona, and the Byzantine Empire in Istria; two, the small Christian kingdoms of northern Spain, the Anglo-Saxon kingdoms of Mercia and Wessex which had relations with the Carolingian Empire, the countries of Wend, Czech, Avar, and Serb populations, and the territories occupied by Magyars and the Bulgarians which existed under the pull of the Byzantine Empire; and, three, the Islamic territories under the Imperial authority of Baghdad. The three great powers entered into treaties[36] and practiced customary principles.[37]

This composition changed by the beginning of the tenth century. In the Iberian peninsula on the western Mediterranean, the Emirate of Cordoba broke ties with Baghdad and became a caliphate in its own right, occupying almost the entire peninsula by the end of the tenth century. North of the Pyrenee mountains, the Carolingian Empire was partitioned after the death of Charlemagne by the Treaty of Verdun of 843 and, again, by the Treaty of Meersen of 870, whereunder the Kingdom of France occupied the region allotted to it, to which the Carolingian sovereign succeeded. The Carolingian dynasty was overthrown toward the end of the tenth cen-

---

35. The point is powerfully made by Judge Ago. R. Ago, *supra* note 1.

36. For example, treaties of truce, peace, peaceful settlement of disputes, alliance, neutrality, recognition of title or possession, renunciation of claims, transfer of territories, delimitation of frontiers, allocation of spheres of influence, establishment of family bonds among sovereigns for granting special rights and privileges, subventions, etc. F.L. Ganshoff, "Le Moyen Age," in P. Renouvin, ed., *Histoire des Rélations Internationales*, Vol. I, 22, 36 ff. (1958), cited in R. Ago, *supra* note l (*Italian Yearbook*), 14, n.25. See also, E. Nys, "Le droit des gens dans les rapports des Arabes et des Byzantins," 26 *Revue de droit international et de législation comparée* 461, 485 (1894).

37. For example, customary practices concerning the protection of diplomatic missions and immunities of the envoys, the procedures for adoption and authentication of treaties, the treatment of hostages, the dependency relationships with major powers, and so on. F.L. Ganshoff, *supra* note 36, 49 ff.; R. Ago, *supra* note 36, 15.

tury and Hugh Capet was crowned as the first king of the Capetian dynasty. Thereafter, the country was almost continually involved in fights with Normans and wars with the Kingdom of Germany. Norse invasions occurred upon the Anglo-Saxon kingdoms of England during the ninth century. By the beginning of the eleventh century, England, Denmark, and Norway were united under the Danish Empire of Canute, the Great. After his death, England became independent. Due to the weakness of the royal power, the kingdom of Germany was divided into five duchies of Saxony, Bavaria, Franconia, Swabia, and Lorraine. The monarchy expanded eastward, taking Bohemia, the Pole settlements, the Hungarian settlements, eastern Prussia, and the Austrian Mark, although, by the end of the tenth century, it had to pull back westward due to the Slavic reaction. Bohemia remained under Germany, but Poland and Hungary were founded as independent kingdoms. The kingdom of Italy, the third part of the partitioned Carolingian Empire, was added to the German crown by the Saxon kings and this body of states was christened as the Holy Roman Empire. In southern Italy, the Arabs conquered western and central Sicily about the middle of the ninth century. This produced shifting alliances between the Saracens and the Cities of Gaeta, Naples, and Amalfi against the Byzantines, and between these Cities and the Byzantines. Interventions were made by the Cities of Pisa, Venice, and Rome and by the Longobard duchies of Benevento and Salerno.

The Empire of Constantinople re-established itself over Puglia and Calabria in the second half of the tenth century. It took the Longobard duchies under its protectorate and created special relations with the coastal cities. Venice remained under the Byzantine vassalage. The German Emperors tried but failed to regain their lands from the Byzantine and Arab powers. As a result, the Holy Roman Empire had to coexist with them on the Italian peninsula.

In the latter part of the tenth century and the early part of the eleventh century, the Byzantine Empire took Crete from the Arabs, captured the Balkans from the Russians, and subjugated the Bulgarians. It reached north of the Black Sea into the Crimean peninsula and established relations with the principality of Novgorod-Kiev. It entered into relations with western European states as well as the Muslim principalities. It expanded into Asia Minor in a major way, annexing Anatolia, Armenia, Georgia, Cilicia, and much of Syria. The Caliphate of Baghdad broke up into independent principalities and ceased to exist except as a theocratic authority. Eastern Iran, western Iran, lower Mesopotamia, and Arabia came to be ruled by their own dynasties. The Fatimid Caliphate of Egypt became the major Muslim power of the eastern Mediterranean and extended its control over the remainder of Muslim Syria and over the northern African shore, including Tunisia.

Berber-Islamic dynasties existed along the African coast west of Tunisia, including Fez that bordered on the expanses of the Caliphate of Cordoba.

This culturally pluralistic community engaged in a variety of international relations, including negotiations,[38] exchange of diplomatic missions,[39] immunity of the envoys, right of passage for foreign missions, treaty procedures,[40] treaties on various subjects (including treatment of aliens[41] and regulation of commerce[42]), settlement of permanent colonies of foreign nationals,[43] capitulations,[44] use of reprisals for securing performance of treaty obligations, vassalage and dependence, war, and peaceful settlement of disputes through negotiations, mediation, and arbitration. These relations were entered into not only among Christian powers but between Christian and Muslim powers as well. Therefore, one can "realize the historical error made by those authors who, while rightly placing the beginnings of the present international Community in the Early Middle Ages, have nevertheless seen this Community as limited, at its origin, to the States of the German-Roman Christian world, with the exclusion, therefore, of both the Byzantine world and the Islamic world."[45]

---

38. These negotiations were bilateral as well as multilateral. Often, multilateral conferences were organized on neutral or border territories. However, the Byzantine Emperors and the Caliphs of Cordoba and Cairo preferred the venue at their own courts. F.L. Ganshoff, *supra* note 36, 120.

39. These missions were exchanged between the big powers, namely, the Caliph of Cordoba, the German-Roman Emperor, the *Basileus* of Constantinople, the Fatimid Caliph of Egypt, the King of France, the Prince of Kiev, and the King of Hungary, as well as between the smaller powers, such as the maritime Republics of Italy, the Emirate of Sicily, and the Saracen Kingdom of Tunisia. Even the Pope sent legatees. R. Ago, *supra* note 36, 22.

40. Such as duplicate texts to be delivered by one party to the other.

41. For example, the Treaty of 987 between the Empire of Byzantium and the Fatimid Caliphate. Cited in R. Ago, *supra* note 36, 22.

42. For example, rights and privileges of foreign merchants and foreign ships, duties and taxation on them, duration and conditions of their sojourn, trade restrictions, etc.

43. The first Venetian and Amalfian colonies were established in Constantinople and Alexandria.

44. The agreements of capitulations, so named because they were divided into numbered *capitula* (brief chapters), were in the nature of a unilateral grant by the Muslim ruler whereunder he permitted the citizens of the foreign country to practice their own law and administration within their settlement in the territory of the Muslim ruler. These capitulations were transformed into unequal treaties of commerce in the eighteenth and nineteenth centuries. W. Hyed, *Histoire du commerce du Levant au Moyen Age*, tr. from German by F. Raymond, Vol. I, 386 (1923); G. Depping, *Histoire du commerce entre le Levant et l'Europe*, Vol. II, Ch. X (1830); F.R. Sanborn, *Origins of the Early English Maritime and Commercial Law*, 42 (1930); N. Susa, *The Capitulatory Regime in Turkey* (1933); S.P. Sinha, *New Nations and the Law of Nations*, 19–20, fn. 20 (1967).

45. R. Ago, *supra* note 36, 25–26.

Thus, a universalist argument for the origin and growth of international law can be constructed on the basis that (1) there are antecedents of principles and institutions which are part of this law, (2) there are other systems of law which deal with matters that concern this law, (3) there existed international communities prior to the international community of this law, and (4) there existed a cultural pluralism at the inception of this community.

And, yet, we shall show below that, in spite of these facts, international law is a very particular system invented to govern relations of the modern state system of Europe, the final stage of which system's emergence was marked by the Peace of Westphalia of 1648. International law developed in a very European way in the centuries following this event.

This does not mean that the roots of the modern state do not go back in times prior to the Peace of Westphalia. Quite to the contrary, the pattern of political units upon whose basis the modern state came into being emerged in Western Europe from A.D. 1100 to 1600. That pattern consisted of "the appearance of political units persisting in time and fixed in space, the development of permanent, impersonal institutions, agreement on the need for an authority which can give final judgments, and acceptance of the idea that this authority should receive the basic loyalty of its subject."[46] This state, however, did not derive directly from the states of ancient India, China, Greece, or Rome, mentioned above. Nor did it issue from the Germanic Kingdoms that appeared in the wake of the fall of the Roman Empire, for those kingdoms were based on loyalty to persons, not on concepts and institutions, and they lacked temporal continuity and territorial stability. The later Frankish kingdoms of the eighth and ninth centuries and the Anglo-Saxon kingdoms of the tenth and eleventh centuries were more durable and displayed a more stable territorial connection.[47] But the state was yet to emerge.

Eight factors contributed[48] to its emergence:

One, the spread of Christianity[49] brought the elements of Church organization to prominence, pointing to enduring institutions, administrative techniques, and even a Papal sovereignty, elements which would eventually become attributes of a state.[50]

---

46. J. R. Strayer, *On the Medieval Origins of the Modern State*, 10 (1970).

47. F.L. Granshoff, *Frankish Institutions under Charlemagne*, 71–97 (1968); J.E.A. Jolliffe, *Constitutional History of Medieval England*, 57–74, 107–127 (1937); F.M. Stenton, *Anglo-Saxon England*, 289–296, 485–495, 538 (1943).

48. See, in this connection, Strayer, *Modern State*.

49. It was not until the end of the tenth century that Western Europe became fully Christian under the Church, as distinguished from nominal Christians existing hitherto without any significant contact with the Church.

50. For the theory of Papal sovereignty, see W. Ullman, *The Growth of Papal Government in the Middle Ages*, 275–300, 414–438 (1955).

Two, the gradual stabilization of Europe at the end of a period of migration, invasion, and conquest enabled temporal continuity and territorial stability which, in turn, made permanent institutions possible.[51]

Three, some of the feudal institutions, practices, and incentives, which survived the destruction of the Frankish Empire, paved the way for state-building. These included the separation of the people in political roles from the rest of the community, the artificial creation of political structure (the county, the office of the count, the county court, etc.), the separation of the government from the folkways of the community, the opportunity for political experimentation due to the fact that feudalism made it unnecessary to hold on to non-viable political units, and the incentives on the part of the feudal lord to improve methods of government in order to earn greater income and achieve greater security.

Four, the reorganization of the European political structure in the wake of the Investiture Conflict further assisted in the emergence of the state. The growth in prosperity and population following the year 1000 produced tensions between politics and religion, between a better government and a more Christian way of life.[52] The relationship between the secular and the religious had hitherto been intermingled,[53] but, in the eleventh century, it became

---

51. Until the year 1000, kingdoms fought and destroyed each other almost continually. Thus, the early Germanic kingdoms tore the Western Empire apart and, thereafter, began tearing up each other. The rival kingdoms of Gaul and Germany were conquered by the Franks who, in turn, were torn by civil war and by attacks by the Northmen. The Visigoths were destroyed by a Muslim invasion, the Ostrogoths and the Vandals by the Eastern Empire, and most of the Anglo-Saxon kingdoms by the Danes. Only after the year 1000 did enduring entities establish themselves in the shapes of the Kingdom of England, the Kingdom of the West Franks (later to become France), and the Kingdom of the East Franks (later to become the essential core of Germany).

52. For example, the Peace Movement in Central France in the tenth century was the Church's attempt to organize peasants and non-combatants against the violence of feudal lords and it failed because, firstly, the sophisticated armies of the lords prevailed over the ill-equipped armies of the Peace Associations and, secondly, the people were suspicious about the Church's involvement in the secular matters of war and criminal justice. The Peace Movement came in handy in Normandy when, after the Church accepted a secondary role, the dukes and the counts used it to intervene in local affairs for suppressing violence. See, G. Molinie, *L'organization judiciare, militaire et financière des associations de la paix* (1912); J. Yver, "L'interdiction de la guerre privee en Normandie," 1927 *Travaux de la semaine d'histoire de droit Normand* 307 (1928); H. Pentout, "La treve de Dieu en Normandie," 6 *Memoires de l'Académie de Caen* 1 (1931); L.C. Mackinney, "The People and Public Opinion in the Eleventh Century Peace Movement," 5 *Speculum* 181 (1930).

53. For example, the Kings appointed abbots, bishops, and often Popes. Charlemagne even intervened in doctrinal matters. E. Amman and A. Dumas, *"L'Église au pouvoir des laigues 888–1057*, Book I, Ch. 2, Book II, Chs. 2, 3, Book III, Ch. I (1948); J.W. Thompson, *Feudal Germany*, Chs 1, 2 (1928); Kantorowicz, *King's Two Bodies*, Ch. 3 (1981).

a matter of fundamental disagreement. The Church, most notably Pope Gregory VII (1073–1085), took the position that in order for Europe to be truly Christian, it must have Christian leadership. The lay rulers contested that position. Thus ensued the Investiture Conflict that lasted for nearly five decades. It resulted in a sharp separation of the Church from secular authorities, in its independence at the highest level, and in a considerable measure of its autonomy at lower levels.[54] From the point of view of state-building, this meant the dismissal of the revived Western Empire's claim to universal domination. The other rulers were able to settle their disputes with the Church reformers independently of the Emperor. Each kingdom or principality was recognized as a separate entity and the function of the lay ruler was primarily that of a guarantor of justice.

Five, the fact that the only *raison d'etre* for the lay rulers now was the enforcement of justice meant a strong emphasis on law and the strengthening of the codes of law and judicial institutions.

Six, the growth of educated men during the twelfth century[55] facilitated the creation of permanent impersonal institutions through the device of written records and official documents.

Seven, concentrating attention on the development of internal institutions, such as courts of justice and treasury departments, rather than foreign offices and departments of defense, went hand in hand with the secular ideals of justice and rule of law. The fragmented and weak situation of the European political units forced them to concentrate on internal, rather than foreign, affairs. This resulted in improved estate management, which, in turn, led to central financial institutions.[56] Since profits of justice, such as fines, made significant contribution to the revenues, the administration of justice and the collection of revenue remained closely connected.[57] Soon, however, the courts were seen as a means for asserting and enhancing the

---

54. G. Barraclough, *The Origins of Modern Germany*, 127–155 (1949); N. Cantor, *Church, Kingship, and Lay Investiture in England*, Chs. 1, 5 (1958); A Fliche, *La réforme grégorienne*, 55–64, 76–83 (1946); G. Tellenbach, *Church, State, and Christian Society at the Time of the Investiture Conflict*, 147–161 (1940); Ullman, *Papal Government*, 272–299.

55. D. Knowles, *The Evolution of Medieval Thought*, 71–171 (1962); C.H. Haskins, *Renaissance of the Twelfth Century* (1927); B. Pare, A. Brunet, P. Tremblay, *La renaissance du XIIe siecle* (1933); R. W. Southern, *The Making of the Middle Ages*, Ch. 4 (1987).

56. The reeves and shire-reeves (sheriffs) of England, the *prevots* of France, and the ministerials of Germany centralized the revenues of their territories and turned them over to their kings. L. Delisle, "Des revenues publics en Normandie au XIIe at XIIIe siècle," *Bibliotheque de l'Ecoles des Chartes*, X, XI, XII (1848–1949, 1852), cited in Strayer, *Modern State*, 28, n. 16. See also, F. Lot and R. Fawtier, *Le premier budget de la monarchie française: Le compte général de 1202–1203* (1932); B. Lyon and E.E. Verhulst, *Medieval Finance* (1967).

57. Judges were often used as revenue collectors. See, W. Stubbs, *Select Charters*, 251–257 (1921).

ruler's authority. Their jurisdiction was augmented through various techniques, such as reserving serious crimes for the court of the king or the duke or the count, [58] or bypassing the local lord in civil litigation and approaching the royal or ducal or comital court directly, which intervened to preserve peace.[59] Another technique was assuming appellate jurisdiction.[60] The process of increased jurisdiction of the king's court led to solidifying territory within which the final authority resided in one ruler, rather than being fragmented among many lords.

Eight, the need to coordinate the activities of various departments, such as courts, revenue collectors, prelates and barons, led to the establishment of the office of the chancery, which also handled such matters as communications with other kings and Popes.

These eight factors appeared during the period between 1000 and 1300 and assisted in the emergence of the sovereign state in Western Europe. During the period 1300–1450, the European states suffered a great economic depression, accompanied by its concomitant famine and plague (the Black Death). They waged many wars. Their weakened position revived the power of barons, prelates, and self-governing towns, who used the legal procedures to defeat the government's power. Representative assemblies grew into a means for limiting the power of the government.[61] The bureaucracy could not respond to the new needs. It became preoccupied with perpetuating itself as a semi-autonomous body. The gap between policy-makers and bureaucrats widened.[62] Nevertheless, in spite of these weaknesses, the states survived.

In the period after 1450, the economic and political situation changed for the better. International conflicts became less intense after the end, in 1453, of the Hundred Years' War. The New Monarchs strengthened their governments and by and large enjoyed the support of their subjects. A new and more professional bureaucracy began to crystallize, although its efforts were often not well coordinated and it frequently had conflicts with the old bureaucracy as well as with regional authorities. Even the king was wary of its cutting into his power. It took two or three centuries for the new

58. As in the Pleas of the Crown or Pleas of the Sword. Glanville, *De legibus et Consuetudines Regni Angliae* (1187), ed. by G.E. Woodbine (1932), 42.

59. As in seisin. F. Polock and F.W. Maitland, *History of English Law*, 145–149 (1923).

60. F. Lot and R. Fawtier, *Histoire des institutions française en Moyen Age*, Vol. II, 296–323 (1958).

61. G. Post, *Studies in Medieval Legal Thought*, Chs. 3, 4 (1964); E.B. Fryde, "Parliament and the French War, 1336–1340," in T.A. Sandquist and M.R. Powicke, *Essays in Medieval History Presented to Bertie Wilkinson*, 250–269 (1969); R. Cazelles, *La société politique et la crise de la royaute sous Philippe de Valois*, 224–225, 427–428 (1958).

62. Strayer, *Modern State*, 69–88.

bureaucracy to overcome these obstacles and establish itself. The structure of state varied from being fairly well organized, as in seventeenth-century France, to being very weak, as in seventeenth-century Russia. Eventually, most European states became very much alike in administrative structures. In addition to achieving organization, the state also gained the loyalty of its subjects, not on the basis of divine rights of monarchs but on the basis of nationalism.[63]

The modern state system, whose law international law came to be, emerged, as mentioned above, through the process of emergence of politically sovereign and juridically equal states in Europe that began with the Peace of Basel of 1499 and culminated with the Peace of Westphalia of 1648, at the end of the Thirty Years' War. International law developed in the centuries following this event.

Whatever coincidences this law may have had with its antecedents, whatever likeness it may possess with principles of international conduct followed previously, and whatever sources may be of its ideas, its own body of principles came into existence only through its own law-creation technique of custom as practiced in this particular, European, state system and none other. The practice of states which was consulted in using the twin principles of this technique, namely, *usus diuturnus* (general and concordant practice of states over time) and *opinio juris sive necessitatis* (conviction that they are bound to follow it by law), was none other than that of the European states. Peoples, territories, rulers, and political entities did exist for it in the world outside of Europe and in civilizations other than European. The practice of states that was considered relevant to the creation of international custom in the formative centuries of international law was the practice of independent, sovereign, and juridically equal states which, in the definition of this system, were only the states of Europe. States elsewhere would later emerge, until, in our times, the entire world is comprised within this system,[64] making international law a universal law and enriching its law-creation techniques.[65] But that was to happen only later.

In its origin, therefore, and for the most part of its growth, international law has been centered exclusively in Western civilization. Today, however, it applies to states of all civilizations. An important question now arises as to how does this diversity of civilizations affects this law. We shall explore this question in Chapter 4 but, first, we must see what this diversity is. That we shall do in the next chapter.

---

63. K. Deutsch and W.J. Foltz, eds., *Nation-Building* (1963).

64. S.P. Sinha, *New Nations and the Law of Nations*, 26 (1967).

65. S.P. Sinha, "Identifying a Principle of International Law Today," 1973 *Canadian Yearbook of International Law* 106; S.P. Sinha, *Asylum and International Law*, 244 (1971).

Chapter 3

Civilizational Pluralism

First, we shall demonstrate history's tenacity to civilizational pluralism. The consequent lesson is that it is misleading to proceed as if there exists, or is soon going to exist, one world of a single, pulverized civilization, a single set of values at the most fundamental level.

Next, in Chapter 4, we shall show how different civilizations have developed different principles of life and social organization as a result of their particular history, so that the culture of law (*nomos)*, for example, is fundamental to Western civilization but not to other civilizations. The consequent lesson is that it is misleading to proceed as if the values of that culture are a universal value.

At any given period of time through world history, there have always existed three to four civilizations, which remains true even today in spite of the global approach to many of our contemporary problems. We shall demonstrate this tenacity through various periods of history.

A. From the Beginning to 500 B.C.

By 500,000 B.C., humans and proto-humans appeared on earth. By 30,000 B.C., *homo sapiens* (modern human types) appeared. Grain agriculture began in the Middle East by 7500 B.C. and in Mexico by 7000 B.C. The earliest civilization emerged between 4000 B.C. and 3000 B.C. in the land of Sumer, along the lower stretch of the Tigris and Euphrates rivers.

Sumerian priests planned big projects and the multitudes of men carried them out, making specialization possible. Invented were bronze metallurgy, wheeled vehicles, wheel-spun pottery, sculpture, sailing vessels, the plow, weaving, dyeing, a distinctive art style, the art of measurement, the measurement of time, a systematic doctrine about gods ruling the world, a method of recording spoken words, which later became cuneiform, the engineering of water into irrigation, and, eventually, a military organization that competed with the priestly leadership. Stable empires came into being, even though guarding borders from barbarian invasions and keeping peace among the cities were continual problems. Techniques of bureaucracy, law, and market were established. Akkad began to dominate Sumer by the time of Sargon (2350 B.C.). Sumerian language was replaced shortly after 2000 B.C. by various Semitic languages, primarily the Akkadian.

By the time of Hammurabi (1700 B.C.), Babylon became the capital of Mesopotamia. In Egypt, along the Nile, King Menes united Upper and Lower Egypt about 2850 B.C. While the gods of Sumer were invisible, even though they possessed human-like needs, character, and behavior, the gods of Egypt were personified in the godking or the Pharaoh. The ideals of the Old Kingdom (2600–2200 B.C.) took such a hold in the valley that, even after two hundred years of political division, the expanse of Egypt was united again in 2000 B.C. by the Middle Kingdom. It broke up when the Hyksos, the barbarian invaders from Asia, conquered Egypt. In the Indus valley, civilization flourished in the urban capitals of Harappa and Mohenjodaro from about 2500 B.C. The Aryans, who were barbarian invaders from the north, destroyed these cities completely by about 1500 B.C.

Thus, three centers of civilization existed contemporaneously until 1700 B.C. With the transition to irrigation agriculture from rain-water agriculture, satellite civilizations spread around them in the borderland of Mesopotamia, namely, the Hittites in Asia Minor, the Canaanites in Syria and Palestine, and the Hurrians and the Elamites in the north and east of the Tigris valley. An early sea-borne civilization developed on the Minoan Crete in the Mediterranean which, by 1900 B.C., possessed its famous Palace, its own form of writing, its pottery, its metallurgy, its art style, and so on. Another center of high culture existed on the island of Malta, which was the center of the megalithic religion. The megalithic proto-civilization expanded to the Far West from about 2500 B.C. to about 1700 B.C., at the end of which period invaders from Eurasian steppe reached the Atlantic coast and conquered the megalithic builders. Between 3000 and 1700 B.C., a distinct, loess-cultivating farming population emerged in the middle region of the Yellow River valley. Populous communities arose from Bengal to China that practiced a garden-style cultivation. Hunters that came across the Bering Straits into the Americas spread all over by about 8000 B.C. and, by 7000 B.C., maize cultivation appeared in southwestern United States, central Mexico, and other parts of South America.

Civilizational pluralism is also found during the period 1700 B.C. to 500 B.C.

Thus, chariot warfare, developed in Iran or Azerbaijan shortly after 1700 B.C., enabled the barbarian conquerors to overrun the existing centers of civilization. While their effect was less drastic in the more deeply rooted civilizations of Mesopotamia (invaded by Kassites) and Egypt (invaded by Hyksos), Crete and India were devastated by the Achaean and the Aryan invasions, respectively. The conquerors began to construct their own styles of civilization. Born were the classical Greek and Indian civilizations. The chariot warriors began the Shang dynasty in China where the Hsia, the first rulers of China, had previously governed only the neolithic village communities. In the Middle East, the conquerors set themselves as masters of pre-existing populations. Local leaders soon revolted. In Egypt, a prince of Thebes drove the Hyksos out by about 1570 B.C. In Mesopotamia, the king of Assyria drove the Kassites out in about 1380 B.C. The Hittites emerged as a third great power. These Empires existed as loosely consolidated states. The king's power was restricted by his warrior nobles. His daughters were given in marriage to form alliances. Charioteers commanded the core of the fighting forces. Mercenaries were recruited for the army. Peasants and servitors were oppressed ruthlessly. Akkadian cuneiform was used as the diplomatic language.

The Bronze Age Empires were invaded again by the barbarians, who now possessed iron weapons. The Empires had been weakened by deep divisions between masters and subjects and they toppled before the psychological cohesion of the egalitarian communities of the barbarians, in which every man was free to become a soldier. Free peasantries grew in parts of the Middle East as a result of the more efficient tools made from the new metal of iron. They traded their surplus for artisan products, which promoted economic specialization and exchange of goods. Tribal struggles enabled reappearance of large territorial states. The nomads of the steppes mastered horseback riding between 850 and 700 B.C. and invented the new power of cavalry. Shortly after 700 B.C., the Cimmerians and the Scythians launched cavalry raids against the Middle East. The Assyrian state was overthrown in 612 B.C. by a combined assault of the Babylonians from the south, the Medes of the Iranian highlands in the east, and the Scyths from the north. The Scythians returned to the steppe with their loot, but the Medes and the Babylonians stayed behind and split the Assyrian Empire with Egypt. The victors, in turn, began fighting among themselves, most notable of which struggle was between Babylonia and Egypt for the control of Palestine and Syria. The Persian conqueror Cyrus (ruled 559–530 B.C.) appeared from the eastern highlands and took over nearly all of the Middle East. Cambyses (ruled 530–521 B.C.) and Darius (ruled 521–486 B.C.) extended the Persian Empire over Egypt and India. Although the Persians initially restored local freedoms, religions, laws, and authority of the Egyptian and the Babylonian priests, they were faced with revolts and soon returned to the old ways of the Assyrian administration.

Three major features characterized the Middle Eastern civilization between 1700 and 500 B.C. One, the technique of empire evolved. It included a political order based on bureaucratic administrators, a professional standing army, and a legal definition of the rights and privileges of merchants, which facilitated trade between alien peoples over long distances. Two, alphabetic writing was invented. By about 1000 B.C., Aramaic became the common language used by merchants and officials in interregional affairs. A more simple mode of writing than the hieroglyphic and the cuneiform was experimented with in the region between Sinai and the Taurus mountains. Alphabetic writing appeared in Syria by about 1300 B.C. and soon spread in every direction, although it was repudiated by the scribes of Mesopotamia and Egypt and the sacred writing was still done in hieroglyphics and cuneiform. Three, monotheism rose. Since divine Pharaoh's will was no longer found supreme, nor Sumer remained the gods' principal concern, people sought a new definition of their relationship with the supernatural in which, although traditional polytheism did not vanish entirely, tendencies for monotheism surfaced strongly, their most evocative expressions being the Judaism of Palestine and the Zoroastrianism of Iran.

In India, after the Aryan invaders finished destroying the Indus cities about 1500 B.C., they switched from herding to agriculture and they expanded into new ground with their slash-and-burn style of cultivation. The aristocratic chariot-age was displaced about 900 B.C. with the use of a cheaper metal, iron, that resulted in a spread of weapons and emergence of small states. Iron tools helped clear the jungles of the Ganges valley to grow rice. Permanent villages and towns grew with the diking, digging, and terracing needed to irrigate the paddy fields. In contrast with tribal groupings of the Indus valley, only occasionally united by a suzerain, centralized monarchies flourished in the Ganges valley. They sustained professional administrators and soldiers, supported courtly centers of high artisan skills, promoted inter-regional trade, and resumed, about 800 B.C., sea-borne trade with Mesopotamia. A unique life-style developed after 800 B.C. that centered around caste and ascetic transcendentalism. It is not clear if the caste principle already existed in the Indus valley civilization or if it resulted from the antipathy between the Aryan invaders and the local people. In any case, the principle consisted in the idea of ceremonial purity. That produced a hierarchy of castes, in which higher-caste people limited their association with lower-caste people in order to prevent their contamination by the latter. One was born to a caste and stayed within it. This system enabled people to maintain their particular customs and identities generation after generation, instead of surrendering them to the established or conquering groups. Brahmanical teaching recognized four castes (Brahman, Kshatriya, Vaisya, and Shudra, in the descending order), but hundreds of castes existed in fact. People identified themselves primarily with their caste. Therefore, political administration played a less important role. The tolerant hospitality of this system, under which new groups were easily brought in by merely being assigned to a new caste, without requiring major changes in habits and customs, produced an uniquely Indian approach to religion wherein different doctrines easily blended through logical enunciation. Priests recited texts of the Vedas at sacrifices and ceremonies. As Sanskrit, the language of the Vedas, became less of an everyday language, the emphasis shifted from learning the substance of the texts to memorizing them and pronouncing them exactly. The act of worship, rather than the Aryan gods, became more important in religion. This led to a heightened power of the priests, whose claims were propounded in the texts called Brahmanas, which were supposedly commentaries on the Vedas. These claims were not widely accepted. The Upanishads, another body of oral literature, expressed a different religious theme in which the release of the soul from the cycle of rebirth is achieved not by obeying priests and observing ceremonies but by self-discipline, mediation, and ascetism. The Brahmans, in turn, reconciled the doctrines of Upanishads with their own religion by a remarkable argument that the approach of the Upanishads was quite appropriate for the end of a man's life, after having observed ceremonies and honored the priests in the preceding stages of life. The Brahmanical religion was challenged more seriously by Jainism and Buddhism about 500 B.C. Both made the escape from the cycle of rebirth through personal annihilation as the ultimate goal, with, of course, important differences of detail between the two. Buddha taught a less severe way of cultivation of inner holiness through the eight-fold path of right views, right aspirations, right speech, right conduct, right livelihood, right effort, right mindedness, and right rapture.

In Greece, the earliest invaders of the Aegean region conquered Knossos in Minoan Crete and settled in the island and on the mainland. A raid from Mycenae, the new capital of the Greek mainland, destroyed Knossos. Mycenaean ships raided all over the Mediterranean coast for the next two hundred years. Shortly after 1200 B.C., the Dorians from the north invaded the Mycenaean centers. Mainland refugees fled across the Aegean and settled upon the coast of Asia Minor. There, they invented a set of laws and a system of government that effectively created the earliest Greek city-states, the polis. With growth in population, new Greek settlements sprang amid barbarian populations as far as Sicily and southern Italy and along the northern Aegean and Black Sea coasts. Oil and wine were traded for grain and raw materials. Coined money, invented in the Kingdom of Lydia during the sixth century B.C., further helped trade. The phalanx was invented in the military about 650 B.C., wherein members of a densely-massed infantry formation of the depth of eight ranks ran and charged at once. It was, obviously, absolutely necessary in this to conform very closely to a norm. Soon, this principle was adopted in civilian life. Competitive self-assertion yielded to collective concerns of the polis. The polis dominated all walks of life. Public cult ceremonies of the polis provided the principle of reconciliation between the Olympian gods brought from the north and the ancient goddesses of fertility worshipped prior to the Greek arrival. Requirements of public temples shaped art, such as the cult statues, wall decorations, pediment decorations, and portrayal of gods and heroes. The polis-dominated drama emerged after 500 B.C. In Ionia, the first philosophers explained the phenomenon not in terms of gods but natural law as the ruling force of the universe. Claims of polis clashed with personal holiness, well illustrated by the tumultuous history and the fateful end of the Pythagorean Order.

In China, neolithic settlements, such as of the Black pottery culture, flourished in the mid-region of the Yellow River valley. The Hsia were the first rulers of China. The warlike and aristocratic Shang dynasty ruled between 1523 and 1028 B.C. It supported a small group of skilled artisans, practiced human sacrifice, and worshipped gods that were embodiments of natural features, such as the mountain, the lake, or the river. It was overthrown by the Chou from the western borderlands. The Chou suffered a barbarian attack in 771 B.C. that destroyed their capital in the Wei valley. A year later, the Eastern Chou dynasty was inaugurated at Loang. It was characterized by a continuous struggle for power among the rival princes, especially in the Age of the Warring States (403–221 B.C.), during which the Chinese civilization spread into the coastal regions of North China and to the South in the Yangtze Valley. The Chou conquerors stopped human sacrifice practiced by the Shang. They claimed that Heaven, which was somewhat of an anthropomorphic deity, granted the Son of Heaven (the Emperor) to rule the earth. The Emperor was dutybound to behave in accordance with the prescribed rites in order to achieve a harmony between the earth and the heaven that was necessary to produce human welfare. Nobles held feudal tenure. Their sons were given training in military skills, rites, and the Chinese script, thereby combining skills of the ruler, the warrior, the priest, and the scribe. The later Chou, weak in central authority, were surrounded by powerful kingdoms that developed bureaucratic government in both civil and military spheres. The warring pressures for maximization of state power challenged the older beliefs of observing traditional rites as the source of welfare and these beliefs were repudiated by the Legalists. In the end, however, the more conservative Confucianism came to prevail. Confucius (551–479 B.C.) explained that in the happy days of the early Chou, the Shang, the Hsia, and the legendary Divine Emperors earth and Heaven were situated in a harmonious relationship. This was lacking in a bad world. In such a world, the wise man, he taught, should live by pursuing virtue in the circumstances of his life. The Five Classics of that learning were compiled by his disciples during his lifetime. The Confucianist moderation and self-discipline was balanced by magical charms and rituals of the Taoism. Together, they provided for a complete life.

Thus, by 500 B.C., four major civilizations had established themselves.[1] They present to us four distinct expressions of life-styles and fundamental

1. For prehistory, see R. Ardrey, *African Genesis* (1961); J.G.D. Clark, *World Prehisto-*

values, namely, the Middle Eastern, the Indian, the Greek, and the Chinese. This was accompanied by the development of high barbarism in the steppes, western Europe, southern China, north Africa, and possibly southern India.

---

ry: A New Outline (2d ed., 1969); J.G.D. Clark, *The Stone Age Hunters* (1967); W.E. LeGros Clark, *The Antecedents of Man* (1960); J.M. Coles and E.E. Higgs, *The Archaeology of Early Man* (1969); C.S. Coon, *The Origin of Races* (1962); C. Gabel, *Analysis of Prehistoric Economic Patterns* (1967); W.H. McNeil, *A World History* (2d ed., 1971); M.F.A. Montagu, ed., *Culture and the Evolution of Man* (1962); K.P. Oakley, *Man the Tool-Maker* (4th ed., 1958); S. Tax, ed., *Evolution After Darwin*, 3 vols. (1960). For the ancient Middle East, see W.F. Albright, *The Archaeology of Palestine* (rev. ed., 1960); B. Albrektson, *History and the Gods: An Essay on the Idea of Historical Events as Divine Manifestations in the Ancient Near East and in Israel* (1967); V.G. Childe, *What Happened in History* (1943); G.E. Daniel, *The First Civilizations: The Archaeology of Their Origins* (1968); D. Diringer, *The Alphabet: A Key to the History of Mankind* (3d ed., 1968); J. Finegan, *The Light from the Ancient Past: The Archaeological Background of Judaism and Christianity* (2d ed., 1959); R.J. Forbes, *Metallurgy in Antiquity* (1950); H. Frankfort, *The Birth of Civilization in the Near East* (1951); I.J. Gelb, *A Study of Writing* (rev. ed., 1964); D. Harden, *Culture and Character* (1963); S. Moscati, *The World of Phoenicians* (1968); O. Neugebauer, *The Exact Sciences in Antiquity* (2d ed., 1957); A.T. Olmstead, *A History of Assyria* (1923); A.T. Olmstead, *A History of the Persian Empire* (1948); A.L. Oppenheim, *Ancient Mesopotamia, Portrait of a Dead Civilization*, (3d ed., 1968); T.H Robinson and W.O.E. Oesterley, *History of Israel*, 2 vols. (1932); H.H. Rowley, ed., *The Old Testament and Modern Study* (1951); C. Singer, *et al*, eds., *A History of Technology, I: From Early Times to Fall of Ancient Empires* (1954); W.S. Smith, *Interconnections in the Ancient Near East: A Study of the Relationships Between the Arts of Egypt, the Aegean, and Western Asia* (1965); G. Steindorf and K.C. Steele, *When Egypt Ruled the East* (rev. ed., 1957); J.A. Wilson, *The Burden of Egypt: An Interpretation of Ancient Egyptian Culture* (1951); R.C. Zaehner, *The Dawn and Twilight of Zoroastrianism* (1961). For Europe, see S. Alexiou, N. Olaton, and H. Guanella, *Ancient Crete* (1968); K. Branigan, *The Foundations of Palatial Crete: A Survey of Crete in the Early Bronze Age* (1970); R. Block, *Origins of Rome* (1960); V.G. Childe, *The Dawn of European Civilization* (6th ed., 1958); J.G.D. Clark, *Prehistoric Europe: The Economic Basis* (1952); G.E. Daniels, *The Megalith Builders of Western Europe* (1963); E.R. Dodds, *The Greeks and the Irrational* (1957); J.D. Evans, *Malta* (1959); M.I. Finley, *The World of Odysseus* (1954); C.F.C. Hawkes, *The Prehistoric Foundations of Europe to the Mycenean Age* (1940); R.W. Hutchinson, *Prehistoric Crete* (1962); S. Hood, *The Home of the Heroes: The Aegean Before the Greeks* (1967); T.G.E. Powell, *The Celts* (1958); C.G. Starr, *Origins of Greek Civilization 1100–650 B.C.* (1961); B.H. Warmington, *Carthage* (1960); A.E. Zimmern, *The Greek Commonwealth* (5th ed., 1931). For the Eurasian Steppe, see V.G. Childe, *The Aryans: A Study of Indo-European Origins* (1926); W.M. McGovern, *The Early Empires of Central Asia* (1939); T.T. Rice, *The Scythians* (1957); M. Rostovtzeff, *Iranians and Greeks in South Russia* (1922); G. Verandsky, *Ancient Russia* (1943). For India, see B. Allchin and F.R. Allchin, *The Birth of Indian Civilization: India and Pakistan Before 500 B.C.* (1968); A.L. Basham, *The Wonder That Was India* (1954); J.H. Hutton, *Caste in India: Its Nature, Functions, and Origins* (1946); R.C. Majumdar and A.D. Pulaskar, eds., *History and Culture of the Indian People, I: Vedic Age* (1951); R.E.M. Wheeler, *Early India and Pakistan, to Ashoka* (1959); R.E.M. Wheeler, *The Indus Civilization, The Cambridge History of India,*

B. Between 500 B.C. and A.D. 1500

During the 2000 years between 500 B.C. and A.D.1500, the above four civilizations remained autonomous, despite cross-cultural borrowings and disturbances.

In Greece, Persian-Greek wars began with the rebellion of 499 B.C. in Ionia against the Persian rule that invited the punitive expedition of Darius in 490 B.C. against Athens and Eretria that aided the Ionian rebels. These wars ended in Greek victory over Xerxes in Salamis in 480 B.C. and at Plataea in 479 B.C. Since then and until the outbreak of the Peloponnesian War in 431 B.C., great cultural achievements took place. Poets Aeschylus (526–456 B.C.), Sophocles (495–405 B.C.), and Euripides (484 or 480–406 B.C.) transformed ancient goat songs into the drama of tragedies in which they explored relation of gods to men, of fate to free will, of private to public duty, and so on. Philosophers carried forth reflection. At first, they were resented. Anaxagoras (500?–428 B.C.) was exiled from Athens for arguing that the sun was a red-hot stone, not a god. Later, however, the Sophists were better accepted, since they trained men in the art of rhetoric and the rules of government. Socrates (d. 399 B.C.) employed the Sophists' tools of linguistic and logical analysis for supporting traditional values and finding universal truth behind conventions of the moment. Plato (427–347 B.C.) explored the relation of soul and body, knowledge and opinion, idea and reality, and he speculated upon the nature of the good, the true, and the beautiful. Aristotle (384–322 B.C.) provided a comprehensive philosophy for everything important. Geometry received attention from Plato and other philosophers. Physics was systematized by Aristotle. A school of medicine was founded by Hippocrates of Cos (460–370 B.C.), who believed that disease was caused by an imbalance of fluids ("humors") and not by evil spirits. The discipline of history was created by Herodotus of Halicarnassus (d. 425 B.C.). Thucydides (d. 400 B.C.) wrote a detailed analysis of Athens' downfall. Architecture and sculpture blossomed, led by Phidias (d. 431 B.C.), who made the cult statues of Athena in Athens and of Zeus at Olympia and who planned the sculptural decorations of the Parthenon.

Supplementary Volume (3d ed., 1968). For China, see L. Chi, *The Beginnings of Chinese Civilization* (1957); H.G. Creel, *The Birth of China* (1936); H.G. Creel, *The Origins of Statecraft in China* (1970); H.G. Creel, *Confucius: the Man and the Myth* (1949); J. Gernet, *Ancient China from the Beginnings to the Empire* (1968); L.C. Goodrich, *A Short History of Chinese People* (3d ed., 1959); G.F. Hudson, *Europe and China* (1931); W. Watson, *China: Before the Han Dynasty* (1961); G. Clark, *Space, Time, and Man: A Prehistorian's View* (1992); W.E. LeGros Clark, *The Antecedents of Man* (1963); G. Clark, *Aspects of Prehistory* (1970); G. Clark, *World Prehistory in New Perspective* (1977); N.R.E. Fisher, *Hybris: A Study in the Values of Honour and Shame in Ancient Greece* (1992).

The Peloponnesian war ended in 404 B.C. with Sparta vanquishing Athens. In turn, Sparta was defeated by Thebes in 371 B.C. The semi-barbarian kingdom of Macedonia won the battle of Chaeronia in 338 B.C. and, as a result, the city-states ceased to exercise genuine sovereignty thereafter. Macedonian Alexander (ruled 336–323 B.C.) pushed Hellenism eastward, conquering Persia and invading northwestern India. After nearly half a century of warfare, he was succeeded by the Ptolemies in Egypt, the Seleucids in Asia, and the Antigonids in Macedonia. As a result, massive Greek immigration penetrated the Middle East. Before long, cultural borrowing became mutual. For example, the religions of Mithra and Serapis intermixed with Greek rituals, although the Jews' hatred of Greek customs made the interaction with Judaism difficult. Or, the Greeks took the Babylonian data of astronomical events and constructed a geometric explanation of heavenly motions. Hellenistic astronomy enabled the development of astrology at Alexandria in Egypt.

In Rome, the royal Etruscan rule ended in 509 B.C., replaced by an aristocratic Republic. Rome expanded, albeit with occasional setbacks, finally winning at the battle of Zama in north Africa in 202 B.C., conquering Macedonia and Greece in 146 B.C., Seleucid Asia in 64 B.C., and Egypt in 30 B.C. The Republic was broken down by wars and rivalry and was replaced by a long period of military dictatorship of the Roman Emperors, beginning with Julius Caesar (d. 44 B.C.). The Empire reached out as far as Rhine and Danube (Augustus, crowned 30 B.C., Domitian, reigned A.D. 81–86), Britain (Claudius, reigned A.D. 41–54), Dacia in modern Hungary and Rumania (Trajan, reigned A.D. 98–117), and Mesopotamia (Trajan). Hellenistic culture spread to Italy, Gaul, and Spain, even though the preferred language now was Latin, not Greek. Lucretius (d. 55 B.C.), Cicero (d. 43 B.C.), Virgil (d. 19 B.C.), and others used Latin to express Greek ideas in philosophy, rhetoric, and poetry. Sculptors used Hellenistic skills to create realistic portraiture of Roman taste. Provinces within the Empire were organized into a series of city-states. Even the early Christianity bore a distinctive imprint of Greek life-style.

In Asia, most of the Ganges valley had been united under the kingdom of Magadha by the time Alexander invaded the Indus valley in 327 B.C. Shortly thereafter, Chandragupta Maurya, the King of Magadha (reigned 321–297 B.C.), added the Indus region to his kingdom. His grandson Ashok (reigned 274–236 B.C.) extended the Empire to central and southern India and, eventually, became a Buddhist. There is a speculation among historians that Mauryan sculpture and the Mauryan concept of universal empire may have been influenced by the Persian and Hellenistic models. After Ashok's death, his Empire broke up into warring pieces. New invaders came from central Asia (Greeks, Shakas, Kushans, and Parthians) due to the conflict caused in the steppes by the new unification of China.

In China, the ruler of Ch'in defeated all rivals in 221 B.C. and became the first emperor (Shih Huang-ti) of the Ch'in dynasty. He divided the country into provinces and prefectures, prescribed a uniform script, completed the construction of the Great Wall, and repudiated Confucianism, since its doctrines put limits to his power. A civil war ensued upon his death in 210 B.C., resulting in the establishment of the Han dynasty in 202 B.C.. It ruled until A.D. 220, except for a brief period during A.D. 9–22. The Han Emperors promulgated Confucianism as the official ideology. A new style of heavy armored cavalry stabilized civilized governments in central Asia by keeping the unarmed nomads out. This made an organized trade route possible between China and Rome. A sea route developed from Red Sea to southern India, from India to Malaya across the Bay of Bengal, and, through a short portage across the isthmus of Kra, all the way to China.

In spite of trade and travel, no fundamental modifications occurred in any of these civilizations and they continued to follow their own particular patterns. Thus, in China, the rival schools of learning that had risen to dispute Confucianism and Taoism were absorbed into Confucianism after the establishment of the Han dynasty. In India, development continued toward the linkage of priestcraft, courtly elegance, and ascetic discipline, which achieved a classical expression in the Gupta period ((A.D. 320–535). The Gupta kings shared traditional Indian values and patronized Hinduism, whose doctrines about various caste duties were compiled in law books called Dharma Shastras. Culture blossomed as a result of patronization by royal courts and temples. A school system revised the Sanskrit language and expanded knowledge. The Decimal was invented about A.D. 270. So was the numerical system of notation, known to the West as Arabic numerals. Panini wrote his classical grammar. The epics of Mahabharata and Ramayana achieved their final form. Sanskrit drama flourished. Kalidas (A.D. 400–455), the great master of Sanskrit literature, lived in this period. Buddhist art and sculpture attained their own heights. In Iran, the Seleucids were replaced by the Parthians in 171 B.C. as overlords of Iran and Mesopotamia, but that did not bring about any fundamental cultural change. A purely Iranian life-style persisted, finding its political expression in the establishment of the Sassanian Empire in A.D. 226.

The inter-civilizational communication promoted some cross-fertilization of art styles but, more profoundly, it provided a climate for the development of new cosmopolitan religions, namely, Hinduism in southern India where Aryan, Dravidian, and Greco-Roman influences converged, the Mahayan Buddhism in northwestern India where Indian, Greek, and steppe influences converged, and Christianity in the Greek-speaking regions of the Roman Empire. Indian civilization spread eagerly in southeast Asia, as in

Burma, Sumatra, Java, Malaya, Siam, and Viet Nam, and selectively among the Chinese, Persian, and Greco-Roman populations north of the mountains. North of the mountains, Buddhism spread in a massive way in China, Korea, and Japan between A.D. 200 and 600. Iranian and Roman parts of the civilized world were also influenced by the Indian civilization. Witness, for example, the adoption by the Christian ascetics of details of devotions developed by the Indian sages, or the adoption by the early Egyptian and Syrian monks of the Indian ascetic disciplines and withdrawal from the world. Ideas of Upanishads were adopted by philosopher Plotinus (d. A.D. 270) in his new themes, especially in his mystical emphasis.

The Chinese, the Romans, and the Persians suffered disturbances from the nomads of the Eurasian steppe, but they reestablished their respective unity in the sixth century. Thus, in China, the Juan-juan confederacy, which was formed in outer Mongolia about A.D. 350 and exerted its power from Manchuria to Lake Balkhash, was destroyed by the Chinese in 552 A.D. with assistance from the Turks. The new ruling family broke up in a dynastic feud in A.D. 572 and the Turkish confederacy was divided between the east and the west. China was reunited by the Sui dynasty in A.D. 589, succeeded by the T'ang dynasty (A.D. 618–907). As the Juan-juan swept westward along the steppes, peoples fled from their homes. One such people, the Huns, appeared in southern Russia in A.D. 372 and defeated the ruling Ostrogoths there. The neighboring Visigoths fled to the Roman frontiers, sacked the city of Rome in A.D. 410, and set up a kingdom in Spain that lasted until A.D. 711. The Huns established themselves in the Hungarian plain. The Hunnic confederacy broke up with the death of Attila in A.D. 453, whereupon some of the subjugated Germanic peoples fled south and west to establish Germanic kingdoms of western Europe, bringing Goths, Burgundians, Vandals, Franks, Anglo-Saxons, and other Germanic people to the Roman soil between A.D. 378 and 450. During the period A.D. 235–84, the Romans suffered the first prolonged crisis of civil war and invasion. Emperor Constantine (ruled A.D. 306–337) established a new capital at Byzantium, renaming it Constantinople, and made Christianity the favored religion of the state. Emperor Theodosius (d. A.D. 395) made Rome officially Christian by prohibiting all rival faiths. Emperor Justinian (A.D. 527–565) attempted to reunite the Roman Empire by launching campaigns against German kings and succeeded in winning North Africa, Italy, and parts of Spain. The Epthalites erupted in eastern Iran just about the time when the Huns appeared in western Europe. From there they invaded northwest India. However, civil war disintegrated their power in India by A.D. 549 and they were destroyed in the north of the mountains by A.D. 554. The Persian kings of the Sassanian dynasty overthrew the Epthalites in A.D. 554. Furthermore, they succeeded in pushing the frontier of the Persian Empire to the Oxus River, thereby reuniting all of Iran. The Sassanians ruled Persia and Mesopotamia until A.D. 651. Their state structure was based on baronage, sustained by an appeal to the greatness of the Persian Empire and by the Zoroastrian faith. The divergent traditions of Zoroastrianism were standardized in the scripture Avesta. Occasionally, other religious movements surfaced, such as that of Prophet Mari (A.D. 215–273) and, three hundred years later, of Prophet Mazdak. The Romans adopted some of the attributes from the Persians, such as the crown and the scepter (Diocletian, reigned A.D. 284–305) as symbols of royalty, or the technique of heavily-armed cavalry, but they preserved their own social structure. Justinian (A.D. 527–565) codified their own principles and practices of administration. The Byzantines actively differentiated themselves from the Persians, the differences being further underscored by the development of Christianity, although the Christendom itself was deeply divided between the Greek, the Latin, the Syriac, and the Coptic Churches.

Prophet Mohammed (d. 632) preached Islam and unified Arabia by both diplomacy and war. Subsequent Arab conquests brought a large stretch of territory under the Muslim rule. It included the entire ancient Middle East (except for Asia Minor), the desert region of lower Indus valley (by A.D. 715), North Africa, and Spain (A.D. 711–715). Defeats began after A.D. 715. A Turkish force pushed the Muslims out of eastern Iran by 715. The city of Byzantium suffered a siege in 717–718. In 732, the Franks defeated a Muslim party at the Battle of Tours in central Gaul. From Mohammed, the leadership passed to Abu Bakr (d. 634), and then to Omar (caliph 634–644). The Ommayad family succeeded to it after Omar's assassination in 644 and made Damascus (Syria) the capital of its caliphate. They were overthrown by the Abbasids in 750, who made their capital in Baghdad in Mesopotamia. They abandoned the previous practice of combining the religious authority with military-political leadership and transferred religious jurisdiction to experts in Islam, collectively known as Ulema. Much of government concerning private persons was transferred to the religious experts. While this resulted in far-ranging autonomy to other religious communities as well, namely, the Christians and the Jews, it also produced a doctrinal intolerance that required acceptance of Islam in its entirety or not at all. The Muslims themselves were divided into the Shi'a and the Sunni sects. In spite of Islam's pious injunctions, a courtly style of life developed among the Arab fighting men. And in spite of the self-evident truth that all that man needed to know was in Koran and traditions, the knowledge of astronomy and medicine was developed. Greek and Indian works of science and philosophy were translated into Arabic. The decimal notation was borrowed from the Indians to produce algebra. Strides were made in alchemy and mathematical optics.

Pressures from the spread of Islam were felt in China, India, and Europe. China felt it the least. The Sui dynasty was succeeded by the T'ang dynasty (618–907), which was followed by the Sung dynasty (960–1279). They did not suffer any major military challenge from the Muslims, losing only some unimportant oases to them in the Battle of Talas in 751. Although central power was disrupted after 755 and the barbarian masters took over direct administration of north China, trade continued to flourish, painting became the principal art, and poetry assumed its classical form, as seen in the works of Li Po (705–762) and Tu Tu (712–770). Buddhism was systematically persecuted after 845. By 1000, Neo-Confucianism was already under way, representing a philosophically sophisticated reinterpretation of the Classics.

India was affected more. It lost Sindh to the Muslims by 715 and, soon, the seaways of the Indian Ocean. Unable to repel them by force, the Hindus attempted to conserve their culture by erecting a philosophic system, as in the system of Shankara (788–850), which rebutted the Muslim reproaches to Hindu idolatry by explaining how the rites of the Hindus were in fact an aid to a pure and transcendental monism. Tantrism was elaborated in an attempt to defend everything that was own against that which was alien. Social and economic activity continued at a high level. The society even expanded in the border regions of Bengal and Kashmir.

However, Europe responded to Islam with a military, rather than intellectual, fight. In the process, it transformed its own fundamental institutions. Europe confronted invasions from the barbarians as well as the Muslims. Shortly after Justinian's death, the Avars from Russia drove into the Hungarian plains. The Muslims besieged Constantinople in 717–718. Emperor Leo III, the Isaurian (717–741) reorganized the Byzantine power and kept the Arabs at check at about the Taurus mountains, but he and his successors failed to prevent a massive Slavic infiltration of the northern and the central regions of the Balkan peninsula. After 568, the German tribe of Lombards displaced the Byzantines in Italy. The Bulgarian Empire consolidated itself on the lower Danube after 679. The Carolingian Empire did the same in the far west after 687. The Franks, too, followed a somewhat similar development. Their Charlemagne was ultimately crowned by the Pope as the Emperor of Romans in 800. Friction between the Byzantines and the Franks rallied around the role of images in Christian worship. In the end, in 843, the Byzantine Emperors restored icons to the churches. Such a divided Christendom faced another barbarian invasion from the Magyars (or, the Hungarians), who crossed the Carpathian passes in 896. Shortly thereafter, the Muslim states of north Africa brought ruination to the Byzantine naval power. However, about 1000, Italian shipping asserted itself in the Mediterranean. Also, Russia converted to Christianity in 989, Hungary in 1000, and Denmark, Sweden, and Norway between 831 and 1000. In the east, the Byzantine Empire developed a feudal system. In the west, Charlemagne's Empire developed a system of knights with military and political leadership in order to defend the Empire from the Vikings and the Magyars. This system of knighthood, accompanied by the spread of the mouldboard agriculture and the growth of an aggressive mercantile population, produced for the Far West a unique set of local institutions. However, it suffered setbacks in art, literature, and learning, lending truth to the characterization of this period as the Dark Age.

After about 900, Turkish mercenaries and tribesmen dominated the political life of Islam. They extended the Muslim frontiers. They penetrated deep into India, as far south as Vijayanagar, which capitulated in 1565. They advanced against the Byzantines until they conquered Constantinople in 1453. This Turkish offensive produced the Ottoman Empire. Sufism, drawing upon the mysticism of Indian origin, grew to bring important changes in the Islamic culture, attempting to merge the rationalist tradition with the sacred tradition. It was disseminated through Persian poetry of such poets as Rumi (d. 1273), Sa'di (d. 1291), and Hafiz (d. 1390). It was accompanied by a distinctive Muslim style of painting and architecture. The Muslim conquest of India produced a version of Islam that was quite distinct from that of the Middle East. Although Hindu temples were sacked and the Sanskrit language was discarded, religious innovators such as Kabir (d. 1518) attempted to synthesize Hinduism and Islam. However, since Sufi mystics provided no more vivid vision of God than the Hindus did, Islam's attraction was limited only to the fringes of the Indian society.

In China, important socio-economic changes took place during the brief Mongol period (early 13th century), but the old Confucian forms re-established themselves and continued to flourish. The existing social order continued to be strengthened with the new inventions of printing (756), gunpowder (about 1000), and magnetic compass (early 12th century).

Two new civilizations arose during 1000–1500. On the eastern end of the civilized world, Japan arose. On the western end adjacent to Byzantium, Western Europe arose. Although the early courtly culture of Japan had imported the anti-militaristic culture from the T'ang China, the border barons developed a warrior code of manners and ideals and expanded the Japanese society to the north. In time, this code of the Samurai became binding. A Japanese feudalism developed. By 1300, townsmen and sailors began asserting their prominence. When, in 1430's, the Chinese withdrew from the seas, the Japanese took over the southwest Pacific. With the rise of towns, a new social milieu surfaced which produced a high culture, a unique style of painting, and such refinement of Samurai manners as the tea ceremony. Zen Buddhism, though initially imported from China, was integrated with the Samurai ideal. The Pure Land Buddhism began to develop from about 1200. While the cult of the Sun Goddess had previously been assimilated to Chinese patterns of ancestor worship, after 1400 it was remodeled into the Shinto cult and acquired a metaphysical theology that compared with Buddhist doctrines. On the western end, Latin Christendom expanded in Western Europe by the year 1000 across every frontier. This came about as a result of various factors, namely, the growth of a numerous knightly class, the development of a manorial agriculture based upon the mouldboard plow, the emergence of an enterprising set of townspeople, and the growth of a Church with an elaborate theological doctrine. Norway and Iceland were converted in 1000. The Anglo-Norman knights invaded Wales and Ireland in 1171. The German knights conquered a broad territorial belt across the Elbe River. Others conquered Prussia, Livonia (modern Latvia), and Estonia, although they failed (1241–1244) to conquer Russia. Poland and Hungary held their ground against the German pressure only by copying the German armament made with the artisan and mercantile services of the imported German and Jewish townsmen. Southern Italy and Sicily succumbed to the Norman conquest (1059–1091). The Muslims were gradually pushed out of Spain and Portugal until, finally, Moorish Granada fell in 1492.

The medieval Europe consolidated itself economically, politically, and culturally. Economically, interregional trade was made possible in articles of wide consumption (such as, woolen cloth, grain, herring, and iron), and not merely in fine articles for the rich, due to the cheap water transport facilities available to very large parts of Europe. Politically, the Emperor (*i.e.*, the ruler of Germany who derived his title from Charlemagne's usurpation) first tried to keep local sovereignties under control. However, in 1054, the Papacy began to strip him of his right to appoint Bishops in Germany and parts of Italy. By 1254, the Imperial power finally collapsed and the Papacy claimed the universal government of Latin Christendom. However, soon the Papal authority began to be challenged. It collided against the Kingdoms of France and England. In Germany, Rudolf of Hapsburg was elected Emperor in 1273. The Papal authority suffered further setbacks with the establishment of rival Popes in Avignon and Rome (1378–1417), after Pope Clement V and his successors moved their residence to Avignon (1307). Representative and parliamentary government grew as a distinctive political institution, since money matters became a major subject of consultation between the prince and his followers. Culturally, until about 1200, the Arabic and Byzantine traditions were creatively received and Roman law was dutifully studied for resolving confusions of the local law. Monumental Romanesque architecture was developed. The tensions between faith and rational faculties between 1200 and 1300 gave a further upthrust to culture. St. Thomas Aquinas (d. 1274) and St. Albert the Great (d. 1280) attempted to reconcile faith and reason in theology. Christian knighthood was counterpoised with a romantic ideal, heresy with the piety of Franciscan and Dominican friars. Literature expressed diverse thought and feelings in Latin as well as in vernaculars, the most important literary figure of the time being the Florentine exile Dante (d. 1321). Gothic architectural style became decoratively complicated. However, this medieval cultural synthesis waned after 1300 and a new art style was born in the Italian towns, where the Renaissance style deliberately modeled itself on ancient example. Since ancient examples were not available that much in painting, a more original style came to fore in that field. The region north of the Alps, however, remained culturally static due to the Hundred Years' War (1337–1453) between France and England.

Thus, civilizational pluralism existed during this period (500 B.C.–A.D. 1500) as well.[2]

C. *Between 1500 and 1850*

Civilizational pluralism continued to characterize the world between

2. For Europe, see J.B. Bury, *History of Greece to the Death of Alexander the Great* (3d ed., 1951); A.R. Burn, *Persia and the Greeks: The Defense of the West* (1962); M. Bloch, *Feudal Society* (1961); G. Barraclough, *The Origins of Modern Germany* (1947); G. Barraclough, *The Medieval Papacy* (1968); M. Cary, *History of Rome Down to the Reign of Constantine the Great* (2d ed., 1954); E. Cassirer, *et al.*, eds. *The Renaissance Philosophy of Man* (1948); C. Dawson, *The Making of Europe* (1932); T. Frank, *et al.*, *An Economic Survey of Ancient Rome*, 5 vols (1933–1940); W.G.G. Forrest, *The Emergence of Greek Democracy* (1966); G.T. Griffith, ed., *Alexander the Great: The Main Problems* (1966); F.M. Heichelheim, *Ancient Economic History*, 3 vols. (1958); C.H. Haskins, *The Normans in European History* (1915); C.H. Haskins, *The Renaissance of the Twelfth Century* (1927); J. Huizinga, *The Waning of the Middle Ages* (1924); A.H.M. Jones, *The Greek City: From Alexander to Justinian* (1940); D. Knowles, *The Evolution of Medieval Thought* (1962); P.O. Kristeller, *Renaissance Thought: The Classic, Scholastic, and Humanistic Strains*, 2 vols. (rev. ed., 1961); R.S. Lopez, *The Birth of Europe* (1967); McNeil, *World History*; R.F. Morrison, *Tradition and Authority in the Western Church, 300–1140* (1969); C.H. McIlwain, *The Growth of Political Thought in the West* (1932); H. Pirenne, *Economic and Social History of Medieval Europe* (1937); S. Runciman, *A History of the Crusades*, 3 vols. (1951–1954); P.H. Sawyer, *The Age of the Vikings* (1962); C. Stephenson, *Medieval Feudalism* (1942); W.W. Tarn and G.T. Griffith, *Hellenistic Civilization* (3d ed., 1952); H. Trevor-Roper, *The Rise of Christian Europe* (1965). For eastern Europe, see N.H. Baynes and H. St. L.B. Moss, eds., *Byzantium* (1961); J.H. Billington, *The Icon and the Axe, An Interpretative History of Russian Culture* (1966); S. Runainan, *Byzantine Civilization* (1933); N.P. Kondakov, *The Russian Icon* (1927). For Islam see, T.W. Arnold, *The Caliphate* (1924); T.W. Arnold, *The Preaching of Islam* (2d ed., 1913); A.J. Arberry, *Sufism: An Account of the Mystic of Islam* (1950); A. Christensen, *L'Iran sous les Sassanides* (2d ed., 1944); N.C. Debevoise,

1500 and 1850.

During 1500–1648, Europe was partitioned into monarchical states due to the violent deeds associated with Reformation, although that partition was also inspired by the Italian political practices north of the Alps. Federalism developed in the Netherlands following the Dutch revolt against Spain (1568–1609). Parliamentarianism grew in England following the English civil wars (1642–1648). Although Charles V of Hapsburg was crowned as the Holy Roman Emperor in 1519, the sovereignty of the local German princes was acknowledged in the Treaty of Westphalia of 1648. However, the Papacy retained its power in Europe. Spain retained most of its Empire in Europe and in the Americas. The Austrian branch of the Hapsburg family consolidated its control in Austria, Bohemia, and Hungary. Europe discovered its capacity to mobilize its resources for political and economic purposes. It traded with and colonized far parts of the world. Following navigational improvements made by Prince Henry of Portugal (d. 1460), historical voyages were undertaken by Christopher Columbus in 1492, Vasco da Gama in 1498, and Ferdinand Magellan in 1519–1522. The Portuguese established themselves in Goa (1510), Malacca (1511), and Macao (1557). The Spanish established themselves in Mexico (1519–1521), Peru

---

A Political History of Parthia (1938); R.N. Frye, *Heritage of Persia* (1963); H.A.R. Gibb, *Mohammedanism: An Historical Survey* (2d ed., 1953); R. Ghirshman, *Iran from the Earliest Times to the Islamic Conquest* (1961); G.E. von Grunebaum, *Medieval Islam: A Study of Cultural Orientation* (2d ed., 1955); B. Lewis, *The Arabs in History* (1950). For Central Asia and the Steppes, see R. Grousset, *The Empire of the Steppes* (1970); W.M. McGovern, *The Early Empires of Central Asia* (1939); A.K. Narain, *The Indo-Greeks* (1957); T.T. Rice, *The Scythians* (1957); M.I. Rostovtzeff, *Iranian and Greeks in South Russia* (1922); W.E. Tarn, *The Greeks in Bactria and India* (2d ed., 1951). For India, see Basham, *Wonder*; K.A.N. Sastri, *A History of South India from Prehistoric Times to the Fall of Vijayanagar* (3d ed., 1966); E.H. Warmington, *Commerce Between the Roman Empire and India* (1928). For southeast Asia, see J.F. Cady, *Southeast Asia: Its Historical Development* (1964); D.G.E. Hall, *A History of Southeast Asia* (1955); H.G.Q. Wales, *The Making of Greater India: A Study in Southeast Asian Culture Change* (1950). For China and Japan, see L.C. Goodrich, *A Short History of the Chinese People* (3d ed., 1959); W. Eberhard, *Conquerors and Rulers: Social Forces in Medieval China* (1952); G.B. Sanson, *Japan: A Short Cultural History* (rev. ed., 1962); J.K. Shryock, *Origin and Development of the State Cult of Confucius* (1932); F. Wright, *Buddhism in Chinese History* (1959). For the Americas, see H.E. Driver, ed., *The Americas on the Eve of Discovery* (1964); G.R. Wiley, *New World Prehistory*, Smithsonian Institute on Report for 1960 (1961); G.M. Bongard-Levin, *Ancient Indian Civilization* (1985); J. Coleman, *Ancient and Medieval Memories: Studies in the Reconstruction of the Past* (1992); A.L. Dellapiccola, ed., *Vijayanagara: City and Empire* (1985); T.B. Jones, *From the Tigris to the Tiber: An Introduction to Ancient History* (4th ed., 1989); M. Melko, *Peace in the Ancient World* (1981); N.H.H. Sitwell, *The World the Romans Knew* (1984); C.G. Starr, *A History of the Ancient World* (4th ed., 1991); T. Yuge and M. Doi, eds., *Forms of Control and Subordination in Antiquity* (1988).

(1531–1535), and the Philippines via Mexico (1571). The East India Companies of the Dutch and the English were created in 1600 and 1601. The English came to India. The Dutch pushed the Portuguese out of Malacca and Ceylon and established themselves in Java. In the Americas, English colonies were established in Virginia (1607) and Massachusetts (1620), a Dutch colony in New York (1626), and a French colony in Quebec (1608). By 1640 or so, the English, the French, and, to a lesser degree, the Dutch took over the rich Caribbean trade from the Portuguese and the Spaniards.

In Europe, the Renaissance drew from the Greco-Roman past and moved thought and sensibility toward secularism, whereunder beauty was created by human skill and truth was discovered by exercise of human faculties (Leonardo da Vinci, d. 1519; Niccolo Machiavelli, d. 1527). The Reformation drew its inspiration from the Judeo-Christian traditions and reasserted religious concerns which produced Protestantism (Martin Luther, d. 1546; John Calvin, 1509–1564), along with its many sects and subsects. Others devoted themselves to science, such as the mathematically sophisticated physics and astronomy (Galileo Galilei, 1564–1642), a mathematically rigorous philosophy (Rene Descartes, d. 1650), a new medicine based upon exact observation of anatomy (Paracelsus, d. 1541, Andreas Vesalius, d. 1564, William Harvey, d. 1657), a mathematical formula for elliptical motions of planets (Johannes Keppler, d. 1630), and new instruments of observation and experimentation, such as the telescope (1608), the microscope (1590), the pendulum clock (1656), the thermometer (1654), and the barometer (1643). Cultural pluralism asserted itself in intellectual matters, literature, painting, and, to a lesser extent, architecture.

Russia became an outlier of Western European civilization. The Khans of the Golden Horde continued their suzerainty over Russia until 1480, when Ivan III renounced his allegiance to them and declared himself the Tsar. Ivan IV, the Terrible, conquered the Khan capital of Kazan in 1552 and, four years later, conquered Astrakhan in the lower Volga. The Russians crossed the Urals, overthrew the Khanate of Sibir, and established themselves along the middle reaches of the Ob River. In 1638, the Russian explorers finally reached Okhotsk on the Pacific. Since the Tatars were no longer a threat, the Russians rapidly settled themselves in the new lands along the Volga, in the Ukraine, along the lower Don, and in the Ural regions. However, the centralized regime of autocratic Moscow had to be maintained in order to meet the military threat from the West, *i,e,,* the Livonian War with Sweden (1557–1582) and the Polish-Lithuanian offensive during the Time of Troubles (1604–1613). European religions came to the Russians as a result of their controversy with the Roman Catholic Jesuits in the wake of the Russian assertion of their Orthodox Church being the last stronghold of true Christianity after Constantinople fell to the Turks in

1453. In architecture, new heights were achieved when stone-masonry imported from Italy interacted with the wooden church architecture of the older Russian style. Painters used Italian and Byzantine skills to their icon paintings.

Likewise, the Americas, too, became an outlier of Western European civilization. The Amerindian culture collapsed swiftly and the Spaniards replaced the priests and warriors of the Aztecs and the Incas. Mexico and Peru were Christianized. Spanish legal forms were adopted to govern personal relations in cities and towns. European architecture was copied. Native depopulation from disease meant collapse of the old subsistence agriculture, and that provided the Spanish settlers with badly needed labor. The Indians died away rapidly on the Caribbean and the Brazilian coasts. As a result, Negro slavery became quite important. The Spanish exploitation was tempered by the missionary concern for converts but no such inhibitions existed for the Portuguese, English, French, and the Dutch, whose economies were based on slavery. The French did make some missionary effort in Canada which, ironically, brought smallpox and other diseases to the missions. Eventually, Amerindian societies were destroyed along the coast of North America and in Brazil.

Islam expanded spectacularly during 1500–1700. The last major Hindu state of Vijayanagar in southern India fell to the Mughals of the north in 1565. Practically all of peninsular India came under the Mughal rule of Emperor Aurangzeb (1658–1707). Hindu Java in southeast Asia was overthrown by a coalition of Muslim coastal states in 1513–1526. Islam spread as far as Mindanao (the Philippines) and Borneo (Indonesia). In West Africa, Bornu, Morocco, Timbuctoo, and Sokoto emerged as Muslim states. The Turks conquered most of Hungary by 1543. Until 1683, they enjoyed dominance in their border wars with Poland and Austria.

The Ottomans lost most of Hungary to Austria in a long war with it in 1683–1699. The Russians overthrew the Muslim Khanates of Kazan, Astrakhan, and Sibir. The Tibetan Lamaism displaced Islam between 1550 and 1630 in central Asia around the Ili River. However, the Turks prevailed against the Spanish and the Portuguese in the Mediterranean and in the Indian Ocean. In 1502, the Shi'a leader Ismail Safavi proclaimed himself Shah in Tabriz and proceeded to conquer Baghdad and Bokhara. He was defeated by the Ottomans at Chaldiron in 1514 but, since the Ottoman janissaries refused to move further on, a truce was concluded in 1638 between the Safavids and the Ottomans.

The Shi'a-Sunni split had interesting consequences for the Mughals of India. While the first Mughal Emperor Babur (d. 1530) and his son Humayun (ruled 1530–1556) embraced the Shi'a faith in order to secure aid from the Shah, a stronger Akbar (ruled 1556–1605) renounced it for the Sunni faith.

He even claimed independent religious authority. Since Hinduism no longer enjoyed state support, it took to the streets and was revived most ardently by saints (Chaitanya, d. 1527) and poets (Sur Das, d. 1563, Tulsi Das, d. 1623). It remained the religion of the overwhelming majority of the Indians. Buddhism resisted Islam in Ceylon, Burma, and Siam.

In China, the Ming dynasty continued to rule until the Manchus came to assist Peking in suppressing a rebellion in 1644 and ended up replacing the Ming dynasty itself by their own Ch'ing dynasty. In 1689, China and Russia concluded the Treaty of Nerchinsk which created a no-man's land between the two in the main part of the steppe in outer Mongolia and central Asia. China launched its campaign against the Mongols and the Kalmuks of the buffer zone when they entered into religious and diplomatic relations with Tibet, and the Kalmuk confederacy succumbed in 1757. During this rather peaceful period, population grew rapidly, trade with European merchants increased, and commercial activity expanded. Cultural attitudes became highly conservative. Intellectuals examined the Classics to re-establish old Confucian texts and discouraged bold reinterpretations of the New-Confucianist kind.

Japan suffered a civil war until Hideyoshi (d. 1598) united the country. He even attacked Korea twice, though unsuccessfully. After his death, power went to Ieyasu of the Tokugawa after a battle. The Tokugawa shoguns used two means to secure themselves. First, they regulated and eventually forbade sea-faring, which eliminated a haven for the defeated samurai clan leaders. Second, they banned missionaries and eventually destroyed the Christian community, crushing the Christian revolt of 1637 in Kyushu. Then they ruled for more than two hundred years. Their government remained rigid and austere, but the country's economic and cultural life changed significantly due to the decline of the samurai and the emergence of an active market economy.

During the period 1648–1789, Western European powers fought limited wars, such as the campaigns of Louis XIV (reigned 1643–1715) to win the Rhine and Pyrenees, the wars between England and France over North America and India, and the Wars of Spanish Succession (1701–1714). Power realigned more drastically in Eastern Europe. Austria and the Brandenburg-Prussia competed with Russia for the Swedish and Polish territories (1648–1721) and swallowed entire Poland among the three of them (1772–1795). In England, parliamentarianism acquired its own definition; it began calling itself Great Britain when Scotland and Ireland united with it in 1707. In Prussia, Frederick William, the Great Elector (ruled 1640–1688), consolidated the kingdoms of Prussia. The territory was much enlarged by Frederick II, the Great (reigned 1740–1786).

The European economy grew rapidly with improvements in mathematical measurement and invention of the steam engine. The steam engine was invented by Thomas Newcomen in 1712 and improved by James Watt in 1769. Geometry and algebra merged to produce analytic geometry which, in turn, produced calculus that refined the power of mathematical reasoning and advanced the study of physics. The geometrician's deductive reasoning from axioms was applied to questions of human condition, as by Rene Descartes (d. 1650), Baruch Spinoza (d. 1677), Thomas Hobbes (d. 1679), and Gottfried Wilhelm Leibnitz (d. 1716). Isaac Newton (d. 1717) proposed a mystic force called gravitation to explain the behavior of moving bodies operating according to a definitive mathematical formula, whereunder gravitation diminished between any two bodies with the square of the distance. In biology, a great deal of information was collected. Carl Linnaeus (d. 1778) invented a system of classifying plants which is used even today. Physiocrats in France and Adam Smith (d. 1790) in Scotland tried to deduce the effect of individual's natural behavior on trade and industry if that behavior were not interfered with by governments. A new theory of social contract was developed for political legitimacy, wherein people in a state were assumed to have made an agreement as to the forms and powers of government. This theory was used to justify both the sovereign's absolute power (Thomas Hobbes) and the people's right to rebellion (John Locke, d. 1704, Jean-Jacques Rousseau, d. 1778). Techniques of historiography were perfected (Jean Mabillion, d. 1707) and more accurate histories were written (Edward Gibbon, 1737–1794, Voltaire, d. 1778, David Hume, d.1776). Philosophy turned empirical (John Locke, David Hume, Immanuel Kant, d. 1804). Music blossomed anew (Johann Sabastian Bach, d. 1750, Wolfgang Amadeus Mozart, d. 1791). However, classicism prevailed in architecture (Christopher Wren, d. 1723) and literature (Pierre Corneille, d. 1684, Moliere, d. 1673, Jean Racine, d. 1699), although it was interlaced with the romantic point of view.

Russia abandoned its old ways between 1654 (when Patriarch Nikon began his church reform) and 1725 (when Tsar Peter died) and emerged as a full and powerful member of the European type of civilization. Prosperity and economic development continued in the reign of Catherine II, who assumed the throne in 1762 after killing her husband. Black Sea coast was annexed as far as the Dniester River. A large part of Poland had gone to Russia at its first partition of 1772, mentioned above. In the subsequent partitions of Poland in 1793 and 1795, the Russian frontier expanded to the Vistula River. Trade and manufacture grew. Ukraine was settled rapidly. Obligations of the serfs to the landowners were tightened. The peasant uprising in the south and the west (1773–1775) was totally crushed.

In the Americas, civilization grew in the European style. First, the Americas were divided into spheres of influence of the European countries. Then followed the colonial struggles. Between 1654 and 1664, the Dutch lost Brazil to the Portuguese loyalists and New Amsterdam (New York) to the British. The French surrendered Canada to the British in 1763. The American colonists, in turn, won their war of independence against the British (1775–1783). Along the Pacific coast, Captain Vitus Bering of the Russian Navy discovered Alaska between 1728 and 1741 and the Russian fur traders established their settlements there. To counter this, the Spaniards pushed northward and established their missions at San Francisco in 1775 and at Nootka in 1789. In Spanish America, population began to grow again after 1650. Coastal trade prohibitions among the American ports of the Spanish Empire were lifted in 1774–1778. All this spurred commercial activity and brought prosperity. However, cultural development made no noteworthy strides due, partly, to the exclusion of the Indian peasantry from high culture.

The Asian civilizations reacted to the Western ascendancy in various ways. The Ottomans lost practically all of Hungary to the Austrians in the Peace of Karlowitz of 1699 and suffered defeats from the Russians between 1768 and 1774. They surrendered important territories along the Black Sea by the Treaty of Kutchuk Kainardji (1774) and gave Russia the right to protect Orthodox Christians that lived under the Turkish rule. The Muslims reacted to such reversals by attempting religious purification through the Wahhabi movement (Mohammed ibn Abdul Wahhab, 1691–1787) and by modernizing their armies with borrowed European techniques, but, eventually, after some small successes, both attempts failed. The Christian populations of the Balkans welcomed the fall of the Ottomans. They began their entry into the Western society with the Serbian revolution (1803–1815) and the Greek revolution (1821–1830). In Iran and Turkestan, in spite of the spectacular exploits of Nadir Shah (ruled 1736–1747) and the Afghan Chieftain Ahmad Shah Durani (1747–1773), the power among local rivals came to depend, by early nineteenth century, upon the military subsidies from the British and the Russians and upon the latters' punitive raids, such as the British raid of Kabul in 1839.

In India, the British activities began in 1600. As the Maratha and the Sikh revolts weakened the imperial power of the Mughal Emperor Aurangzeb (d. 1707), the European trading companies began enlisting Indian soldiers (sepoys) under European officers. In a struggle between France and England (1756–1763), the British succeeded in excluding French participation in the Indian economic and political affairs. Indians were also ravaged by the Afghans, who defeated the Marathas at Panipat (1761). Whenever a choice had to be made between these two alien invaders, most

Indians opted for the British. The British crushed all military rivals, defeating the Marathas in 1818. The Hindus reconciled with the Europeans by putting them in another caste. In the early nineteenth century, an interaction began between the two cultures with the establishment of missionary colleges. Some Indians, most prominently Ram Mohan Roy (d. 1833), opened up to the British world and showed not only that all religions conveyed the same message but also that that message was discovered by the Hindu philosophers long before the advent of Christianity and Islam. This gave rise to an enthusiastic study of the Vedas and Upanishads by Western scholars. Such research by the Hindus and the Europeans produced a demand for reforms among the educated Hindus. However, after a few initial successes with reform, the British stopped meddling in the traditional customs. The great majority of people remained passive to the activities of these educated Hindus.

China remained largely unaffected by European ways throughout the eighteenth century, partly because the rites controversy among the Christian missionaries discredited the Europeans generally and convinced the Chinese that the missionaries were nothing but agents of the Pope. However, dynastic decay began with the rebellion of 1774, that lead to the Taiping rebellion of 1850, and with conflicts with the British. Conflicts with the British began when the British abolished East India Company's monopoly of China trade in 1834 and introduced European patterns of commerce at Canton. This clashed with China's own regulation of trade. The Chinese forbade import of opium. This was a very lucrative trade for the British and the Europeans. So, it continued illegally. When the Chinese sent a commissioner to Canton in 1839 to stop it, war ensued between the British and the Chinese. China lost. By the Treaty of Nanking (1842), it ceded Hong Kong to the British, opened four more ports to the European trade, and admitted British Consuls to all of these ports. In the wake of this, other Europeans extracted exemption from Chinese law.

Japan's reaction to the Western ascendancy was unique. Throughout the eighteenth century, Japan had thrived in peaceful isolation, keeping its population down through infanticide. A duality of culture prevailed in the Tokugawa regime wherein austere aesthetics of the samurai tradition existed alongside the vigorous vulgarity of the sensuous world of the towns. Artists experimented with the Chinese, the Western, and the Japanese elements. Intellectuals studied Western and Chinese knowledge in spite of the Tokugawan prohibition against studying philosophies other than Neo-Confucianism. This underground found particular protection in the outlying parts of the archipelago, where the ancestors of the Outside Lords had been rivals to the Tokugawa family. It nurtured reverence for the Emperor, Japanese patriotism, and Western knowledge. Therefore, when Commodore Perry of the United States demanded the right to use Japanese ports and the Tokugawa Shogun accepted it with proper reluctance, the Japanese had already proceeded on their path to master the technical and political secrets of the West.

Thus, while the Western civilization rose to dominate the world by 1850, other civilizations did not vanish.[3] Civilizational pluralism continued.

---

3. For the West, see R. Boxer, *Four Centuries of Portuguese Expansion, 1415–1825*, (1961); J.H. Clapham, *The Economic Development of France and Germany* (4th ed., 1936); P. Deane, *The First Industrial Revolution* (1965); D.K. Fieldhouse, *The Colonial Empires* (1966); P. Gay, *The Enlightenment, An Interpretation* (1966); C.H. Haring, *The Spanish Empire in America* (1947); E.J. Hobsbawm, *The Age of Revolution, 1789–1848* (1963); H. Kohn, *The Age of Nationalism: The First Era of Global History* (1962); D.F. Lach, *Asia in the Making of Europe, I: The Century of Discovery* (1965); McNeil, *World History*; G. Mosse, *The Culture of Western Europe: The Nineteenth and Twentieth Centuries, An Introduction* (1961); J.H. Parry, *Europe and a Wider World, 1415–1715* (1949); J.H. Parry, *The Age of Renaissance: Discovery, Exploration, and Settlement, 1450–1650* (1963); R.R. Palmer, *The Age of the Democratic Revolution: A Political History of Europe and America, 1760–1800*, 2 vols. (1959, 1964); L.S. Stavrianos, *The Balkans Since 1453* (1965); W.B. Willcox, *Star of Empire: A Study of Britain as a World Power, 1485–1945* (1950). For Islam, see G. Antonius, *The Arab Awakening* (1938); P. Avery, *Modern Iran* (1965); H.A.R. Gibb, *Modern Trends in Islam* (1947); H.A.R. Gibb and H. Bowen, *Islamic Society and the West, I: Islamic Society in the Eighteenth Century*, 2 parts (1950, 1957); G.E. von Grunebaum, ed., *Unity and Variety in Muslim Civilization* (1955); B. Lewis, *The Arabs in History* (1966); B. Lewis, *The Emergence of Modern Turkey* (1968); W.C. Smith, *Modern Islam in India: A Social Analysis* (rev. ed., 1947); W.C. Smith, *Islam in Modern History* (1957); Z.N. Zeine, *The Emergence of Arab Nationalism* (1966). For India see, W.H. Moreland, *India at the Death of Akbar: An Economic Study* (1920); W.H. Moreland, *From Akbar to Aurangzeb: A Study in Indian Economic History* (1923); K.M. Panikkar, *A Survey of Indian History* (3d ed., 1956); P. Spear, *India: A Modern History* (1961); V.A. Smith, *The Oxford History of India* (rev ed. by P. Spear, 3d ed., 1958). For China and Japan see, G.M. Beckman, *The Modernization of China and Japan* (1962); W.T. deBary, ed., *Sources of Chinese Tradition* (1966); R.N. Bellah, *Tokugawa Religion* (1957); C.R. Boxer, *The Christian Century in Japan, 1549–1650* (1951); C. Chang, *The Chinese Gentry: Studies in Their Role in Nineteenth-Century Chinese Society* (1955); J.K Fairbank, ed., *Chinese Thought and Institutions* (1957); J.K. Fairbank, ed., *The Chinese World Order: Traditional Chinese Foreign Relations* (1968); P. Ho, *The Ladder of Success in Imperial China: Aspects of Social Mobility, 1368–1911* (1962); E.O. Reischauer, J.K. Fairbank, and A.M. Craig, *A History of East Asian Civilization, II: East Asia: A Modern Transformation* (1965). For Africa see, B. Davidson, *Black Mother: The African Slave Trade* (1961); Fage, *West Africa*; Hallett, *Africa*; L. Marquard, *The Story of South Africa* (1955); Oliver and Matthew, *East Africa* (1963); E. Williams, *Capitalism and Slavery* (1944); E. Chaney and P. Mack, eds., *England and the Continental Renaissance: Essays in Honor of J.B. Trapp* (1990); Di Cesare, ed., *Reconsidering the Renaissance* (1992); M.S. Haynes, *The Italian Renaissance and Its Influence on Western Civilization* (1991); W.L. Langer, ed., *Western Civilization* (2d ed., 1975); W.H. McNeill, *The Rise of the West: A History of the Human Community* (1990); V.S. Naravane, *A Cultural History of*

D. *Since 1850*

During 1789–1914, the Western civilization was extensively transformed by two revolutions: the industrial and the democratic. Industrial revolution was characterized by a vast expansion of scale in every aspect of manufacture, commerce, and economy, an intensification of transportation both on land and sea, and an intensification of the communicative systems of mail, electric telegraph, and wireless telegraphy. It resulted in vastly increased wealth, an accelerated growth of population, and a shift from village to the city. The democratic revolution had at its heart the principle proclaimed by the American rebels in 1776 against King George III that governments derived their just powers from the consent of the governed. The idea had a strong appeal in many countries, but it was in France that it actually produced a revolution against monarchical absolutism. The revolution began in 1789 and ended in bringing about a republic. The Consulate was established in 1799 under Napoleon. Democratic doctrines and ideals of popular government spread across Europe, although they were much diluted in the process and produced a checkered history of the subsequent decades. They established that governments were man-made, that they were, consequently, amenable to manipulation according to plan, and that government could command a far greater power than hitherto by winning support of the majority of the population. These two revolutions (industrial and democratic) heightened the military, economic, and intellectual power of the West.

They also intensified its dominance in the world. Japan deliberately appropriated Western technology and mastered the Western skills to defend its own land. China, however, watched helplessly as the Western adventurers swarmed into the treaty ports with their machine-made goods, unable to resist the Western pressures. The three Muslim Empires, namely, the Ottoman, the Mughals, and the Persians, were subdued by the West. Although the Ottoman Turks won the Crimean War against Russia (1854–1856), the Empire could survive only with the support of one or another major European power. The Sultan remained under the tutelage of the Germans by the 1890's. In India, the British crushed the Sepoy revolt of 1857 and formally terminated the Mughal Empire. The Persian and Afghan courts became mere puppets of the British or the Russians.

Western-style reform became the official policy of the Ottoman Empire since 1839, but it lacked support in the society. Sultan Abdul Hamid reversed the reform policy between 1878 and 1908, calling for a return to the old ways. Since his claim of being the Caliph was never taken seriously, the

---

Modern India: Nineteenth Century (1991); S. Ozment, ed., *Religion and Culture in the Renaissance and Reformation* (1989); N.G. Wilson, *From Byzantium to Italy: Greek Studies in the Italian Renaissance* (1992).

Muslim sentiment failed to rally behind his policy. The Young Turks of his modernized army overthrew him in 1908. The Empire lost its Balkan territory in the Balkan Wars (1912–1913). The victorious powers of World War I (1914–1918) partitioned the Empire among themselves. Mustapha Kemal (1881–1938) led the Turks in defending their Anatolian homeland and succeeded, in 1923, in obtaining European powers' agreement to his repossession of Constantinople. He launched radical reforms that shook the traditional life. However, while the nationalism promoted by his policy did reach the general population, this nationalism also brought forth the values of the Turkish Islamic tradition. In Iran, Reza Pahlavi seized power in 1925 and started secular reforms along the Turkish lines. However, Islam here remained even stronger than in Turkey. Such was also the case in Afghanistan.

In the Arab world, while the more affluent parts were assigned to the French and the British, Abdul-Aziz ibn-Saud (1880–1953) consolidated his victories in Arabia by 1925. He introduced Western businessmen in the land to exploit oil and make him rich. Roads, airfields, and telegraph lines were constructed in order to centralize his power. Egypt, Syria, and Iraq, too, witnessed a rise of secularism, even though the nationalists dreamed of a return to the glorious days of early Islam. Islamic Africa came under European rule, southern Philippines under the Americans, Indonesia under the Dutch, and central Asia under the Russians. In spite of such setbacks, however, Islam continued to be the living faith of one-seventh of humankind, gaining converts in parts of central and west Africa.

In China, the French and the British seized Peking in 1860 and burned the Imperial Palace in retaliation for imprisonment of their diplomats by China. Land beyond Amur River was ceded to Russia in that year. Other areas of traditional dominance were lost as well: Indo-China (Viet Nam, Cambodia, Laos) to France in 1885, Burma to England in 1886, Korea to Japan during the 1870's, as well as Formosa (Taiwan) and other islands to Japan. Foreign control was established over Chinese customs (1863), postal services (1896), and railroad construction (1888). Outraged by the government's concessions to foreigners, secret societies sprang up for overthrowing the Manchu dynasty. The semi-secret society of Boxers, so-called by the Westerners after their calisthenic exercises, rose to take action against the hated foreigners. The Western powers responded by occupying Peking in 1900. They forced a settlement whereunder the Chinese government had to pay damages caused by the Boxers. Because of these factors, it did not take much bloodshed to replace the Manchu dynasty by a Chinese republic in 1912. In 1915, Japan made its Twenty-one demands on China for special privileges, no doubt prompted by the post-revolutionary lack of effective government in China and the outbreak of World War I. The United

States kept Japan under control over China and new power arrangements were worked out for the Pacific at the Washington Conference (1922), comparable to the settlement reached in Europe in 1918–1919. Within China, rival warlords sprang up. The revolution changed its own character when a large number of Chinese youth took to Western education in institutions at home and abroad. Sun Yat-sen (d. 1925) founded the Kuomintang Party which fought against the local warlords, the Japan-supporters, and the Communists during 1911–1949. Military Commander Chiang Kai-Shek and the Kuomintang succeeded in destroying the warlords by 1928 but the Communists, who had organized their Party in 1921, survived. Japan occupied Manchuria in 1931 and invaded China in 1937. Chiang Kai-shek fled to Chungking up the Yangtze River. Mao Tse-tung and his Communists settled down in the northwest near the Russian border. After the end of World War II, the two renewed fighting. The conflict ended in Communist victory in 1949. During this period, the Chinese intellectuals came in close contact with Western ideas, science, and technology, but the bulk of the population remained immured in its poverty, overpopulation, and political instability. Only after 1949 did they come under real contact with new ideas and techniques.

The Japanese overthrew the Shogun in 1868, restored the Emperor, and launched a vigorous effort to strengthen their military power through producing military material within the country. This spurred industrialization. At first, factories were started by the government. Later, they were turned over to private management. Even when substantial private industry came to be established, profit did not become the all-consuming end. National policies were carried out in industry along the old samurai values, wherein firms sought honor and managers served the nation, obeying their superiors and protecting their inferiors. Big firms farmed out jobs to artisan family enterprises. Even though this transformation brought about unpopular changes in the familiar ways, such as opening up the country to the foreigners, it succeeded due to the traditional loyalty to the Emperor and the nationalistic appeal of Shinto that regarded the Emperor as divine. Clan ownership of land and feudal duties and privileges were abolished in order to break up potential rivals among the dissatisfied clans of the samurai. A new type of armed forces was created along the line of universal military service that did not limit the right to bear arms to the samurai alone. However, the samurai traditions and values were actively embraced by the new military class. In 1889, Emperor Meiji (1868–1912) promulgated a German-style Constitution. Universal male suffrage was needed for elections to the Diet, which introduced a democratic element into the Japanese politics. In cultural matters, although Western ideas and styles were massively juxtaposed to the Japanese traditions of art, drama, architecture, and Shinto, the two never achieved a synthesis.

After the conquest of Manchuria in 1931 and China in 1937–1941, Japan attacked the American fleet at Pearl Harbor in 1941 in order to gain time for seizing the oil fields of Borneo, since the Americans had put trade embargoes on Japan for oil and scrap iron in order to check its conquests. The United States dropped atomic bombs on Hiroshima and Nagasaki in 1945. Japan surrendered. Thereupon began another transformation of Japanese society and economy, this time without the necessity of building military strength.

In Africa, a very active state-building took place during the nineteenth century, resulting from suppression of the slave-trade and introduction of the American crops of maize, peanuts, and sweet potatoes. While slave-trade had helped the kings of Dahomey in west Africa and the Sultan of Zanzibar in east Africa, it had deleterious effect upon African wealth and population. With its abolition in the west by 1833 and in the east by 1897, various raw materials, palm oil, and ivory came to be traded for European products and armament. The new weapons upset the African political systems by diminishing the power of such older military systems as that of the spear-wielding Zulus of Natal or the armored horsemen of Bornu in the west.

Islam continued to spread into new regions of Africa. Muslim legal doctrines assisted in state organization in a large part of east and west, for example, in the Ashanti Kingdom (Ghana). Conflict with the Europeans resulted in renewed Muslim movements, such as the brotherhood of Sanusi, founded by a native of Algiers near Mecca in 1837, which led the resistance against the French and the Italians in eastern Sahara. Religious leader Mohammed Ahmed of Sudan declared himself the Mahdi (the restorer of Islam) in 1881 and led a rebellion against the Turkish-Egyptian authorities of the Upper Nile Valley. His forces were destroyed in 1896–1898.

Christian missionary activity increased, too. European penetration, however, remained modest, except in Algeria in the north and the Boer republics in the south. Most of the interior was ruled by the Africans, such as the thousand-year old Kingdom of Bornu or the newly-founded (1817) military government of the Zulus.

By 1914, all of Africa came under European domination, with the exception of Ethiopia where Emperor Menelik II defeated Italy in 1896. The colonization effort was led by France and Britain, followed by Germany, Belgium, and Portugal. The patterns of colonization varied from extensive white settlements, as in South Africa and Algeria, to indirect rule in which the Europeans acted as distant overlords. Sometimes, a local ruler would set himself up under the protection of a European administration, as in the Kingdom of Buganda. Or, sometimes a European administration would rescue an African territory from destruction, as in Basutoland, where the English intervened in 1868 to save the tribe from destruction by the Boer settlers. However, the older structures of society, such as kinship groups, village communities, and tribal ties, remained intact.

Only minor disturbances occurred during World War I. The German colonies were easily divided up between the victorious French and British. During the inter-war period, as well, rebellions and inter-colonial conflicts were few. The Union of South Africa, Liberia, and Ethiopia continued to exist as independent states. Egypt was granted independence by the British in 1922. However, Italy conquered Ethiopia in 1934 in order to get even with it for its defeat in 1896. During the inter-war period, a significant number of Africans acquired European skills and knowledge. either through serving in European armies or receiving education at mission schools and other institutions of higher learning. Many left their villages to work and live in towns. When strangers from different tribes converged in urban areas, they needed a new basis for governing their relationships. That basis was found in the European models, which were more in tune with urban and industrial living than the other available model of the Islamic patterns.

Since the end of World War II, the erstwhile colonies of European powers have attained independence everywhere. The new states are seeking conscious modernization, which means selective Westernization. They are engaged in political, military, intellectual, cultural, and economic interrelationship of the sort which has led some historians to describe this an age of global cosmopolitanism.[4] Many of our contemporary problems are approached in a global manner. Nevertheless, this has not resulted in the elimination of civilizational pluralism. In spite of the apparent Westernization of the globe, there persist different cultures pursuing different life-styles along different value-systems.

For example, in today's China ancient traditions are followed inasmuch as education and persuasion, rather than the principle of Western legality, are used as the instrument for social peace, so that conflicts are resolved by appeal to conscience of the parties rather than by pursuing rights in Western-style courts of law. In Japan, the law made in imitation of the West governs a very small segment of social life, namely, the middle class individuals who fashion their relations on the basis of freedom and liberty. The majority of the people continue to live according to the traditional ways, following the Confucian idea of hierarchy based on natural order, ordering their personal relations along the traditional *giri-ninjo* (rules of behavior). In Africa, although there has been a noticeable activity of modernization along Western models, eighty or ninety percent of the population

4. McNeill, *World History*, 403.

continues to live according to the ancient custom, largely unaware of the cities' institutions and generally unaffected by the reform legislation, using traditional procedures of conciliation for their disputes, rather than state courts. Although the Muslim countries vary in social conditions, traditions, and pervasiveness of Islam, their peoples continue to pursue life in accordance with the Islamic concept of personal morals and societal order as applied to their own particular conditions. Among the Hindus, who constitute nearly eighty-five percent of the population of India, life for the most part moves along in the traditional ways of *dharma* and the joint-family continues to exist as the fundamental unit of social order.

Thus, civilizational pluralism continues to be a basic fact of human life on this planet, even in this age of global cosmopolitanism.[5] Although techniques of the West, even its life-styles, are being adopted in various parts of the world in varying degrees, ranging from mimicking to genuine conversion, there continue to exist various value-systems among the various peoples of the world. These systems are characterized by their own particular

5. For the West, see H. Blakemore, *Latin America* (1966); *Cambridge Modern History*, 12 vols. (1956–); J.E. Fagg, *Latin America: A General History* (2d ed., 1969); H.C. Herring and H.B. Herring, *A History of Latin America: From the Beginning to the Present* (3d ed., 1968); R.A. Humphreys, *Tradition and Revolt in Latin America* (1969); W.L. Langer, *The Rise of Modern Europe*, 20 vols. (1936–); McNeil, *World History*; S.E. Morrison and H.S. Commager, *The Growth of the American Republic* (6th ed., 1969); R.R. Palmer and J. Coulton, *A History of the Modern World* (3d ed., 1965). For India see. R. Gopal, *How India Struggled for Freedom: A Political History* (1967); K.M. Panikkar, *The Foundations of New India* (1963); V.B. Singh, ed., *Economic History of India 1857–1956* (1965); H. Tinker, *Experiment with Freedom: India and Pakistan, 1947* (1967). For China and Japan see, J.C. Abegglen, *The Japanese Factory: Aspects of Its Social Organization* (1957); H. Borton, *Japan's Modern Century* (1958); J.K Fairbank, *The United States and China* (1958); P. Ho and T. Tsou, eds., *China in Crisis, I: China's Heritage and the Communist Political System* (1968); I.C.Y. Hsu, *The Rise of Modern China* (1970); Ssu-yu-teng, J. Fairbank, *et al.*, *China's Response to the West: A Documentary Survery, 1839–1923* (1954); C. Tse-tsung, *The May Fourth Movement: Intellectual Revolution in Modern China* (1960). For Islam see, Antonius, *Arab Awakening*; Avery, *Modern Iran*; Gibb, *Modern Trends*; von Grunebaum, ed., *Unity and Variety*; G.S. Hodgson, *The Venture of Islam*, 3 vols. (1971–1972); G. Kirk, *The Middle East, 1945–1950* (1954); Lewis, *Arabs in History*; E. Monroe, *Britain's Moment in the Middle East* (1963); W.R. Polk and Richard L. Chambers, eds., *Beginnings of Modernization in the Middle East: The Nineteenth Century* (1968); smith, *Modern Islam in India*; Smith, *Islam in Modern History*; Seine, *Arab Nationalism*; Z.N. Zeine, *The Struggle for Arab Independence* (1960). For Africa see, Fage, *West Africa*; Hallett, *Africa*; Marguard, *South Africa*; Oliver and Matthew, *East Africa*; R. Oliver and A. Atmore, *Africa Since 1800* (1967); T.O. Ranger, ed., *Aspects of Central African History* (1968); R. Robinson and J. Gallaghar, *Africa and the Victorians* (1961); B. Davidson, *Africa in History: Themes and Outlines* (rev. ed., 1992); Langer, *Western Civilization*; McNeill, *Rise of the West*; D. Rothermund and S.K. Saha, eds., *Regional Disparities in India: Rural and Industrial Dimensions* (1991); C. Schirokauer, *A Brief History of Chinese and Japanese Civilizations* (2d ed., 1989).

concepts of social order, their own particular notions about the fundamental unit of society (individual, family, or the tribe), and their own particular modes of dispute-resolution. Civilizational pluralism persists. In light of the tenacity of history to this diversity, it is misleading to proceed as if there exists, or is about to exist, one, single civilization in the world.

What is the consequence of this fact for international law? We shall analyze that in Chapter 5. Before that, in the next Chapter, we shall take a closer look at this civilizational diversity.

Chapter 4

Civilizational Diversity

Different civilizations have developed different principles of life and social organization. This has been the result of their particular historicity. We shall see below how that happened, using the examples of the Western, the Chinese, the Indian, and the African ways of life as they developed in history.

1. The Western Way of Life

The Western civilization found its roots in the ancient Greeks, whence it grew in its own particular historicity and gained its own definition of its way of life, value systems, and social organization.

A. The Greek Period

In the Archaic Age of the Greek civilization (1100 B.C.–650 B.C.), Hellas spread from the southeastern end of the Black Sea to almost the Atlantic Ocean. Probably the pre-Hellenic people, but certainly the Hellenes and the Greco-Italic people, entertained those notions of marriage, family, and property rights that formed the social foundations of the Greek life, shaped by a primal religion which worshipped ancestors and venerated the hearth. Veneration of the hearth and graves produced the right to own land.

Soon, the racial community (the *genos*) disappeared, except as an awareness of a common ancestry. The *polis* (loosely translated as city-state) emerged as a small independent state which consisted of a central city and its surrounding territory that tolerated no competing stronghold and no independent citizenry. It was a community of free men in which residents of foreign birth (*metics)* and slaves had no rights. Cripples were not to be brought up. Self-sufficiency (*autarkeia*) was maintained by agriculture, trade and industry, and an army of *hoplites*. Those who governed, as by holding an office or serving on the tribunal, and those who were governed formed the citizenry. The citizen realized his capacities in the service of the state. The individual was completely subordinated to the general policy. *Nomos* was the guardian of every civic virtue. Social life was dominated by competition (*agon*).

The Greeks first sought learning from the East. Disappointed by the discordance among the priestly experts of the Middle East, they, in Iona, employed their own imaginative reason to face the fundamental questions. They rejected gods as the ruling force of the universe and they sought an explanation of the phenomenon in the natural law.

Greek thought evolved through four stages: the Heroic, observing concrete experiences of the physical sense and garnishing it with fantasy and myth, as in Homer's epics; the Visionary, seeking ordering through ideas woven into senses, as in the poetry and drama of Pindar, Aeschylus, and Sophocles; the Theoretical, using analytical powers to discover more than what was apparent on the surface, as seen upon emergence of Athens after the Persian Wars; and the Rational, exploring the concepts of rational order, as in Plato and Aristotle. The world-view was now expressed by the concepts of *logos* (word) that conceptualized the instrument for truth and justice by thinking and discussing issues, *arete* that conceptualized man's special worth as a reasoning creature, and *metron* (measure) that conceptualized measurement and proportion for the purpose of avoiding *hubris* (excess). Man was possessed of reason, freedom of choice, and the ability to make decisions. He no longer lived for the sake of some exalted human being or a supernatural power. The political consequence of this individualism was the independence of the polity whose citizens possessed political and legal rights. Law was the instrument for realizing those rights.

Aristocracy, tyranny, democracy, and oligarchy evolved as the forms of government. Aristocracy not only represented various class rights and interests but was also a social force and a moral system, whose ethos was characterized by *kalokagathia*, which represented the individual fusion of a moral, aesthetic, and material dedication to an idea. Tyrannies were opposed to the *kalokagathia* and they ruled more severely, banishing or killing the rich and distributing their property to the tyrant's followers. Democracy began with the reforms of Cleisthenes in Athens in 507 B.C. As the Peloponnesian War ended in the subjugation of Athens by Sparta and the rule of the Thirty Tyrants, secret oligarchic clubs emerged. A coalition of such clubs succeeded in 411 B.C. in imposing an oligarchic constitution (the Oligarchy of the Four Hundred).

This was followed by a democratic restoration in 410 B.C., followed by the second oligarchy in 404 B.C., followed in turn by the second democratic restoration in 403 B.C.. In the middle of the fourth century B.C., the Athenian society was no longer that extravagantly individualistic as previously at the end of the fifth century, nor did it indulge into radical questioning of accepted values as previously. The *polis* came to an end with the Macedonian conquest in 338 B.C.[1]

Nomos,[2] which eventually became law, is probably the most fundamental principle of the Western way of life. The word first appeared in Hesiod (8th century B.C.) to denote law laid down for men. In Homer (8th century B.C.), as well in later compositions of Hesiod, there is a concept of *themis* (that which is laid down and established). *Themistes* (plural of *themis*) were divine ordinances of Zeus granted to man for his benefit. The king was entrusted with them. As the self-consciousness of man grew, the emphasis shifted from *themis* to *dike* (order, right, judgment, that which is right) and eventually to *nomos*. The king had to exercise his power in light of *nomos*.

In Hesiod, *nomos* appeared in three aspects: an entity ordained by Zeus in place of *themis*, an independently established practice or usage, and that which conformed to nature's regularities. In it, thus, there was a notion of pre-existing natural phenomenon whose regularity governed man's actions, as well as a notion of the given way of life, whether given as divine directives or as human usages. Soon, *nomos* assumed the meaning of *thesmos*, or authoritatively laid down law for the benefit of the community. Its divine aspect faded with the growth of the rule of *logos* and abstract meaning. Pre-Socratic thinking moved toward searching for an *arche* (first principle), i.e., what *is* at its beginning and in its basic sense. Thus, Anaximander

1. A. Andrews, *The Greeks—The History of Human Society* (1967); G.W. Botsford, *Hellenistic History* (1926); J. Fran. P. Burckhardt, *History of Greek Culture* (1963); J.K. Davies, *Democracy and Classical Greece* (1978); M.I. Finley, *Early Greece* (1981); M. Hadas, *Hellenistic Culture* (1959); J.A. John, *Manners and Customs of Ancient Greece*, Vol. III (1971); M.Pope, *The Ancient Greeks* (1976); C.E. Robinson, *Everyday Life in Ancient Greece* (1947); M. Rostovtzeff, *The Social and Economic History of the Hellenistic World*, Vol. II (1941); C.G. Starr, *The Origins of Greek Civilization, 100–650 B.C.* (1961); A. Zimmen, *The Greek Commonwealth* (1924); J.B. Bury and R. Meiggs, *A History of Greece* (4th ed., 1975); N.G.L. Hammond, *A History of Greece to 322 B.C.* (1959); R. Sealy, *A History of the Greek City States* (1976); V. Ehrenberg, *The Greek City States* (1976); V. Ehrenberg, *The Greek State* (2d ed., 1969); N.R.E. Fisher, *Social Values in Classical Athens* (1976); V.R. d'A. Desborough, *The Greek Dark Ages* (1968); A.M. Snodgrass, *The Dark Ages of Greece* (1971); A.R. Burn, *The Lyric Age of Greece* (1960); A. Andres, *The Greek Tyrants* (1956); R. May, *Law and Society East and West: Dharma, Li, and Nomos* (1985); M. Ostwald, *Nomos and the Beginnings of the Athenian Democracy* (1969); V. Ehrenberg, *Aspects of the Ancient World* (1946); J.W. Jones, *The Law and Legal Theory of the Greeks* (1956); D.M. MacDowell, *The Law in Classical Athens* (1978); R.J. Bonner and G. Smith, *The Administration of Justice from Homer to Aristotle*, 2 vols. (1930); W.K.C. Guthrie, *A History of Greek Philosophy*, Vol. I (1962); J.C. Stobart, *The Glory That Was Greece* (1911, 1978); J. Ferguson, *Moral Values in the Ancient World* (1958); V. Ehrenberg, *From Solon to Socrates* (1968); N.R.E. Fisher, *Hybris: A Study in the Values of Honour and Shame in Ancient Greece* (1992).

2. See R. May, *Law and Society East and West: Dharma, Li, and Nomos* (1985).

(611?–547? B.C.) proposed that whatever existed did so in being exposed to the order of time. Heraclitus (540–475 B.C.) distinguished between *nomos theios* (divine *nomos*) and *anthropeioi nomoi* (human *nomoi*). *Nomoi*, in this way, comprised the cosmic totality of both human usages and natural phenomena. *Nomos* was now very much of this world, not of the domain of gods. Pindar (522?–443 B.C.) regarded it as the supreme ruling authority and poets Aeschylus (525–456 B.C.), Sophocles (496?–406 B.C.), and Euripides (5th century B.C.) extolled the ancient custom which, in effect, referred to an unwritten *nomos*.

The substantive meaning of *nomos agraphos* was a constitution of the *polis* that pleased the gods, deviation from which resulted in the decaying of the good order (*eunomia*). In the 6th and 5th centuries B.C., unwritten customary rules (*nomoi agraphoi*) and equity rules lost ground to codified laws. The Sophists of the mid-5th century held that neither customary regulations (*nomoi agraphoi*) nor written regulations (*nomoi gegrammenoi*) provided sufficient foundation for an order of justice. The divine *dike* (order) was replaced by the abstract conception of *dikaiosyne* (righteousness, justice).

Nomos was contrasted with *physis* (nature, natural form of a person or thing), a concept that had already been introduced by such pre-Socratic thinkers as Xenophanes (6th century B.C.) and Heraclitus. It denoted not a product of culture but an elementary phenomenon. *Physis* was real, *nomos* unreal. *Physis* was necessary and grown, *nomoi* arbitrary and conventional. As a real order of things, *physis* could disclose true basis for justice for moral and legal conduct. It could form the basis for ethos (*nomos agraphos*) and statute law (*nomos gegrammenos*).

The *nomos-physis* controversy produced the natural *nomos*. Democritus (460?–362? B.C.) thought that men must obey *nomoi* for their own welfare because of their natural tendency to hurt each other. Plato (427–347 B.C.) considered *nomos* as participating in the idea of good and justice. The divine *nous* (intellect) was the *physis* in which *nomoi* participated. Aristotle (384–322 B.C.) rejected the position that Plato granted to *nous* as a participation in good and justice but he, like Plato, considered *nomoi* inevitable for man in order for man to exist differently from wild beasts. He distinguished between the *nomos idios* (special) and *nomos koinos* (universal). *Nomos* became natural law. There was a general idea of just and unjust in accordance with nature. Man-made conventions were just so long as they did not contravene the natural order of things present under the rule of God (*theos*) and reason (*nous*). In its final development, *nomos* came to denote a constituted order of society comprising individual rights and duties. The thought is basic to the Western way of life.

B. The Roman Period

In the early part of the Roman period, i.e., the period under the kings, political and social institutions were characterized by *gentes* (a class of persons related to a common ancestor, to which were attached the *clientes* (clients) in a relationship of dependence), *familia* (a sub-division of the *gens* comprising all that fell under the power of the *paterfamilia*, namely, children, slaves, cattle, land, etc.), *plebs* (conquered and transplanted people), and *patriciate* (the *gentes* that emerged from the mass of people). In the period of the Republic, the *clientela* system continued to govern the personal relationship of mutual obligation between the *patronus* (patron) and his dependent *clientes*, fostering the power of the nobility and inhibiting the growth of democracy. Civil servants were recruited from the members of the equestrian order (the *equites*), who had already shown business abilities. Freedmen, too, provided the needed talent. In the period of the Principate, slaves and freedmen of many races and languages mingled with the freeborn. The imperial court grew lavishly. A new form of clientage developed on the basis of voluntary association of the master and the paid retainer. Slave-holding continued, with progress toward humane treatment and eventual manumission. Workers included hired laborers, freedmen, and slaves. The freeborn engaged more in agriculture than industry.

Municipal life was free from central power. Communities were allowed to follow their own traditions so long as they were not offensive to the state. Only the Christian communities were persecuted. Most Roman communities possessed charters granted by the Roman Government providing for magistrates, a council of elders or of *decuriones* (local senators), a popular assembly, and law courts. In Rome itself, the Emperor, his ministers, and the Senate exercised absolute control. The people who directed the social and economic life of the Empire lived in towns and the capital.

The period of Enlightened Despotism ended with the reign of Emperor Commodus (A.D. 180–192). A new period of bloodshed and misery began. People began concentrating on the inner life of man. The worsening of the social and economic crisis changed the institutions as well. Thus, the idea of the *principate* as power exercised by the First Citizen faded. So did the privileged position of the Roman citizen. The Emperor became a military despot. Civil freedom disappeared.

After decades of anarchy and war, Emperor Diocletian restored order by strengthening the hands of the ruler, reforming the methods of government, and regenerating the army. Reforms cost money, whose burden fell on the people who were already impoverished by the civil wars of the third century. A population of serfs lived and worked for the government.

Diocletian abdicated. Civil wars followed, from which emerged Emperor Constantine. He seized upon the realization that religion was the only sanction of despotic power and created a structure of authority that sustained for centuries. He created a single state religion to buttress the imperial authority of a despotic and hereditary power. The old Roman state of Senate and the people died. So did the Graeco-Roman ideal of citizenship and freedom.[3]

C. The Christian Period

With Christianity, a shift was made from natural philosophy to revelation. Both spiritual and secular orders were sustained by the power of God. Man found meaning to his existence only to the extent it reconciled him with his Maker. A divinely-ordained unity maintained order in Europe in the Medieval times. Its coherence and harmony became the subject of discovery for both the theologian as well as the scientist. Gratian (1140) argued

3. F.F. Abbott, *A History and Description of Roman Political Institutions* (1963); F.E. Adcock, *Roman Political Ideas and Practice* (1959); E. Badian, *Roman Imperialism in the Late Republic* (1968); R. Bloch, *The Origins of Rome* (1960); A.E.R. Boak and W.G. Sinnegan, *A History of Rome to A.D. 565* (1969); J. Carcopino, *Daily Life in Ancient Rome* (1975); J. Crook, *Law of Rome* (1967); S. Dill, *Roman Society from Nero to Marcus Aurelius* (1956); D.R. Dudley, *The Romans, 850 B.C.–A.D. 337* (1970); W.W. Fowler, *Social Life at Rome in the Age of Cicero* (1908); T. Frank, *A History of Rome* (1923); L. Friedlander, *Roman Life and Manners Under the Early Empire*, trans. by L.A. Magnus (no date); P. Garnsey, *Social Status and Legal Privilege in the Roman Empire* (1970); S. Goodenough, *Citizen Rome* (1979); M. Grant, *The World of Rome* (1960); W.C. Green, *The Achievement of Rome* (1933); A.M.J. Grenridge, *Roman Public Life* (1922); J. Heurgon, *The Rise of Rome* (trans. J. Willis, 1973); H. Mattingly, *Roman Imperial Civilization* (1959); T. Mommsen, *The History of Rome* (1959); M. Rostovtzeff, *Rome*, trans. by J.D. Duff (1960); H.H. Scullard, *A History of the Roman World from 753 to 146 B.C.* (1969); G. Showerman, *Rome and the Romans* (1931); C.G. Starr, *The Emergence of Rome as a Ruler of the Western World* (2d ed., 1953); N. Lewis and M. Reinhold, *Roman Civilization*, 2 vols. (1951–1955); M. Hadas, *A History of Rome* (1956); M. Rostovtseff, *Social and Economic History of the Roman Empire* (2d ed., 1957); E.T. Salmon, *A History of the Roman World from 30 B.C. to A.D. 138* (3d ed., 1957); F. Poulsen, *Glimpses of Roman Culture* (1950); E. Barker, *From Alexander to Constantine: Passages and Documents Illustrating the History of Social and Political Ideas* (1956); J.B. Bury, *History of the Later Roman Empire*, 2 vols. (1957); F. Lot, *The End of the Ancient World and the Beginnings of the Middle Ages* (1931); S. Katz, *The Decline of Rome and Rise of Medieval Europe* (1955); F.W. Walbank, *Decline of the Roman Empire in the West* (1947); H. Hill, *The Roman Middle Class* (1952); M. Last, *Family and Social Life in the Legacy of Rome* (1923); M. Cary and T.J. Haarhoff, *Life and Thought in the Greek and Roman World* (1940); F.F. Abbott, *The Common People of Rome* (1931); H.W. Johnston, *The Private Life of the Romans* (1903).

the merits and demerits of discordance within the laws of the Church and Irnerius (d. 1130) offered Roman Law for solving confusions in local laws.

The individual was subordinated to a collective world-order in which obedience to authority was what was emphasized. The work-ethic was characterized by collective ends as its goal.

D. The Renaissance

With Renaissance, man returned to the center of things. While in the primary economy of the medieval times the individual was dependent upon and closely linked to his community group, he now became mobile due to the new money economy. Men of money got rid of the medieval barriers to free entrepreneurship. The Medieval burgher was replaced by the early capitalist. The elite capitalists separated themselves from the middle class and from the workers. The great merchants (*haute bourgeoisie*) needed the support of the middle and small bourgeoisie in order to defeat the feudal aristocracy but once that was achieved, the real power went to a select plutocracy, not to the middle class represented by the lower guilds.

The new spirit of enterprise was introduced not only in economic matters but in political and military matters as well. Business and politics became interdependent. Politics became rational, governed by the considerations of means-and-ends for bourgeois aims. Justice meant abolition of traditional privileges. The principle of statecraft was no longer blood relationship, neighborhood, or relationships of service but social organization of a methodical, objective, and scientific kind. Since money capital and the time to use it became important, success required industriousness, economical expenditure, and an orderly plan. A cooperative relationship emerged between God's grace and man's performance. Religion lost its power and became only a matter of formal observances. Individual freedom displaced the Church leadership. Rationally calculable principles became the tool of organization. The concept of an absolute law in nature as well as in politics (Machiavelli) provided the presupposition needed for this free competition. Bourgeois empiricism opposed clerical speculation and transformed the individual's relation to the cosmos, leading to a secularized view of the world. As the money economy called for the ideal of exact numerical calculation, so the methods of mathematical equations became the method of interpreting the world itself, employing impersonal, abstract, interchangeable, and measurable quantities. Man, instead of being the object of domination, became the instrument of domination. Human labor became free, therefore open to exploitation. The new sciences took up all relationships for analysis of reason, no longer content with leaving them unexplained in divine origin. Understanding the laws of nature became a means of mastery over nature. Humanism came to the fore with its methodic insight (Petrarch) that humanities, poetry, history, and moral philosophy were intellectual instruments for attaining and expressing knowledge of subjective reality. Historical writings showed that the major turning points in the culture of man were found immanent in human history and not introduced by an eternal Divine plan. Ethical writings believed that return to the forms of ancient thought would restore man's natural virtue, which resulted in the pursuit of classical studies as a means of achieving what is specifically human.

Experience mediated between man and nature. It was governed by necessity. Leonardo grasped this necessity of nature by the rule of a proportional correlation and laid the methodic foundations of experimental science. Empirical interest in the phenomenal world was combined with mathematical techniques. Direct relations were established between natural knowledge and humanistic learning. Mathematical ideas interpenetrated with technical practice. The humanistic, the artistic, and the scientific were significantly interrelated, as exemplified in the Copernican Revolution in science. Humanism worked to restore the classic view of nature and, in turn, drew its basic historical and ethical ideas from the original creativity of the human spirit. The spiritual creativity of the humanists produced a completely secular concept of soul.

The Church became very worldly, fully exploiting money and credit economy to secure its material power, which made the clergy increasingly secular in outlook. The bourgeois interest in it became primarily political. The rationalist and humanist view of human *virtus* (that man can achieve everything by his own power) produced an ideological reaction that, as Martin Luther taught in his doctrine of *servum arbitrium*, salvation could be had by faith alone. This ideological reaction was accompanied by the proletariat's reaction against a worldly Church and its connection with the upper class. It turned to sectarianism and was suppressed by the stronger powers, both religious and secular. The passive and powerless middle class was ready to compromise with anything, including Erastian Protestantism. It supported Reformation because Reformation reacted against the capitalist mode of thought and idealized the primary producer and the artisan, as done by Luther, who himself was the son of a peasant. The anti-capitalist bias was evident in Calvinism as well. Puritanism originally favored the peasant and the artisan, although eventually it accepted the concept that the bourgeois way of life was compatible with a state of Grace. Reformation and Counter-Reformation were, thus, a reaction to the Renaissance.[4]

4. E. Cassirer, *The Individual and Cosmos in Renaissance Philosophy* (1927, trans. 1964); M. Chambers, *et al.*, *The Western Experience* (1974); V. Cronin, *The Florentine Renaissance* (1967); R. Ergrang, *The Renaissance* (1967); M.P. Gilmore, *The World of Humanism,*

E. The Early Modern Period

New commodities after 1600 increased food supply and the European population increased in a major way from 1500 to 1800. It became mobile as well. The middle class became prominent. The bourgeois determined the trend of cultural development more than any other class. It was not until the end of the nineteenth century that its rival, the industrial proletariat, appeared.

The theoretical pretensions of the Church failed to stop the supremacy of the secular state and philosophical justifications for it were found, firstly, in the doctrine of Roman law for claims to political absolutism, secondly, in the theory of the divine right of kings, and, thirdly, in the conceptions of a social contract (Locke, Pufendorf, Rousseau) that located the origin of civil society in an assumed agreement, on the one hand, among those who left the pre-social state of nature and, and on the other, between the rulers and the subjects.

With the growth of Rationalism and religious liberalism (Protestantism), the old struggle between the political state and the Roman Catholic Church faded. Jurisprudence divorced law from revelation and grounded it in human experience. Natural law doctrines were developed to sanctify personal lib-

---

1453–1517 (1952); G.R. Potter, ed., *The New Cambridge Modern History*, Vol. I (1967); A. von Martin, *Sociology of the Renaissance* (1963); G. Renard and G. Weulersse, *Life and Work in Modern Europe (Fifteenth and Eighteenth Centuries)* (1926); J.W. Thompson, *Economic and Social History of Later Middle Ages* (1931); P. Boissonade, *Life and Work in Medieval Europe* (1927); H.E. See, *Modern Capitalism: Its Origins and Development* (1928); J.A. Hobson, *Evolution of Modern Capitalism* (1926); H. Pirenne, *The Stages in the History of Capitalism* (1953); E. Lucki, *History of Renaissance, Vol. I: Economy and Society* (1964); R. Weiss, *The Dawn of Humanism in Italy* (1947); W.J. Bouwsma, *The Interpretation of Renaissance Humanism* (1959); P. Kristeller, *The Classics and Renaissance Thought* (1955); P. Kristeller, *Renaissance Thought: The Classic, Scholastic, and Humanistic Strains* (1961); E. Cassirer, P. Kristeller, and J.H. Randell, Jr., ed., *The Renaissance Philosophy of Man* (1953); J. Burckhardt, *The Civilization of the Renaissance in Italy* (1958); D. Hay, *The Italian Renaissance in Its Historical Background* (rev. ed., 1977); J.A. Mazzeo, *Renaissance and Revolution: The Remaking of European Thought* (1969); E. Garin, *Italian Humanism: Philosophy and Civic Life in the Renaissance* (1941, trans. 1965); G.R. Elton, *Reformation Europe, 1517–1559* (1963); A.G. Dickens, *Reformation and Society in Sixteenth Century Europe* (1960); O. Chadwick, *The Reformation* (1963); E. Chaney and P. Mack, eds., *England and the Continental Renaissance: Essays in Honor of J.B. Trapp* (1990); E. Cochrane and J. Kirshner, eds., *The Renaissance* (1986); Di Cesare, ed., *Reconsidering the Renaissance* (1992); M.S. Haynes, *The Italian Renaissance and Its Influence on Western Civilization* (1991); G.W. McLure, *Sorrow and Consolation in Italian Humanism* (1991); S. Ozment, ed., *Religion and Culture in the Renaissance and Reformation* (1989); J.N. Stephens, *The Italian Renaissance: The Origins of Intellectual and Artistic Change Before the Reformation* (1990); N.G. Wilson, *From Byzantium to Italy: Greek Studies in the Italian Renaissance* (1992).

erty and private property (Locke). Comparative jurisprudence (Montesquieu and others) applied conceptions of English common law to all peoples. Historical jurists (notably Edmund Burke) viewed law as an outgrowth of the organic culture of the nation. Later Rationalists stressed that law was the product of reason applied to specific social problems. The Utilitarians (chiefly Bentham) regarded rational jurisprudence as a science of social reform for increasing the happiness of the largest possible numbers. Legal codification was initiated in France and was followed in other European countries. International law rose.

The activities of the Rationalists helped curb cruelty and abuses of the regime and promoted social reform to uphold human dignity in man's earthly setting. The Romanticists vigorously attacked the Rationalist reaction to political and social problems and argued for tradition and authority. There emerged, too, the social and revolutionary doctrines and the Utopias of social change affecting the lower classes. Efforts were made to provide public relief to the poor, the first major example of which is found in the poor-law legislation of England from 1536 and 1796. The idea of state's responsibility for education came to be accepted, although free and compulsory public education did not appear in any significant manner until the nineteenth century. Vernacular literature grew considerably. Literature and art became predominantly middle-class in character.

F. The Modern Period

The modern civilization of Europe was achieved through a remarkable series of achievements in science, engineering, machinery, factory system, industrial and commercial cities, industrial capitalism, imperialism, democratic government, national spirit, and escape from the destruction of the World War. Industrial Revolution denoted a broad conception to include all economic changes that resulted in contemporary material culture as well as the consequent changes in social institutions. It proceeded in three main phases, namely, (a) the revolutionary changes in the technical methods of manufacturing, transportation, and communication, (b) the rise of the factory system as a new method for the organization of industry and use of labor, and (c) the economic, social, political, and cultural effects resulting from the new technology.

The civilization shifted its basis from rural to urban. The modern industrial areas produced new social problems. New methods of communication informed the individual of the world. Class consciousness in the worker stimulated free public education for the masses. Culture became standardized. The laborer became just a cog in the industrial machine. The middle class became politically all-powerful and protected itself through constitutions and legislation guaranteeing property rights. The rising proletariat challenged that class and became an important participant in the democratic process. Increased productivity promoted search overseas for new colonies, raw materials, and markets. producing the modern national imperialism. The concept of corporation separated ownership from management. Price system and profit motive controlled business ideals. The larger scale of business resulted in a marked concentration of control, as, for example, in the shift in American economy after about 1870 from early industrial capitalism to monopoly capitalism.

This capitalism resulted in inhumane conditions in the factory and the mine. That produced both an apology for capitalism in the form of Economic Liberalism as well an attack upon it. Economic Liberalism used its *laissez-faire* concepts to defend the new capitalist order and prevent remedial legislation for social ills. Founded by the French Physiocrats[5] of the mid-eighteenth century and supported by the French economist Turgot (1727–1781) and the Scotch philosopher Adam Smith (1723–1790), its English followers included Thomas Robert Malthus (1766–1834, arguing that the proletariat created its own misery through an excessive birthrate), David Ricardo (1772–1823, propounding his subsistence theory of wages whereunder wages tended toward a level that allows the working class to exist and perpetuate itself without either increase or decrease), James Stuart Mill (1773–1836, arguing that the Utilitarian ideal of the greatest good for the greatest numbers could be achieved only through the principles of Economic Liberalism), John Ramsay McCulloch (1789–1864, proposing his wage-fund doctrine whereunder only a certain amount of money could be diverted into wages without destroying the whole industrial process), and Nassau William Senior (1790–1864, warning against shortening of hours of labor since profits were made only in the last hours of the day). Such doctrines were promoted in France, Germany, and America as well.[6] Herbert Spencer (1820–1903) invoked the new agnostic naturalism to defend the individualistic doctrine of Economic Liberalism.

Economic Liberalism was opposed by six main sources. First, the economists argued that the value of an economic, social, or political policy cannot be judged by the criterion of wealth of particular individuals or classes,[7] that economics must assume responsibility for general prosperity and

---

5. So named after the title of a book by one of them, Dupont de Nemours, *Physiocracy or the Natural Constitution of that Form of Government Most Advantageous to the Human Race* (1767).

6. France: Jean Baptiste Say (1767–1832), Frederic Bastiat (1801–1850). Germany: Johann Heinrich von Thunen (1783–1850), Karl Heinrich Rau (1792–1870). America: Henrey C. Carey (1793–1879).

7. For example, Lord Lauderdale (1759–1839) and John Rae (1786–1873).

social reform,[8] that protective tariffs were needed for self-sufficiency and prosperity,[9] and that economic theories must change with economic changes in history.[10] Second, the political parties opposed to business elements helped produce remedial legislation for social reform. Third, the early Christian Socialism contrasted the social doctrines of Christ with traditionalism and ritualism of the historical church.[11] Fourth, the representatives of the literary and artistic standards of the age attacked Economic Liberalism in their so-called esthetic revolt.[12] Fifth, the Utopian Socialism of the first half of the nineteenth century denounced the assumptions of Romanticism, individualism, and Economic Liberalism and revived the notions of the French Revolution that regarded human intelligence and ingenuity quite capable of creating a new social and economic order. Sixth, the Transitional or Revolutionary Socialism[13] argued that labor was cheated under the capitalist society and the only effective help can come to the proletariat from their own effort.

Revolutions erupted in the winter and spring of 1848 throughout central, southern, and western Europe in which the masses sought political participation, but they all failed. That failure promoted the growth of the revolutionary Marxian Socialism.

The first Industrial Revolution resulted in a gradual transition of the Western civilization from an agricultural to an urban basis, net gains in population as a result of medical science, the widespread success of the bourgeoisie in its power struggle against the old agrarian vested interests, the proletarian challenge to capitalism, a new system of social classes based on wealth, the popular belief in the existence of equality of opportunity, the growing independence of women and change in their status, the psychological strains on people from having to deal with a profoundly changed

8. Notably, Jean Charles Leonard (Simonde) de Sismondi (177301842).

9. Adam Heinrich Muller (1779–1829); Friedrich List (1789–1846), Henrey C. Carey (1793–1879).

10. Richard Jones (1790–1885), Brune Hildebrand (1812–1878), Wilhelm Roscher (1817–1894), Karl Knies (1821–1898).

11. Pioneered by Henri de Saint-Simon, *The New Christianity* (1825).

12. Prominently, Charles Dickens (1812–1870), Thomas Carlyle (1795–1881), John Ruskin (1819–1900), George Sand (1804–1876), Leo Tolstoy (1829–1910), Matthew Arnold (1822–1888).

13. Its important representatives were the Ricardian Socialists of England, namely, William Thompson (1785–1833), John Gray (d. about 1850), Thomas Hodgskins (1787–1869), and John Francis Bray (about 1840), the French thinkers, namely, Louis Blanc (1813–1882) and Pierre Joseph Proudhon (1809–1865), and the German thinkers, namely, Wilhelm Weitling (1808–1870) and Ferdinand Lassale (1825–1864).

volume and variety of subject matter, a greater amount of leisure time for the masses, and the important position of economics as the basis of contemporary culture.

The First Industrial Revolution ended about 1850 and a Second Industrial Revolution began, which is characterized by remarkable new inventions, considerable modification and systematization of the methodology of invention, discovery and use of new forms of power, especially electricity, development of increasingly complex machines, emergence of precision instruments and machinery, domination of industry by science, increasing replacement of natural materials by synthetic products, a tremendous increase in the volume of industrial production, invention of new means of communication and transportation as well as improvement in the older modes, significant increase in industrial capital, emergence of finance capitalism that combined finance, banking, and industry, new forms of industrial organization, high-pressure advertising, a diffusion of the industrial technique throughout Europe and elsewhere, concentration of industry in suitable geographic areas, politico-economic policies with economic consequences, new problems of life interests and class relationships for the workers, and so on. A Third Industrial Revolution began after 1918.

Between 1871 and 1914, parliamentary institutions developed in almost the whole of western and central Europe, though varying in form and effectiveness. State policies engaged into social problems. Labor became organized. Socialism grew. Modern Scientific Socialism originated in the works of Karl Marx (1818–1883) and Friedrich Engles (1820–1895). The English Fabians (Sidney Webb, Graham Wallace, Bernard Shaw, Chiozza Money, Edward Pease, H.G. Wells, Stewart Headlam) repudiated Marx's fatalism and made socialism an evolutionary, rather than a revolutionary, movement, laying down the tenets of Revisionism. State Socialism proposed reforms but hoped to retain the capitalist system. England, Germany, France, and other European states experimented with social legislation of State Socialism, although the United States lagged behind.

Romantics indulged in personal self-expression and originality in art and literature. Nationalistic movements heightened attention to the historic uniqueness of each nation. However, science remained international. Two rival world-views developed in it: one, the absolute system of scientific truth (Isaac Newton, d. 1727), two, the view of reality as developmental flux (Albert Michelson, d. 1931, Albert Einstein, 1879–1955). Reality could be seized upon unique strategic moments. It became a process of unending change (Georg Wilhelm Friedrich Hegel, 1770–1831). In a world where everything changed, human values of the absolute and eternal kind came to be challenged.

After the First World War (1914–1918), urban patterns increasingly shaped the attitudes toward work, family, and the world. Mass media became influential, enabling less than rational appeals, as in commercial advertising or political movements. Awareness of the irrational dimension of human conduct popularized the investigation of the unconscious mind (Sigmund Freud, d. 1939). Natural sciences did not experience any fundamental new insight but new mathematical and conceptual tools were developed as a result of the quantum mechanics of the 1920s (Werner Heisenberg, Erwin Schrodinger, and others). The technique of deliberate invention reversed the earlier process of invention where the inventor used to invent first before promoting the practical application of his invention. Now, the decision of what kind of a machine or weapon was desired came first and, thereafter, its design and development was assigned to the experts. In socio-economic management, too, the technique of deliberate invention was applied and the inquirer analyzed the process into its components, identified critical points, and applied his ingenuity to come up with an idea that would improve the process. World War II (1939–1945) and its consequences brought more changes.

And the Western civilization continues to flourish in its own particular way.[14]

14. E.H. Barnes, *The History of the Western Civilization*, 2 vols. (1935); R.R. Palmer and J. Colton, *A History of the Modern World* (6th ed., 1984); H. Thomas, *A History of the World* (1979); D. Thomson, *Europe Since Napoleon* (2d ed., 1962); C.J.H. Hayes, *Political and Social History of Modern Europe*, 2 vols. (1916); J.E. Gillespie, *History of Europe, 1500–1L15* (1928); Smith, *History of Modern Culture*; D. Ogg, *Europe in the Seventeenth Century* (1925, 1961); R.B. Mowat, *The Age of Reason* (1934); W. Lecky, *History of Rationalism*; W. Lecky, *The Rise and Influence of Rationalism in Europe*; W.A. Dunning, *History of Political Theories from Luther to Montesquieu* (1905); W.A. Dunning, *History of Political Theories from Rousseau to Spencer* (1920); J.O. Hertzler, *History of Utopian Thought* (1923); F.L. Nussbaum, *History of Economic Institutions of Modern Europe* (1935); J.B. Bury, *The Idea of Progress: An Inquiry into its Origin and Growth* (1921); H.A.L. Fisher, *A History of Europe* (1936); P. Fussell, *The Great World War and Modern Memory* (1975); P. Mantoux, *The Industrial Revolution in the Eighteenth Century* (1961); N.M. Ostan, *An Economic History of Western Europe* (1967); H. Sidgwick, *The Development of European Polity* (1903); W. Sombart, *The Quintessence of Capitalism* (1915); J.R. Talmon, *Romanticism and Revolt: Europe 1815–1848*, (1968); J.H. Robinson and C.A. Beard, eds., *The Development of Modern Europe*, 2 vols. (rev. ed., 1929–1930); F.A. Ogg and Sharp, *Economic Development of Modern Europe* (1968); F.C. Dietz, *The Industrial Revolution* (1927); M. Quennell and C.H.B. Quennell, *The Rise of Industrialism, 1733–1851* (1932); J.F. Scott and A. Baltzly, eds., *Readings in European History Since 1814* (1930); L.H. Haney, *History of Economic Thought* (1911); A. Birnie, *Economic History of Europe* (1930); Meakin, *The New Industrial Revolution* (1928); S. Chase, *Men and Machines* (1929); Mayo, *The Human Problems of an Industrial Civilization* (1977); L.C. Marshall, *Readings in Industrial Society: A Study in the Structure and Functioning of Modern Economic Organization* (rev. ed., 1929); Hall and Beller, *Historical Readings in Nineteenth Century Thought*;

While the above profile of the Western way of life in not an exhaustive treatment of it, hopefully enough has been said to show that this way of life grew in its own particular historicity and, because of that, acquired its own particular profile. Therefore, its patterns are indigenous, not inevitable for other civilizations.

2. *The Chinese Way of Life*

The Chinese way of life, too, grew in the unique soil of its own historicity. We shall view it below in chunks of four periods, namely, the formative age (from prehistory to 206 B.C.), the early empire (from 206 B.C. to A.D. 960), the later empire (960–1850), and the modern period (since 1850).

A. From Prehistory to 206 B.C.

As distinguished from other major peoples of the world, the Chinese entertain no creation myth, no epic legend of ancient migrations. Instead, there are Three Sovereigns, Five Emperors, Three Sages, and Three Dynasties. The Three Sovereigns were Fu-hsi (Ox-tamer, whose reign began in 2850 B.C.), Shen Nung (Divine Farmer, whose reign began in 2737 B.C.), and Huang-ti (Yellow Emperor, whose reign began in 2697 B.C). The legendary Five Emperors began with Huang-ti. The Three Sages consisted of the fourth emperor (Yao, ruled 2357–2256 B.C.), the fifth emperor (Shun, ruled 2255–2205 B.C.), and Shun's successor Yu (ruled 2205–2198 B.C.). The Three Dynasties were composed of the Hsia (2205–1766 B.C.), the Shang (1766–1122 B.C.), and the Chou (1122–256 B.C.). Facts of history apart, the traditional Chinese found in this remote past a golden age of social stability and good government which showed them the "ways of

---

C. Wilson, *The Transformation of Europe, 1558–1648* (1976); R. Davis, *The Rise of the Atlantic Economies* (1973); C.M. Cipolla, *Before the Industrial Revolution: European Society and Economy 100–1700* (1976); C.N. Clark, *The Seventeenth Century* (1929, 1961); W. Doyle, *The Old European Order, 166–1800* (1978); M.S. Anderson, *Europe in the Eighteenth Century, 1713–1783* (2d ed., 1977); R.J. Whyte, *Europe in the Eighteenth Century* (1965); G.L. Mosse, *The Culture of Western Europe: The Nineteenth and Twentieth Centuries* (1961); R.N. Stromberg, *European Intellectual History Since 1789* (3d ed., 1981); W.L. Langer, *Political and Social Upheaval, 1832–1852* (1969); P.S. Robertson, *Revolutions of 1848: A Social History* (1952); N. Rich, *The Age of Nationalism and Reform, 1850–1890)* (1970); C.J.H. Hayes, *A Generation of Materialism, 1871–1900* (1941); J.K. Munholland, *Origins of Contemporary Europe, 1890–1914* (1970); W.H. McNeill, *A World History* (2d ed., 1971).

antiquity" that must be emulated. The form of this belief shaped and reshaped institutions throughout the Chinese history.

By Ch'in times, certain principles of government came to be well established, the foremost of which was the doctrine of the Mandate of Heaven (*t'ien-ming*), whereunder an impersonal but all-powerful Heaven (*t'en*) dominated the cosmos and no man ruled except by the Mandate of Heaven. The ruler was entrusted with the responsibility for "all under heaven (*t'ien-hsia*)." Social organization was characterized by the patrilineal family and the class differentiation. Under the late traditional view, there were four classes: the scholar-officials (*shih*), the farmers (*nung*), the artisans (*kung*), and the merchants (*shang*). The ideological traditions developed during this period were probably the most influential factor in the shaping of the Chinese civilization over the centuries.

Basic to all Chinese thought was the conception that the cosmic universe is one entity with three elements: Heaven, Earth, and Man. Tao, or the Way, is the process according to which all things in the cosmos function through the interaction of Yang (the male element: sun, light, and warmth) and Yin (the female element: moon, dark, and cold). The consequence of a disturbance between the two is not viewed as a question of good-and-bad in an absolute sense but as something inappropriate or harmful. Various kinds of spiritual beings (*shen*) exist that affect material affairs and while the ruler deals with Heaven and Earth on behalf of all human beings, each person deals with the lesser spiritual forces according to his own resources. Consequently, the conception of the universe as a single integrated entity means that everything must be regarded as belonging to its appropriate role in one undivided universe and not, as much of the Western thought regards them, situated in antagonistic polarities. Their polytheism means for them that their apparent contradictions must be accommodated and, therefore, one must not entertain absolute contrasts of right and wrong or good and bad.

The turmoil of the last Chou dynasty produced not a philosophy of despair or notions of refuge in afterlife but an optimistic belief in this life and in the possibility of improving it. Three thoughts emerged, namely, Confucianism, Taoism, and Legalism. Though differing from each other, they were complementary, especially the first two.

Confucianism is a set of ethical and political doctrines developed in the teachings of Confucius (557?–479 B.C.),[15] Mencius (about 372–about 289

15. K'ung Ch'iu was his name. The Chinese revered him as K'ung fu-tzu (Master K'ung). European missionaries latinized that name to Confucius. He was born a generation before Buddha (late sixth century–483 B.C.) and he died a decade before Socrates (470?–399 B.C.) was born.

B.C.),[16] and Hsun-tzu (about 300–about 235 B.C.).[17] These thinkers had their own differences, but they had a common theme which consisted of seven propositions, namely, that an impersonal but willful Heaven (*t'ien*) governs the universe, that Heaven wills men to be happy and orderly in accord with cosmic harmony (*tao*), that the appropriate human contributions to the cosmic harmony is an ethical and virtuous life, that virtue (*te*) is actively developed by and is manifested in proper conduct (*li*), that it is not easy to know Heaven's will or choose between conflicting values in major crises, that proper conduct requires wisdom which can be acquired only by studying the precepts of the sages and the lessons of history and by cultivating oneself accordingly, and that individuals and society are perfectible, so that everyone can be a sage and society can be harmonious for all. Ethically, appropriate virtues were prescribed for the five relationships (*wu lan*) in which the society was ordered. Thus, filial piety was the virtue for father-son relationship, loyalty for ruler-subject, brotherliness for brother-brother, love and obedience for husband-wife, and faithfulness for friend-friend. These constituted *li* (proper conduct) and *jen* (kindness and humanness). *Li* and *jen* connected these virtues to the values of righteousness, resolution, wisdom, sincerity, and a sense of shame. Education, not heredity, was the means for attaining social success. The wisdom of Confucius was recorded by his disciples in the Five Classics, which later became the object of study for the educated man and provided the common core of shared experience from which fundamental values flowed that held the Chinese civilization together until our own times.

That which is called Confucianism is an expression of *li*, which is the essential principle of Chinese life. *Li* originated in the course of a period of 350 years beginning with the early years of the Western Chou dynasty (1122 B.C.), through the Shu Ching (Book of History), the Shih Ching (Book of Poetry, 1122–600 B.C.), and Tsao Chuan ("Spring and Autumn" Annals, 770–464 B.C.). It attained its full meaning through the Lun Yu (Analects) of Confucius, the works of his successors and followers during the Warring States period (463–222 B.C.), and the Li Chi (Book of *Li*) compiled during the early part of the former Han dynasty (206 B.C.–A.D. 8).

In the Book of History (Shu Ching), it indicated ceremonies, religious ritual, and sacrifices usually connected with ancestor worship. In the Book of Poetry (Shih Ching), it indicated correct and proper behavior. It was up to a man to follow that conduct which would maintain harmony between him and nature. In the later documents of the Book of Poetry and in the Spring and Autumn Annals, it became a particular responsibility of the ruler

16. His name was Meng K'o. He was revered as Meng-tzu (Master Meng). His name was latinized to Mencius.

17. His name was Hsun Ch'ing.

to govern in accordance with *li*. Corresponding to the above mentioned five relationships were the five respective lessons of behavior (*wu chiao*). Disregard of one's duty invited appropriate action for restoring the harmony between the human and non-human spheres that had been lost due to that infraction. Corresponding to the five lessons of behavior (*wu chiao*) were five punishments (*wu hsing*). *Fa* (regulations, statutes, laws) was the procedure for enforcement of punishment and was always regarded with suspicion and antipathy, since preference was accorded to personal relations of *li* and its practice in the spirit of benevolence and harmony. With Confucius, *li* became a principle of social organization and control. The moral essence of *li* lay in filial piety (*hsiao*) and it derived its effectiveness from the moral impetus of virtue or excellence in character (*te*) directed toward the expected cultivation of benevolence or humaneness (*jen*), righteousness, in the sense of that which is right to do as one's duty (*i*), wisdom or practical knowledge (*chih*), and confidence (*hsin*). Law (*fa*) was considered hideous. Confucius insisted upon a positive motivation of the people to avoid misconduct detrimental to social relations, conformity to *li*, and avoidance of litigation (*sung*). Finally, the Book of Li (the Li Chi), gave a complete expression of *li*. It was compiled in the early part of the Former Han dynasty, as mentioned above, and it contains 3,300 rules of behavior made concrete in customs, habits, and ceremonies, all designed to maintain an all-embracing social harmony in accordance with the highly valued ancient way of life. Failure in one's duty calls for a socially agreed corrective or a disciplinary sanction and moral education for securing proper conduct in the future. This education includes both exhortation and punishment. In non-criminal matters, as well, reliance is placed on the self-regulating procedure of *li*, so that prevention of litigation is considered better than taking recourse to it.

It is significant to note that *li* was something internal to human conduct, not something imposed from above by a human or divine agency. Its practice was internally enforced as a demonstration of man's personal ability to contribute to the universal harmony and to the cultivation of his being and his society.

Taoism originated in a departure from Confucianism made by Mo Ti, known as Mo-tzu (about 470–391 B.C.) With Yang Chu (440–360 B.C.), it took on an escapist point of view. The main texts of its teachings are the *Lao-tzu* (Master Lao), also known as the *Tao-te-Ching* (The Classic of the Way and of Virtue), and the *Chuang-tzu*. In contrast with the Confucianist moralism, it is a mystic proponence of individualism, quietism, and spontaneity in union with nature (*tao*). It seeks peace of mind by being natural and spontaneous, renouncing obligations issuing from social relationships and institutions. One achieves by non-striving or non-action (*wu-wei*). It, thus, satisfied people's need for that aspect of reality which lies in mystery, magic, and passion and thereby complemented the decorum and self-control of Confucianism. The two, together, almost in a balance, provided the most stable pattern of human thought in history. Though modified and replenished, that pattern was never fundamentally interrupted until the twentieth century.

Legalism disputed the Confucianist-Taoist view that "the ways of antiquity" were the best. It focussed upon what must be done to make the state survive and prosper. Its original proponent was the administrative specialist Kuan Chang in the seventh century B.C. Subsequently, Shen Pu-hai (d. 337 B.C.) elaborated upon administrative techniques (*shu*). Shen Tao (held office about 300 B.C.) emphasized authority (*shih*). Kung-sun Yang (d. 338 B.C.) emphasized law (*fa*). Finally, Li Ssu (d. 208 B.C.) and Han Fei (d. 233 B.C.) provided the Legalist synthesis. It maintained that people in the present were neither worse nor better than their ancestors. A small population of antiquity, which possessed sufficient land for food, changed to a large population whose needs exceeded production. This produced contention and competition. That necessitated strict governmental control. In the sphere of authority what mattered was power, not talent, wisdom, or virtue. What was crucial to administration was not the sentiment of trust but the art of manipulating people. Law had nothing divine to it. It was man-made. It was the only means for ensuring that people (including the ruler) would do what is best for the state. Laws must be promulgated with clarity, be comprehensive in detail, and be enforced strictly through both reward and punishment.However, as demonstrated by the collapse of Ch'in, Legalism proved an unrealistic approach for China.[18]

---

18. K. Chang, *The Archaeology of Ancient China* (2d ed., 1971); H.G. Creel, *The Birth of China: A Study of the Formative Period of Chinese Civilization* (1937, 1954); C.Y. Hsu, *Ancient China in Transition: An Analysis of Social Mobility, 722–222 B.C.* (1965); C.O. Hooker, *China's Imperial Past: An Introduction to Chinese History and Culture* (1975); W. Watson, *Cultural Frontiers in Ancient East Asia* (1971); W. Eichhorn, *Chinese Civilization, An Introduction*, trans. by J. Seligman (1969); W.T. deBary, Jr., W. Chan, and B. Watson, *Sources of Chinese Tradition* (1960); J. Gernet, *Ancient China: From the Beginnings to the Empire*, trans. by R. Rudorff (1968); L. Chi, *The Beginnings of Chinese Civilization* (1957); A. Waley, *Three Ways of Thought in Ancient China* (1939); W. Watson, *China Before the Han Dynasty* (1961); V.G. Childe, *New Light on the Most Ancient East* (1952); E.O. Reischauer and J.K. Fairbank, *The History of East Asian Civilization; Volume One: East Asia, The Great Tradition* (1958, 1960); L.C. Goodrich, *A Short History of the Chinese People* (3d ed., 1959); H.G. Creel, *Confucius: The Man and the Myth* (1949); H.G. Creel, *Chinese Thought from Confucius to Mao Tse-tung* (1955); H. Welch, *The Parting of the Way—Lao Tzu and the Taoist Movement* (1957); H.G. Creel, *The Origins of Statecraft in China* (1970); D. Bodde, *China's First Unifier: A Study of the Ch'in Dynasty as See in the Life of Li Ssu* (1938); N. Nivison and A.F. Wright, eds., *Confucianism in Action* (1959); A.F. Wright, ed., *The Confucian Persuasion* (1960); J.G. Anderson, *Children of the Yellow Earth* Studies in

Thus, Confucianism, Taoism, and Legalism emerged as important principles of social life in the formative period of Chinese history.

B. The Early Empire (206 B.C.–A.D. 960)

The period of early empire was ushered in with the collapse of the Ch'in in 207–206 B.C. and went through the Han dynasty (202 B.C.–A.D. 220), the era of division (220–589), the reunification of 559, the T'ang dynasty (618–907), and the era of the Five Dynasties (907–960) that was made up of the Later Liang (907–923), the later T'ang (923–934), the later Chin 936–947), the later Han (947–951), and the later Chou (951–960).

By the time of the early Han emperors, the landowners had become the dominant class, educated in Confucian teachings and recruited into the imperial bureaucracy. Rival doctrines were repressed or absorbed into Confucianism. The officials and the landowners kept the peasants and the lower ranks where they belonged. There existed, as a consequence, a remarkable uniformity of outlook among the educated class. There was some contact with India and the Middle East, but that did not bring about any changes in the mainstream culture.

In the era of division, weakened government, civil war, and barbarian invasion provided the setting for displacing Confucianism by the ascetic withdrawal from the world preached by the Indian Buddhism. Chinese Buddhism soon took its own distinctive shape and filled the gap in Confucianism and Taoism for mystical enlightenment and withdrawal from civil society.

The reconstituted China emerged even stronger than in the Han times. Although central power was disrupted in 755 and weakened in the era following, it did not inhibit economic progress. Rice cultivation was extended, sustaining a large urban population of craftsmen, landlords, and government officials. Foreigners ran the trade, especially the Uighars and the

Prehistoric China (1934); Y. Fung, *A History of Chinese Philosophy* (1952); Y. Lin, *The Wisdom of China and India* (1942); J. Needham and W. Ling, *Science and Civilization in China* (1956); C.P. Fitzgerald, *China: A Short Cultural History* (1935, 1950); R. May, *Law and Society East and West: Dharma, Li, and Nomos* (1985); N.E. Fehl, *Li: Rites and Propriety in Literature and Life* (1971); A. Waley, *Analects of Confucius* (1938, 1971); D.J. Munro, *The Concept of Man in Early China* (1969); D. Bodde, "Dominant Ideas in the Formation of Chinese Culture," in D. Bodde, ed., *Essays on Chinese Civilization*, 132 (1981); T'ang Chun-i, "Cosmologies in Ancient Chinese Philosophy," 5 *Chinese Studies in Philosophy* 4 (1973); R. Dawson, *The Chinese Experience* (1978); D. Bodde, "Harmony and Conflict in Chinese Philosophy," in A.F. Wright, ed., *Studies on Chinese Thought*, 19 (1953, 1967); Y.P. Mei, "The Basis of Social, Ethical, and Spiritual Values in Chinese Philosophy," in C.A. Moore, ed., *The Chinese Mind*, 149 (1977); Yu-wei Hsieh, "Filial Piety and Chinese Society," *id.*, 167; T.-T. Chu, *Law and Society in Traditional China* (1961); M. Loewe, *The Pride That Was China* (1990).

Arabs. Since merchants were held in a low esteem in the Confucian scheme, the urban classes failed to challenge the traditional dominance of the landowning class in spite of growth in trade. The gentlemanly idea enjoyed a great deal of growth during the T'ang and the early Sung periods.

The Confucianists learned from Buddhism the technique of deriving new meanings from old texts by analogy and interpretation and the Taoists adopted from it monastic organization, schooling, and many aspects of the doctrine. The Confucian Classics were reinterpreted and Neo-Confucianism was launched, supported by the policy of the early Sung rulers that rejected all things alien and embraced all things native.

From Han through T'ang times, society was dominated by great families which were composed of (a) a rich and influential landowner, (b) his agricultural estate, its tenants, independent peasants, and slaves, (d) his guests (*k'o*), including astrologers, scholars, spies, and assassins, and (e) his fighting men (*pu-ch'u*). Feudalistic patterns became even more well established under the Northern and Southern Dynasties. During the fourth and fifth centuries, the large proportion of population was composed of serfs, bondsmen, slaves, and the disesteemed occupational groups of shamams, practitioners of medicine, entertainers, and the like. The respectable citizenry shrunk to a few freehold farmers, artisans, and tribal warriors. The mercantile class practically disappeared. The warrior *shih* class turned into a scholar-bureaucratic *shih* elite.

In the T'ang period, class rigidity and discrimination lessened in favor of a new assertion of individual human dignity. This came about as a result of four major factors, namely, the spread of compassionate Buddhism, the traditional tribal egalitarianism of the nomadic invaders, the efforts of the later Northern Dynasties to expand their political control, and the new civil service procedures of the Sui and T'ang dynasties. Nevertheless, a relatively small group of land-owning class still controlled wealth and political privilege.

Thought was characterized by (a) Han eclecticism, ((b) revived Taoism, and (c) Buddhism.

(a)The eclecticism of the early Han was a mixture of Taoist mysticism and naturalism with the prevailing myths and superstitions, as found in several late Chou works, especially *Li-chi* (Ritual Records), the new appendices to the ancient *I-ching* (Classics of Changes), and most notably the group of works known as *wei* (woof) that opposed the classical *ching* (warp). The forces of Yang and Yin were supplemented by Five Elements (*wu-hsing*) of wood, metal, fire, water, and earth, which were metaphysically correlated to all aspects of life, as Yang and Yin were correlated to the eight trigrams of the *I-ching*. These systems were brought into a synthesis by Tung Chung-shu, who applied numerology and cosmology to Confucianism.

Heaven rewarded good and punished evil. People could alter events by virtuous conduct. However, this belief in virtue was undermined by the disastrous usurpation of Wang Mang who used to be regarded a highly virtuous man. Wang Ch'ung expressed the new mood of pessimism and escapism of the Later Han period by ridiculing the idea that man could influence events and that Heaven dispensed good and ill appropriately. The Legalist arguments were revived by such thinkers as Ts'ui Shih (110–170), who advocated strong laws, strict enforcement, and harsh punishments.

(b) The revived Taoism or the Neo-Taoism of the Later Han period displayed two tendencies: revisionist and hedonistic. The revisionists, or the "discoursers on profundities," most prominently Wang Pi (226–249) and Kuo Hsiang (d. 312), maintained the nothingness (*Wu*) of absolute reality, emphasized non-action (*wu-wei*), and pointed to the wisdom of being content with oneself and letting nature take its course. The hedonists, or the "lyrical" or "romantic" Taoists, most prominently the Seven Sages of the Bamboo Grove, led by Chi K'ang (223–262), maintained that the way to preserve moral integrity was to evade every duty, flout every convention, and indulge in every sensual and intellectual whim. In addition to these two tendencies, various cult groups emerged seeking physical immortality.

(c) Buddhism flourished in the Han times and grew to be the most dynamic force in the intellectual and religious life through the rest of the period of the early empire. It was founded in India by Siddhartha Gautama, the Enlightened (Buddha), born in the late sixth century B.C., who taught that there was neither a cosmic essence (Brahma) nor one's spiritual essence (Atman), that it was only your own craving for existence and self-ness that kept you in this world of illusion through the cycle of birth and rebirth, and that the way to break away from this cycle of suffering and rebirth was to realize that you were in that cycle only because you wanted to be. Conditions in the late Han period were just right for receiving such a doctrine, as they were for inventing the Taoist escapism. However, Buddhism was more attractive because, firstly, its higher teachings were preferred by the Chinese conservatives over the orgiastic practices of the Taoists, and, secondly, it was intellectually bolstered by the continuing vitality of its development in India while Taoism merely reinterpreted the *Lao-tsu* and the *Chuang-tzu*.

Many Buddhist sects sprouted in China. The four major ones were: (i) the T'ien-t'ai (Heavenly Terrace), (ii) the Huayen (Garland), both of which were heavily doctrinal and scholastic and, therefore, not very popular, (iii) the devotional Ching-t'u that preached salvation by faith and whose devotees aspired to go to the Pure Land (Ching-t'u) paradise after death, which was a Western Paradise under the *bodhisattva* Amitabha (A-mi-t'o-of) and attended by the Goddess of Mercy, Kuan-yin, and (iv) the Ch'an or Zen (meditation), developed by the monk Hui-neng (638–713), which taught that enlightenment consisted in un-selfconscious awareness of here and now that happened in a sudden, spontaneous flash, so that one must be receptive to whatever happened and respond to it spontaneously.

There was opposition to Buddhism, ranging from xenophobic arguments against it to the controversy between the Buddhists and Taoists over whether Buddha came first in historical times or Lao-tzu[19] to rational criticisms advanced by the Confucians. There were early persecutions and state proscriptions upon Buddhism, but these did not deter the Buddhist influence, which reached its peak in the T'ang dynasty. It was persecuted again in the last T'ang century. This time the persecution was on such a national scale and with such effectiveness that it never recovered from its devastation. Moreover, although by now thoroughly Sinicized, it lost some of its doctrinal inspiration since, by the end of the T'ang period, it virtually died out in India from where it used to receive its intellectual nourishment. Furthermore, Confucianism was being revived, an effort pioneered by the anti-Buddhist and anti-Taoist official litterateur Han Yu (786–824).[20]

As we shall see below, the period of the later empire witnessed a remarkable growth of the Neo-Confucian movement.

C. *The Later Empire (960–1850)*

The period of the later empire began with the establishment of the Sung dynasty (960–1279), after the long decline and fall of the T'ang. In 1126–1127, the alien state of Chin, ruled by proto-Manchu Jurchen peoples, captured the entire North China, while the southern realm was overrun by the Mongols in the 1270's. Kublai Khan set up his Yuan dynasty.

---

19. Wang Fu, who lived in the 4th century, wrote a book, *Lao-tzu hua-hu ching* (The Classic About Lao-tzu's Civilizing the Barbarians), which argued that Lao-tzu departed from China and went to India where he magically transformed a disciple to the historic Buddha, or, alternatively, he converted Buddha to Taoism, or, yet again alternatively, he became the Buddha himself.

20. Hucker, *Imperial Past*; M. Loewe, *Everyday Life in Early Imperial China* (1968); H.H. Dubs, trans., *History of the Former Han Dynasty (From Pan Ku's Han-sul*, 3 vols. (1938–1955); T.T. Ch'u, *Han Social Structure*, ed. J.L. Dull (1972); W. Bingham, *The Founding of the T'ang Dynasty: The Fall of Sui and the Rise of T'ang* (1941); A.F. Wright and D. Twitchett, eds., *Perspectives on the T'ang* (1973); Goodrich, *Short History*; A.F. Wright, *Buddhism in Chinese History* (1959); W. Eberhard, *Conquerors and Rulers: Social Forces in Medieval China* (1952); F. Yu-lan, *A History of Chinese Philosophy*, trans. by D. Bodde, 2 vols. (1937, 1952); Reischauer and Fairbank, *East Asia*; J.K. Fairbank, ed., *Chinese Thought and Institutions* (1957); A.F. Wright, ed., *The Confucian Persuasion* (1960); W.T. deBarge, *et al.*, Sources of the Chinese Tradition (1960); S. Chan, *Buddhism in Late Ch'ing Political Thought* (1985).

Popular uprising overthrew the Yuan dynasty in 1368, replacing it with the native Ming dynasty (1368–1644). The Ming dynasty was replaced in 1644 by the Ch'ing dynasty of the invading Manchus from the northeast (1644–1912), which was the last of the imperial age. During the Sung dynasty, dramatic growth occurred in population, urbanization, commerce, and technology. That pace slowed down in the Yuan and Ming times. The social structure of the metropolitan areas became much more complex than the cities of the early imperial age. During the course of the Ming and Ch'ing dynasties, great cities generally stopped growing and medium-sized commercial towns sprouted everywhere.

Social status became more and more a function of wealth than heredity. Sub-categories and specialized occupational groups added complexities to the classical stratification of the four classes, mentioned above. Education spread widely. A new elite, nick-named degree-holders, dominated government service and managed society. From the early Sung times on, the old Ch'in-Han aversion to extended families gave way to the flourishing of clan organizations. Secret societies, which date back to the Han period, intervened between individuals and the government. These societies were either religious (*chiao*) or political (*hui*). Popular religion was characterized by a broad eclecticism of Buddhist, Taoist, and Confucian elements into a system of Three Doctrines (*san-chiao*) which, though officially condemned, dominated popular religious practices right into the twentieth century. Other religions were generally tolerated, even Islam, Nestorianism, and Christianity.

Confucianism re-emerged in the Sung times as the dynamic creed of the newly dominant scholar-official class. This Neo-Confucianism, often called *Tao-hsueh* (Study of the Way), was not a reassertion of ancient Confucian values but a fashioning of new truths from old rhetoric. It regarded the world as real, not illusory in the Buddhist fashion. Fulfillment was achieved by participating in it, not by staying aloof in the Taoist mode. It rejected the Buddhist promises of spiritual salvation and the Taoist promises of physical immortality, and it focussed upon self-cultivation in this life and upon social and political reform in this world. In the Sung times, it emphasized reform. In the Ming times, it emphasized self-cultivation of the individual. In the Ch'ing times, it tended toward a conservative scholasticism in reaction to Ming excesses. It was imbued with a strong sense of social-welfare activism. Its reformist activities emphasized practical effort (*kung-li*) and effective government (*ching-shih*). After the Sung reforms, the emphasis shifted to self-cultivation. This self-cultivation, most prominent in the twelfth century, was characterized by two trends. One, Study of the Principles (*li-hsueh*), or the Ch'eng-Chu School, pointed to dualism and rationalism.

Two, Study of the Mind (*hsin-hsueh*), or the Lu-Wang School, pointed to monism and idealism.[21]

D. The Modern Period (Since 1850)

Although the Taiping revolution failed, it shifted the locus of power from the Manchus to the Chinese. It inspired later revolutionaries, notably Dr. Sun Yat-sen (1866–1925). Although the Taiping revolution was suppressed by 1864, other rebellions continued, namely, the Nien Rebellion in north China (1853–1868), the Muslim (Panthay) Rebellion in Yunan (1855–1873), and the Tungan Rebellion in the northwest (1862–1878). However, the Ch'ing government re-established its authority over most of the Empire. Military humiliation and concessions to foreign powers soon followed. The Europeans and the Japanese extracted more and more concessions from the Chinese officials. Such betrayal of national interest prompted proliferation of secret societies aimed at overthrowing the Manchu dynasty. The dynasty fell in 1911. A republic was established in 1912, although an effective government was lacking.

The dual challenge of domestic rebellion and foreign invasion forced a shift from traditional learning to the influx of Western ideas, pioneered by Yen Fu (1854–1921), who exalted Western assertiveness and deprecated Chinese passivity. While the Chinese civilization was stability-oriented (*ching-te wen-hua*), the Western civilization was activity-oriented (*tung-te-wen-hua*). Lin Shua (1852–1924) translated Western works which signifi-

---

21. Hucker, *Imperial Past*; Reischauer and Fairbank, *East Asia*; J.T.C. Liu and P.J. Golas, eds., *Change in Sung China: Innovation or Renovation?* (1969); J. Gernet, *Daily Life in China on the Eve of the Mongol Invasion, 1250–1276*, trans. by H.M. Wright (1962); M. Prawdin, *The Mongol Empire: Its Rise and Legacy*, trans. by E. and C. Paul (1940); E.D. Phillips, *The Mongols* (1969); J.W. Dardess, *Conquerors and Confucians: Aspects of Political Change in Late Yuan China* (1973); C.O. Hucker, *The Traditional Chinese in Ming Times, 1368–1644* (1961); W.T. deBary, *et al.*, *Self and Society in Ming Thought* (1970); F. Michael, *The Origin of Manchu Rule in China: Frontiers and Bureaucracy as Interacting Forces in the Chinese Empire* (1942, 1965); K.C. Hsiao, *Rural China: Imperial Control in the Nineteenth Century* (1960); C.L. Chang, *The Chinese Gentry: Studies on Their Role in Nineteenth-Century Chinese Society* (1955); J. Meskill, ed., *The Patterns of Chinese History: Cycles, Development, or Stagnation?* (1965); Creel, *Chinese Thought*; Y.L. Fung, *A Short History of Chinese Philosophy*, ed. D. Bodde (1948, 1960); deBary, *Chinese Tradition*; W.T. Chan, *A Source Book in Chinese Philosophy* (1963); C.E. Moore, ed., *The Chinese Mind: Essentials of Chinese Philosophy and Culture* (1967); K.A. Wittfogel and C. Feng, *History of Chinese Society, Liao (907–1125)* (1949); E.R. Hughes, *The Invasion of China by the Western World* (1938); F. Michael, *The Origin of Manchu Rule in China* (1942); T.H.C. Lee, ed., *China and Europe: Images and Influence in Sixteenth to Eighteenth Centuries* (1991); K Liu, ed., *Orthodoxy in Late Imperial China* (1990).

cantly influenced the younger generation. The kinship society disintegrated. Inalienable rights of the individual were a matter beyond the control of the family head. Modern schools transferred the responsibility for education from the family to the government. New legal codes replaced the old juridical basis of the kinship society by the inalienable rights of the individual, the equality of sexes, the right of women to inherit property, and so on. The new influx of Western ideas eroded the Confucian precepts of family loyalty, filial piety, the Three Bonds (ruler and subject, father and son, and husband and wife), and the Five Relations (the Three plus brothers and friends). Two new social classes surfaced: the new rich class of the compradores and the new power class of the militarists. Both threatened the earlier scholar-official class and challenged the traditional social stratification of the four classes of the scholar-official (*shih*), the farmer (*hung*), the artisan (*kung*), and the merchant (*shang*).

The New Cultural Movement or the May Fourth Movement (named after the demonstration of 4 May 1919 in Peking) attacked traditional ethics, customs, literature, social relations, and institutions in favor of a new Westernized culture. But the new culture was slow to emerge. Nevertheless, three trends became evident. First, the literary revolution produced revolutionary literature through the establishment of the Plain Language in 1920 and brought it to social consciousness. Second, two conflicting approaches to social construction emerged, one evolutionary, the other revolutionary. The former was adopted by the Nationalist Party, the latter by the Communist Party. The conflict between the two determined the history of China since 1921. Third, a strong reaction arose against foreign imperialism and unequal treaties.

The Nationalist Government was established in 1928. The subsequent decade of 1928–1937 was a decade of internal troubles and external invasion (*nei-yu wai-huan*). The decade itself is well summarized by the Chinese expression *wai-ch'iang chung-kan* (strong on the outside and weak inside). Although there was modernization in finance, communication, defense, and light industry, ignored was the misery of the peasant who constituted more than 80 percent of the population.

The Sino-Japanese war (1937–1945) was primarily won by the Americans. A civil war (1945–1949) within China ended in the Communist victory. The Organic Law of 1949 made the Chinese People's Republic not a dictatorship of the proletariat, as in the Soviet Union, but a democratic dictatorship led by the Communist Party on the basis of an alliance of the four classes, namely, the proletariat, the peasantry, the petty bourgeoisie, and the national bourgeoisie. This period of New Democracy ended in 1953, when a program of Socialist Transformation was launched. In 1956, a new period of Socialist Construction began.

Although the Soviet-style socialist legality was adopted in the Constitution of 1954, the Soviet model was abandoned in 1960 when relations with the Soviet Union were broken off. China reverted to a path of its own where social transformation prevailed over economic growth and the Soviet-style democratic centralism was abandoned. Persuasion was emphasized over force. The adversary was treated as not beyond redemption. The practice of self-criticism was adopted. There has been a return to the ancient traditions, although there are significant departures from the traditional thought. The cosmology of natural phenomena and human behavior is no longer entertained. However, mediation remains as a main means for settling disputes, albeit the former methods of mediation by the family, or the clan, or the neighbors, or the local dignitaries has been replaced by mediation by those politically involved, such as the people's mediation committees. Need to re-establish harmony has been supplemented by the need to assure success of some policy. Legality continues to be repudiated in favor of education and persuasion. Most conflicts are resolved by an appeal to conscience, rather than by pursuit of rights in courts of law.[22]

Thus, the Chinese way of life has grown in its own particular history, which is not that of the individualism of the West and its concomitant legalism.

22. I.C.Y. Hsu, *The Rise of Modern China* (2d ed., 1975); J.K. Fairbank, E.O. Reischauer, A.M. Craig, *A History of East Asian Civilization: Volume Two: East Asia, The Modern Transformation* (1965); G.M. Beckman, *The Modernization of China and Japan* (1962); P.H. Clyde, *The Far East: A History of the Impact of the West on Eastern Asia* (3d ed., 1958); H.M. Vinacke, *A History of the Far East in Modern Times* (6th ed., 1961); O.E. Clubb, *20th Century China* (1964); S. van der Spenkel, *Legal Institutions in Manchu China, A Sociological Analysis* (1962); J.K. Fairbank, *Trade and Diplomacy on the China Coast: The Opening of the Treaty Ports. 1842–1854* (1953); M.C. Wright, *The Last Stand of Chinese Conservatism, the T'ung-chih Restoration, 1862–1867* (1957); M. Banno, *China and the West 1858–1861: The Origins of the Tsungli Yamen* (1964); P.A. Cohen, *China and Christianity: The Missionary Movement and the Growth of Chinese Antiforeignism 1860–1870* (1963); V. Purcell, *The Boxer Uprising, A Background Study* (1963); J.R. Levenson, *Confucian China and Its Modern Fate*, 2 vols. (1958, 1964); C. Tse-tung, *The May Fourth Movement: Intellectual Revolution in Modern China* (1960); S. Chiang, *The Nien Rebellion* (1954); F. Michael and C. Chang, *The Taiping Rebellion: History and Documents*, 3 vols. (1966, 1971); Y. Hao, *The Compradore in Nineteenth Century China: Bridge Between East and West* (1970); S. Teng and J.K. Fairbank, *China's Response to West* (1954); P.S. Ropp, ed, *Heritage of China: Contemporary Perspectives on Chinese Civilization* (1990); G. Wang, *The Chineseness of China: Selected Essays* (1991); J.D. Spence, *Chinese Roundabout: Essays in History and Culture* (1992).

3. *The Indian Way of Life*

The uniquely Indian way of life is the result of its own particular historicity. Like the Chinese but unlike the Egyptian or Mesopotamian civilizations, there is an unbroken continuity of its traditions from the ancient times. We shall observe India in four periods: the ancient or the pre-Muslim period, the Muslim period, the British period, and the period of independence since 1947.

A. *The Ancient Period*

The ancient period is composed of (i) the prehistoric period, which includes the agricultural communities in Baluchistan about 3000 B.C. and the Harappa culture of 2500–1500 B.C., (ii) the Vedic period, which includes the composition of the Hymns of the Rg Veda in 1500–900 B.C., the Mahabharata war in 900 B.C., and the period of the later Vedas, Brahmanas, and early Upanishads from 900 to 500 B.C., (iii) the Buddhist period that begins with Gautama Buddha (563–483 B.C.) and ends with the invasion of Alexander of Macedonia (327–325 B.C.), (iv) the Mauryan period (322–183 B.C.), (v) the age of invasions (190 B.C.–A.D. 388), (vi) the Gupta period (320–647), (vii) the dynasties of northern India (711–1192), and (viii) the dynasties of the peninsula (300–1565).[23]

About 3000 B.C., agriculturists settled in villages in the upland valleys of Baluchistan and the plains of the Makran and the lower Indus. The Harappa Culture extended in a stretch of about 950 miles from north and south of the Indus valley. Outside of it, the Baluchistan's village cultures continued in their own patterns. This civilization was conservative and theocratic, enjoyed a continuity of government, possessed a script of some 270 characters, and had contact with Mesopotamia. Some animals and certain

23. Historian A.L. Basham concludes that "[a]t most periods of her history India, though a cultural unit, has been torn by internecine war. In statecraft her rulers were cunning and unscrupulous. Famine, flood and plague visited her from time to time, and killed millions of her people. Inequality of birth was given religious sanction, and the lot of the humble was generally hard. Yet our overall impression is that in no other part of the ancient world were the relations of man and man, and of man and the state, so fair and humane. In no other civilization were slaves so few in number, and in no other ancient lawbook are their rights so well protected as in the *Arthasastra*. No other lawgiver proclaimed such notable ideals of fair play in battle as did Manu. In all her history of warfare Hindu India has few tales to tell of cities put to the sword or of the massacre of non-combatants. The ghastly sadism of the kings of Assyria, who flayed their captives alive, is completely without parallel in ancient India. There was sporadic cruelty and oppression no doubt, but, in comparison with conditions in other early cultures, it was mild. To us the most striking feature of ancient Indian civilization is its humanity." A.L. Basham, *The Wonder That Was India*, 8–9 (1954).

trees were sacred, as in Hinduism of today. There was a horned god, the Proto-Shiva, who is quite akin to the Shiva of later Hinduism. Phallic worship was prevalent, as in later Hinduism. Harappa people were the first in the world to use cotton, wild rice, water buffalo, and domestic fowl.

The semi-nomadic barbarians inhabiting the steppeland of Central Asia began emigrating by about 2000 B.C. due to the pressure of their population on the exhausted pastoral land. Some remained in their old home and became the ancestors of the later Baltic and Slavonic peoples. Some invaded Europe and became the ancestors of the Greeks, Latins, Celts, and Teutons. Some went to Anatolia and, mixing with the original inhabitants there, became the ancestors of the Hittites. Some moved south to Caucasus and the Iranian tableland, from where they attacked the Middle Eastern civilizations. Those who invaded India called themselves Arya, a word anglicized into Aryan. The ancient Persians called themselves that, too, which name survives in the word Iran. Eire represents the most westerly reach of the Indo-European peoples in the ancient times. The Harappa cities were invaded by the Aryans in about 2000 B.C., or shortly thereafter. Among the invading tribes was a group of related tribes under the chiefhood of the Bharatas, who had perfected a poetic technique of composition of hymns to be sung at sacrifices in praise of their gods. These were handed down orally, collected, and arranged in the early part of the 1st millennium B.C., though not reduced to writing. This collection, called Rg Veda, is the most sacred text of the Hindus which, along with the subsequent oral religious literature of the first half of the 1st millennium B.C., constitutes part of the living Hindu tradition.

The Aryans came to India already possessed of a class division in their tribal structure. Faced with settling among the darker aboriginals, they stressed purity of blood. These class divisions hardened and excluded the Dasas, the hated survivors of the Harappa Culture, as well as those Aryans who intermarried with them. By the end of the Rg Vedic period, the society was divided into four hierarchical classes which, in the descending order, were the priest (*brahman*), warrior (*kshatriya*), peasant (*vaishya*), and serf (*shudra*). This division exists to this day.

The fundamentals of caste had been well established during this period, to which is linked the modern caste organization. The foremost identification of a person was his caste, rather than a state or its king. The caste did not have territorial boundaries or internal administration. As a result, political and territorial administration was only of secondary importance. The basis of kingship lay in human need and military necessity, the king's first duty being to lead his people in war.

The idea of a divine cosmic order already existed in the Rg Vedic period. The later concept of *dharma* became the most important basis for ordering social relations. *Dharma* is an untranslatable word with many meanings, ranging from the general meaning of righteousness to the legal meaning of divinely ordained norm of good conduct or the sacred law. It prevailed over other bases of law, namely, contract, custom, and royal ordinance. The king was the protector of *dharma*, rewarding the righteous and punishing the evildoer. It was the king's duty to maintain *dharma* by *danda* (stick), which meant force, coercion, or punishment.

Although an intense militarism prevailed in external affairs, it did not lead to a permanent, unified empire, with the exception of the Mauryas and the Guptas in north India. That was due to the Indian concept of conquest which, according to Kautilya's famous text on statecraft, the *Arthashastra*, was of three types: (a) righteous conquest (*dharmavijaya*), in which the defeated king is forced to pay tribute and then is reinstated as a vassal, (b) conquest for greed (*lobhavijaya*), in which a large booty is extracted and vast areas of the vanquished territory are annexed, and (c) demonic conquest (*asurvijaya*), in which the conquered kingdom is politically annihilated and is assimilated into the territory of the victorious king. The righteous conquest was preferred and the other two were condemned. The six instruments of policy (*sadgunya*) were peace (*sandhi*), war (*vigraha*), waiting for the enemy to strike first (*asara*), attack (*yan*), alliance (*samshraya*), and double policy (*dvaidhibhava*) of making peace with one enemy and fighting with the other.

Within the Aryan social structure, the dominant fair minority maintained the purity of its group and its dominance over the darker majority by classifying the society into four *varnas*, wherein the dark-skinned people were assigned to the lowest serf class. Even in the Dravidian south, where *varna* was late in coming, the precedential stratification of the four classes eventually succeeded in establishing a sure hold of the society. The three higher classes (*brahman*, *kshatriya*, and *vaishya*), were twice-born (*dvija*), once at birth and then at initiation when they were invested with the sacred thread. The *shudra* were not regarded as Aryan and had no initiation. The *brahmans* had written the texts (such as the *Dharma Shastras*) which laid down the rules of conduct for the four classes, retaining for themselves the highest honor, precedence, and privileges. The *kshatriyas*, also known as *rajarya* in the Vedic period, were the ruling class. The two classes provided a check upon each other's pretensions. This ruling class was made up of all classes and ranks, including those of the invaders as well as those on the margins of the Aryan civilization, such as the Greeks (*Yavana*), the Scyths (*Shaka*), and the Parthians (*Pahlava*). The *vaishya* class was made up of merchants who ranked below the first two, although they were entitled to the sacred thread initiation. It originated in the peasant tribesmen but grew to other occupations than farming and cattle raising, such as dealing in jewels, metals, threads, spices, perfumes, and other merchandise. The *shudras* were not twice-born and were denied initiation. They included groups that refused to accept the rigid customs of the *brahmans* and adhered to the objectionable customs of meat eating, widow remarriage, and so on. The excluded *shudras* (*nirvasita shudra*) were considered outside the society and were assimilated with those who later were regarded as untouchables. The pure or not-excluded *shudras* (*anirvasita shudras*) were assigned the duty to wait on the other three classes and lived off the master's leftover food, cast-off clothing, and discarded furniture. While they could not hear the Vedas, they could hear the Epics (Mahabharata and Ramayana) and Puranas.

Outside this social structure were numerous groups, later called the untouchables or outcasts, such as the *chandala*, who lived outside the boundaries of an Aryan village and cremated corpses and executed criminals, and the *mleccha*, the outer barbarians, who were despised as invaders but for whom an improvement was hoped.

The caste (*jati*) system, although traced in its present-day form to the end of this period, did not develop out of the four *varnas*. It is characterized by (i) endogamy, wherein legitimate marriage is possible only within the caste, (ii) commensality, wherein one receives food or eats it only in the presence of a member of the same or higher caste, and (iii) craft-exclusiveness, wherein one practices the trade of one's own caste and not another. A caste is an association developed over thousands of years on the basis of region, race, profession, or religion. It is independent of government. Its most severe sanction is social ostracism. This has enabled the Hindu to live under the political order of the day imposed from above throughout his history and yet retain his cultural individuality. Attempts to break this system have failed.

Thus, there exist two systems of *varna* and *jati*, and the relationship between the two has never been harmonized.

The family was a joint family, which is still generally the case today. It was a patriarchal family and it included parents, children, grandchildren, uncles and their descendants, collaterals on the man's side, and, sometimes, adopted children. They lived together and held the property in common. The family, not the individual, was the primary unit of society. The present Hindu law of family has two schools: *Dayabhaga*, followed in Bengal and Assam, under which the male head of the family is not an outright owner of the family property but manages it and protects it for his descendants, and *Mitakshara*, followed in the rest of the country, under which sons and grandsons have a right in it even before the death of the head of the family.

The ideal of life followed a scheme of four stages, or *ashrams*, all of which were attended by nearly forty ceremonies. These four stages were the *brah-*

macharin, which began with the second birth at the sacred-thread investiture and in which the boy lived a life of celibacy and austerity at the home of his teacher and devoted himself to the learning of the Vedas and Vedangas, the *grahastha*, in which the individual returned to his parental home, was married, and led a householder's life, the *vanaprastha*, in which the middle-aged man went into the forest to live like a hermit, after having established his family line, and the *sanyasin*, in which the old man left the hermitage and wandered homelessly, totally separating himself from the material world.

The religions of this period included the religion of the Vedas, Buddhism, Jainism, Hinduism, and the non-Indian religions of Christianity, Judaism, Zoroastrianism, and Islam.

The essential principle of individual and communal life of most Indians is *dharma*. As mentioned above, the word is untranslatable, but its concept is certainly not that of law in the Western sense. *Dharma* originated at the very beginning of Indian civilization, when the Aryan tribal community assigned governmental leadership to the king (*raja*) and spiritual leadership to the priest (*brahman*). By the end of the Rg Vedic period, a fourfold division of society came to prevail along the lines of the four *varnas*, described above. A mode of order had been achieved in this way wherein men engaged in actions to ensure the support of gods. *Rta* denoted the universal cosmic order, which was immanent, pre-existent, and independent of any other force. *Vrata* denoted the notion of laws laid down by gods. *Dharma* denoted that which upholds or sustains. *Rta* offered an order to apprehend man's phenomenal surrounding and to structure irregular phenomena into a form of regularity. Gods gave examples of *dharma* to uphold that which existed in order (*rta*), thereby making man conscious of his own active, though ordered, way of life.

The Vedas expressed *dharma* as a complex of action, conduct, ordinance, and principle of regularity in various situations. As such, it had three aspects, namely, an expression of nature's most active parts, an expression of natural and human phenomena, and an expression of abstract as well as concrete relations of pure knowledge and human affairs. The Upanishads shifted the emphasis to the life of man in all its aspects. While they recognized *dharma* as the supreme force of the world, they transformed it into an all-embracing support of life in this world. The Vedic *dharma* was, thus, related to practical necessities of everyday life. The principle of *karma* operated within the all-embracing function of *dharma*, thereby elaborating *dharma* into the many precepts and rules for human affairs. *Karma* sustained by *dharma* led to *moksha*, *i.e.*, the release from the cycle of life, death, and rebirth. The basis for a life of good actions lay in the man's efforts to conform to his duty.

The Vedas, Brahmanas, Aranyakas, and Upanishads constituted the *shruti* (heard) literature. The subsequent *smriti* (remembered) literature elaborated *dharma* further, adapting it to the changing conditions of life. The earliest *smriti* literature on *dharma* consisted of the *dharma sutras*, which were in the nature of manuals of the precepts of *dharma* stated in the form of aphorisms. The subsequent *dharma shastras* presented more detailed compositions in verse form, the most important of which was named after the ascetic Manu as the Manu-Smriti, usually translated in a misleading fashion as The Laws of Manu or the Code of Manu. These *dharma shastras* also included the secularly conceived *Arthashastra* of Kautilya, mentioned above.

All the various teachings of *dharma* addressed themselves to the issue of how to follow a way of life that would be in accordance with *dharma*. The sources of *dharma* were *shruti*, *smriti*, *achara* (good custom), and *atma-tushti* (self-satisfaction). We have mentioned *shruti* and *smriti* abvoe. *Achara* consisted of widespread and unambiguous practice followed by the virtuous upon a firm belief in *shruti* and *smriti*. *Atma-tushti*, or self-satisfaction, was considered unimportant by the authoritative mode of interpretation (*mimansa*). There were three kinds of *dharma*: *svadharma*, which consisted of one's individual duty as determined by his *varna* and *ashram*; *sadharana dharma*, which guided man's conduct for the benefit of the community as a whole and benefitted his own being as part of that whole, and whose most cardinal virtues were *ahimsa* (non-violence or abstention from injury) and *satyam* (truth); *purushartha*, which related to attaining the ends of man, namely *dharma*, *artha* (material possessions), *kama* (pleasure), and *moksha* (salvation).

Thus, in the ancient or pre-Muslim period of India we find the definition and development of the Indian way of life and its fundamental principles which abide to this day.[24]

24. Basham, *Wonder*; B. and F.R. Allchin, *The Birth of Indian Civilization: India and Pakistan Before 500 B.C.* (1968); R.E.M. Wheeler, *Early India and Pakistan, to Ashok* (1959); R.E.M. Wheeler,*The Indus Civilization*, The Cambridge History of India, Supplementary Volume (3d ed., 1968); R.C. Majumdar and A.D. Pusalker, eds., *History and Culture of the Indian People, I: The Vedic Age* (1951); J.H. Hutton, *Caste in India: Its Nature, Functions, and Origins* (1946); K.A. Nilakanta Sastri, *A History of South India from Prehistoric Times to the Fall of Vijayanagar* (3d ed., 1966); S. Dasgupta, *A History of Indian Philosophy*, 5 vols., (1932–1955); V.A. Smith, *Early History of India* (4th ed., 1924); V.G. Childe, *The Aryans: A Study of Indo-European Origins* (1926); V.G. Childe, *New Light on the Most Ancient East* (4th ed., 1952); L. Renou, *Religions of Ancient India* (1965); B.B. Lal, "The Indus Civilization," in A.L. Basham, ed., *A Cultural History of India*, 11 (1975); T. Burrow, "The Early Aryans," *id.*, 20; J.P. Marr, "The Early Dravidians," *id.*, 30; A.L. Basham, "Medieval Hindu India," *id.*, 51; S. Radhakrishnan, "Hinduism," *id.*, 60; B. Sangharakshita, "Buddhism," *id.*, 83; A.N. Upadhyaye, "Jainism," *id.*, 100; S.N. Dasgupta, "Philosophy," *id.*, 111; J.D.M. Derrett, "Social and Political Thought and Institutions," *id.*, 124;

B. The Muslim Period

This period began with Muslim invasions in the early 8th century, culminating into the Mughal Empire, which declined rapidly after the death of Emperor Aurangzeb in 1707 and died out with the ascendancy of the British, although it survived nominally until 1857.

The Indian society's response to the Muslim threat took two directions. First, the intellectuals attempted to neutralize the Islamic reproach of their idolatrous practices by interpreting and classifying the teachings of the Upanishads and by rationalizing the rites as means suitable for simple folks to comprehend a pure theological monism. The philosopher Shankara attempted to demonstrate how the Absolute lay behind every sensory experience. He even justified Muslim rites as helpful to those who could not go beyond the Prophet Muhammed in grasping the Truth. Second, on the less intellectual and popular level, there set in a rejection of all that was alien and a defense of all that was own. This led to the surfacing of all sorts of indigenous cults. Thus, Tantrism was elaborated, so that the supernatural powers which hitherto remained only within the prowess of the ascetics could now be achieved by ordinary men through magic charms and incantations, without the discipline and sacrifice of the ascetic. Tantrism was primarily a private system of rites, although sometimes it involved group practices.

The Hindu social system, characteristically, accommodated the Muslim conquerors by putting them into just another caste. However, the universal and missionary faith of Islam did not accept the caste system, since all men were considered equal before the omnipotence of Allah. Conse-

---

R. May, *Law and Society East and West, Dharma, Li, and Nomos* (1985); P.V. Kane, *History of Dharmashastra*, vols. 1–5 (1930–1962, 2d ed., 1968); J.D.M. Derrett, *Essays in Classical and Modern Hindu Law* (1977); J.D.M. Derrett, "The Concept of Duty in Ancient Indian Jurisprudence," in W.D. O'Flaherty and J.D.M. Derrett, eds., *The Concept of Duty in South Asia*, 3 (1978); F. Edgerton, *The Beginnings of Indian Philosophy* (1965); P.T. Raju, "The Concept of Man in Indian Thought," in S. Radhakrishnan and P.T. Raju, eds., *The Concept of Man: A Study in Comparative Philosophy*, 220 (2d ed., 1966); R. Lingat, *The Classical Law of India*, trans. J.D.M. Derrett (1973); K.V.R. Aiyangar, *Some Aspects of the Hindu View of Life According to Dharmashastra* (1952); G. Tha, *Hindu Law and Its Sources*, Vol.I (1930); N.C. Sengupta, *Evolution of Ancient Indian Law* (1953); J.D.M. Derrett, *Dharmashastra and Juridical Literature* (1973); W. The. DeBary, ed., *Sources of Indian Tradition* (1958); D.N. Majumdar, *Races and Cultures of India* (4th ed., 1961); T.M.P. Mahadevan, *Outlines of Hinduism* (2d ed., 1960); S. Radhakrishnan, *The Hindu View of Life* (10th impression, 1957); E. Conze, *Buddhist Thought in India* (1962); J.L. Jaini, *Outlines of Jainism* (1916, rev. ed., 1940); A.L. Basham, *The Origins and Development of Classical Hinduism* (1989); G.M. Bongard-Levin, *Ancient Indian Civilization* (1985); K. Jettmar, *The Religions of the Hindukush*, tr. by A. Nayyar *(1986)*.

quently, the preachers of Islam attracted the low-caste urban Hindus and the newcomers to Indian civilization along the frontiers of the Indian society, especially in Bengal, who were put by the caste system at the bottom of the hierarchy. The net result was that the Muslim community came to be composed of two segments, namely, first, a small number of rulers, warriors, and landowners, largely Persian in culture and Turkish in origin, and, second, a large number of humble folks brought into the fold of Islam.

The Muslim rule affected Hinduism in a variety of significant ways. First, it became more public and popular, since Muslim rulers drove it out of the temples by pillaging them. The religious ceremonies took to public squares and town/village streets, thereby strengthening the popular emotional excitement which Islam failed to snatch. Second, some thinkers, such as Kabir (d. 1518) or Nanak (the founder of Sikhism), attempted to synthesize Hinduism with Islam by grasping what was the truth in the two systems and repudiating what was false. Finally, the popularization of Hinduism was further strengthened by a shift from the classical Sanskrit language for religious purposes to the vernacular languages, such as Hindi and others. However, while Hinduism thus continued to survive, it no longer enjoyed the patronage of the ruling courts and official culture. Consequently, it declined in its literature and architecture, while its Islamic counterparts flourished.

Muslim rule in India expanded greatly in the period 1500 to 1700. The last independent Hindu state of Vijayanagar succumbed in 1565. Under Aurangzeb (1658–1707), practically all of peninsular India came under the Mughal control.

Hinduism received a new and vigorous adoration through the works of holy men and poets, especially the poets. For example, the saint Chaitanya (d. 1527) repudiated caste distinctions and other objectionable manifestations of the traditional religion. Through a substantial following, he promoted intensely emotional public ceremonies. This, in Bengal, succeeded in stopping conversion to Islam. Therefore, as the Indian society expanded eastward beyond the Ganges delta, it was Hinduism, not Islam, that embraced the new people. While Chaitanya's influence was limited to one sect, the revivifying influence of poets Sur Das (d. 1563) and Tulsi Das (d. 1623) was more widespread. They took themes of the Hindu tradition and developed them in Hindi verse. These verses were quite understandable to the Hindi-speaking population of the north and provided a rich treasure of chants and hymns for use in religious celebrations. These poets did not repudiate the ancient Sanskrit piety and Brahmanical ritual; they simply left them to the professional priests. Sur Das wrote about Lord Krishna and Tulsi Das wrote about Lord Rama. Since both were incarnations of Lord Vishnu, there was no doctrinal conflict.

In the net, the overwhelming majority of Indians remained Hindu, following the traditions of their ancestors and organizing their social life along their indigenous structures.[25]

C. The British Period

The Hindus did not find this change of their masters particularly important. Characteristically, they put the Europeans, too, in yet another caste. The official British policy left the social institutions and relationships alone. For example, the British kept Persian, not English, as the language of administration until 1857.

Dharma was applied to such matters of the Hindus as marriage, inheritance, the caste system, and religious usages and institutions. Correspondingly, Muslim law was applied to the Muslims. In other matters, a newly created territorial law applied to all subjects, regardless of their religious status. The idea of a territorial law, wherein law existed as an autonomous body independently of religion, was an alien concept to Indian traditions.

A distinction was drawn between the Presidency towns of Bombay, Calcutta, and Madras and the rest of India, known as *Mofussil*. English courts operated in the Presidency towns and applied English law as it existed in 1726, modified by regulations of local authorities and subject to its applicability to Indian conditions. Originally, their jurisdiction existed in disputes involving an Englishman or for parties who formally accepted that jurisdiction. In 1781, that jurisdiction was extended to all disputes. These courts were authorized to apply Hindu law to Hindus and Muslim law to Muslims. In the rest of India, the *Mofussil* courts, under the Governor-General's Regulation of 1772 for the Administration of Civil Justice, applied Hindu law and Muslim law in matters of inheritance, marriage, caste, and religious usages and institutions. In other matters, they applied general principles of justice, equity, and good conscience. The Regulation of 1781 created two superior courts for the provinces of Bengal, Bihar, and Orissa: the *Sadar Diwani Adalat* for private law matters and the *Sadar Nizami Adalat* for criminal matters. The Indian High Courts Act of 1861 reorganized the court system throughout the colony.

The first Law Commission proposed in its famous *lex loci* report that there be three codes: one for the Muslim law, one for the Hindu law, and

25. V.A. Smith, *The Oxford History of India* (3d ed., 1958); P. Spear, *India: A Modern History* (1961); W.M. Moreland, *From Akbar to Aurangzeb* (1923); W.H. McNeill, *A World History* (2d ed., 1971); S.A.A. Rizvi, "The Muslim Ruling Dynasties," in A.L. Basham, ed., *A Cultural History of India*, 245 (1975); S.A.A. Rizvi, "Islam in Medieval World," *id.*, 281; J.T.F. Jordens, "Medieval Hindu Devotionalism," *id.*, 266; H. McLeod, "Sikhism," *id.*, 294; R.C. Gupta, *Hindu Society and Influence of the Great Epics* (1991).

one in the nature of the territorial law (*lex loci*) for matters in which Hindu Law and Muslim Law did not apply. These proposals were met with serious objections. A second Law Commission was established in 1853 and made its own proposals. However, it was only after the revolt of 1857 that an intensive legislative activity for India took place. Various Codes were adopted, for example, the Indian Code of Civil Procedure (1859), which was replaced by the Civil Code of 1908, the Criminal Code (1860), the Code of Criminal Procedure (1861), the Limitations Act (1859), the Succession Act (1865), the Contract Act (1872), the Evidence Act (1872), the Specific Relief Act (1872), the Negotiable Instruments Act (1881), the Transfer of Property Act (1882), the Trusts Act (1882), and so on.

All this made for an efficient colonial administration by an imperial power. Some urban Indians became fashionably English in their attitudes and mannerism, although the social contact between the ruling English and the subject Indians was extremely limited. Most Indians continued to live their lives in accordance with their own traditions.[26]

D. The Period Since Independence

The break from the British, though cataclysmic due to partition of the country into India and Pakistan, was not abrupt. Limited self-government had already been established. India became independent in 1947 and adopted a secular Constitution in 1950. This Constitution provides for the maintenance of the former law (Section 372). New legal activity has followed and the tendency has been to replace the religious laws with a secular law. Moreover, India has been engaged in a vigorous activity of industrialization and modernization. There have also been efforts to abolish the undesirable features of such institutions as the caste system. Increased contact with the West has had its influence on life-styles, especially in urban centers. However, about eighty percent of the Indians live in villages and continue to conduct their lives through traditional institutions, traditions, and beliefs.

---

26. Spear, *India*; Smith, *Oxford History*; K.M. Panikkar, *A Survey of Indian History* (3d ed., 1956); K.M. Panikkar, *The Foundations of New India* (1963); R. Thapar, *A History of India* (1966); V.B. Singh, ed., *Economic History of India 1857–1956* (1965); H. Tinker, *Experiment with Freedom: India and Pakistan* 1947 (1967); P. Spear, "The Mughals and the British," in A.L. Basham, ed., *A Cultural History of India*, 348 (1975); J.T.F. Jordens, "Hindu Religious and Social Reform in British India," *id.*, 365; H. Owen, "The Nationalist Movement," *id.*, 391; C.H. Heimsath, *Indian Nationalism and Hindu Social Reform* (1964); J.N. Farquhar, *Modern Religion Movements in India* (1924); S.A. Natarajan, *A Century of Social Reform* (1959); L.I. and S.H. Rudolph, *The Modernity of Tradition: Political Development of India* (1967); V.S. Naravane, *A Cultural History of Modern India: Nineteenth Century* (1991).

Even in urban centers, where the changes are most evident, there has been a peculiarly Indian blend of Western ways with the Indian traditions in which the fundamental principle of *dharma*, the institution of joint family, the social organization of castes, and other traditions and customs are very much alive and practiced.

4. *The African Way of Life*

The history of Africa and the anthropology of its various peoples demonstrate that they possess their own unique way of life, morality, and social structure which are the result of their own particular historical circumstances. We shall observe below some major examples: the Tallensi, the Ashanti, the Hausa-Fulani, the Yoruba, the Ibo, the Tiv, the Ganda, the Lugbara, the Kikuyu, the Nandi, the Arusha, the Nyakyusa, and the Nuer.

(1). The Tallensi

The Tallensi people live in the basin of the Volta Rivers in a social pattern which the anthropologists call segmentary. A segmentary society is characterized by (a) a segmentary series, whether it be of lineages, where smaller lineage units compose larger ones, or of territorial groups, where smaller territorial units compose larger ones, and (b) a continual segmentation, whereunder a group divides in certain contexts but retains its identity in other contexts. The Tallensi are structured in smaller lineage units composing larger units, all made up of generations descending from a common male ancestor. Each unit has a role or a post designated in kinship terms, whose holder exercises authority, performs rituals, and represents the unit in its relations with other units. The basic unit consists of the nuclear family of a man and his sons, or the extended family of a man and his sons and their families, or the families of several sons of the dead father. The head of the extended family sees to the group's welfare, allocates tasks, and distributes the proceeds. As the lineage head, he holds property and valuables. As the ritual head, he has the custody of the ancestor shrines. He, his wife, and his sons have mutual obligations which are enforced not by a legal machinery but by etiquette.

The patrimonial property (*faar*) belongs to the lineage. It can, therefore, be used by its holder but not disposed by him. The individually acquired property belongs to the individual, subject to the rights of his father, until it becomes *faar* upon inheritance. Interdependency has created mutual obligations. Benefit received is accompanied by the duty to make equivalent returns.

Death does not terminate membership and participation in the kinship group. Ancestors, as spirits, influence the affairs of the group. The concept of *Yin* provides an individual's link with his ancestors. His destiny is preordained before birth. His *Yin* ancestors determine the most important aspects of his *Yin*. These ancestors reveal themselves to him in his early manhood.

Ancestors and spiritual forces preserve piety, cooperation, and solidarity of the kinship group. Misfortunes result from one's *Yin*. The earth, or *teng*, determines the fate of the community. Prayers and sacrifices to it prevent calamities and preserve the unity of the community. Chiefs and *tendaanas* are invested not with temporal power but with the function of performing rituals. *Teng* and ancestors provide the sanctions needed to maintain interests and obligations in the land. The cult of ancestors gives a spiritual dimension to the social order and provides the categories of thought and belief for organizing social intercourse. Wrongdoing is punished by the punitive action of the ancestors. The cycle of the Great Festivals provides a link between the ritual, social, and economic aspects of life. The ceremonies concentrate upon peace and harmony. All holders of ritual offices cooperate in their performance. These ceremonies can be interrupted by any complainant demanding settlement of his unresolved grievance. Witchcraft is not very important. Mystical forces redeem the wrong to the extent it remains outside the practical means of the injured person to secure it.

Inter-clan conflicts produce wars between them, but that rarely involves all Tallensi people. An unsettled injury suffered by a member of one clan from a member of another clan, such as adultery, abduction of a wife, or non-payment of a bride-price, provides justification for cattle-raiding. Conflicts within the clan are, for the most part, in the nature of rival claims to priority in exercising the political-ritual rights, which situation often represents a phase in the structural development of a lineage or clan. When a dispute arises, the lineage segments linked with the disputing parties support their respective sides. However, since these segments are themselves linked in a larger lineage common to them, peace is restored due to the demands of integration and harmony within this larger group. Refusal by a member of a clan to perform an obligation of the group is deemed an offense against the ancestors. In such a situation, a diviner is consulted. The diviner, in a public sermon, finds the mystical cause and transmits the commands of the ancestors to put the situation right through sacrifices and reconciliation.[27]

---

27. J. Middleton and D. Taits, "Introduction," *Tribes Without Rulers: Studies in African Segmentary Systems* (1958); M. Fortes, *The Web of Kinship Among the Tallensi* (1969); P.M. Worsley, "The Kinship System of the Tallensi: A Revaluation," 86 *Journal of the Royal Anthropological Institute* 37 (1956); M. Fortes, *Oedipus and Job in West African Religion*

(2) The Ashanti

The world for the Ashanti people possesses both temporal and spiritual nature. The individual is produced by the union of two spiritual elements, namely, the male spirit (*ntoro*) and the blood (*mogya*). The *ntoro* is transmitted in the male line of descent. The female, who receives the *ntoro* from her father, cannot transmit it. The *mogya*, which is the same thing as *abusua* (clan), confers the clan identity upon the child and invests him (or her) with reason. When the child is conceived by the union of the *ntoro* and the *mogya*, the *okra* comes to him as determined by the gods associated with the day of the week of his birth and determines his destiny. When a man dies, the *mogya* survives him as his *saman* (ghost) and exerts *sasa* (spiritual power) upon the living. His *sunsum*, which embodies his distinctive personality, dies with him.

The spirits of the ancestors and the gods influence the lives of humans. God *Onyame* is the supreme being possessed of power to protect people, which he exerts through lesser gods. The Earth is not a goddess but is still possessed of the power or spirit of fertility and makes all things grow. The land belongs to the ancestors, so that the living have only the right to use it. The spirits of the ancestors see to its proper use.

There is an interrelationship between spiritual forces, misfortune, and ritual communication. Contact with *Onyame* is maintained in the household through the household altar (a gourd positioned between the forks of a three-forked stick cut from the Tree of God), the sharing of the ritual of *ntoro*-washing, and the totemic observances and avoidances. Contact with ancestors is made by the lineage through the lineage stool, each lineage having its own stool for the ritual communication. The stool of the elder identifies his authority over the household, the stool of the chief identifies his authority over the tribe, and the Golden Stool of the Asantahene identifies his authority over the nation. The role of the intermediary with the spiritual world is provided by the elder of the lineage, the chief of the tribe, the Asantahene, the medicine man, and the witch doctor.

While the *ntoro* provides the individual his connection with the spiritual world, the *mogya* provides his connection with the physical world. Through the *mogya*, the person becomes the member of the lineage group, which is determined by matriliny. Thereby, he acquires his ritual status and property interests. His connections with his father's lineage group are subordinated to his matrilineal group. The lineage head or the elder is elected by the senior

---

(1983); M. Fortes, *The Dynamics of Clanship Among the Tallensi* (1967); M. Fortes, "Ritual and Office in Tribal Society," in M. Gluckman, ed., *Essays on the Ritual of Social Relations*, 73 (1962); M. Fortes, *Religion, Morality, and the Person: Essays on Tallensi Religion* (1987).

member of the lineage and is entrusted with mediating with the group's ancestors, managing its property, preserving its traditions, and settling disputes among its members. His decisions are arrived at after consulting other members of the household and are supported by religious sanctions.

The Ashanti chief is entrusted with propitiating the spirits and the gods and with leading his tribe in war. Prior to the battle of Feyiase against the Denkyira in 1669, the Ashanti were a people of separate tribes with a common culture. After this battle they emerged as a nation composed of tribes which, in turn, are composed of lineages. The relationship between the nation, the tribes, and the lineages is hierarchical, with a very significant requirement that the *Asantahene* of the nation must obtain the consent of the chiefs of the tribes and the chiefs must obtain the consent of the elders of the lineages. The *Asantahene*, the chiefs, and the elders perform rituals for the good of their respective groups. The council of chiefs appoints or removes the *Asantahene* from his stool.

The village is an economically self-sufficient unit. Its head, the *Odekuru*, is selected from the lineages living there. The chief, with the concurrence of his council of elders and approval of the people, makes levies and receives services for defraying expenses of war, a chief's funeral, or sacrifice of livestock. Communal labor provides public services, such as road repairs and village cleaning.

Land is not owned in any individual capacity, since it was earlier acquired by the common effort of clearing the forest and secured for the tribe by war. The individual has the right to farm a piece of it. This right is derived from his lineage. His specific share is allotted by the elder. Although the land itself cannot be alienated, the right to use it can be mortgaged with the chief's consent. With the consent of the lineage members, a person can leave a part of his right to a son upon his death. A male decedent's property is inherited on the basis of blood (*abusua*). Consequently, his own children cannot inherit because they belong to their mother's *mogya*. His heirs would include his maternal uncle, elder brother, successive brothers in age, mother's sister's son, and his own sister's son. A female descendent's property is inherited by her mother, her sisters by seniority, her daughters by seniority, and her sister's daughters.

A set of norms define deviant behavior, which include interpersonal conflicts as well as threat to the harmonious relations of the group with the spirits. Violation of these norms trigger inquiry in the family and the tribe, as well as in the nation. Severe sanctions are imposed for tribal offenses, since they entail a great risk of harm to the tribe through spiritual forces.[28]

---

28. K.A. Busia, *The Position of the Chief in the Modern Political System of the Ashanti* (1951); K.A. Busia, "The Ashanti," in D. Forde, ed., *African Worlds* (1954); R.S. Rattray, *Ashanti Law and Constitution* (1929, 1956); R.S. Rattray, *Religion and Art in Ashanti* (1927,

(iii) The Hausa-Fulani

The Hausa-Fulani live in north-central Nigeria, their original seven Hausa states being located in the region east of the Niger and west of Lake Chad. The Habe or Hausa are the indigenous inhabitants, a sedentary people living in walled towns and villages. The Fulbe or Fulani are the immigrant group, a nomadic, cattle-herding people. The Arab influence upon them is significant.

The Arabs divided north Africa into the Maghreb (West) and Egypt. The region of North Africa and the Sahara forms *Bilad al Bidan* (Land of the Whites). The region south of the Sahara up to the rain forest is the *Bilad as-Sudan* (Land of the Blacks). Trade routes existed in the west from southern Morocco to the central Niger region and in the east from Tripoli to the Hausa region, as well as from Egypt to the eastern Sudan. Consequently, both the Habe and the Fulani were exposed to the Islamic culture. However, due to the importance in early times of the western trade, the Fulani had a longer contact with Islam and they regarded themselves more faithful to Islam than the Hausa. This greater contact was also due to the fact that stable Negro empires, such as Songhay and Bornu, had first established themselves in western and central Sudan, resulting in increased intercourse with the Maghreb. The Islamic contact of any significance for the Hausa and Fulani began in the fourteenth century. A shift from the western to the eastern trade route occurred in the seventeenth century as a result of wars between Morocco and Songhay at the end of the sixteenth century. The Hausa enjoyed the consequent prosperity. However, the Fulani considered

---

1954); R.S. Rattray, *Ashanti* (1923, 1955); P. Abraham, *The Mind of Africa* (1952); E.L.R. Meyerowitz, *The Sacred State of the Akan* (1951); J.B. Danquah, *Akan Laws and Customs* (1928); M. Fortes, "The 'Submerged Descent Line' in Ashanti," in I. Schapera, ed., *Studies in Kinship and Marriage*, Royal Anthropological Institute Occasional Paper No. 16 (1963); M. Fortes, "Time and Social Structure: An Ashanti Case Study," in M. Fortes, ed., *Social Structure: Studies Presented to A.R. Radcliffe-Brown* (1963); N.A. Ollenu, *Principles of Customary Law in Ghana* (1962); K. Bentsi-Enchill, *Ghana Land Law: An Exposition, Analysis, and Critique* (1964); S.K.B. Asante, "Interests in Land in the Customary Law of Ghana—A New Appraisal," 74 *Yale Law Journal* 848 (1965); M. Manoukian, "Akan and Ga-Adangme Peoples of the Gold Coast," in D. Forde, ed., *Ethnographic Survey of Africa, Western Africa, Part I*, 9 (1950); T. Lewin, *Asante Before the British: the Prempean Years, 1875–1900* (1978); A.A.Y. Kyermaten, *Kingship and Ceremony in Ashanti* (1970); I. Wilks, *Asante in the Nineteenth Century: The Structure and Evolution of a Political Order* (1975); I. Wilks, *Forests of Gold: Essays on the Akan and the Kingdom of Assante* (1993); E.E. Obeng, *Ancient Ashanti Chieftaincy* (1988); D. Owusu-Ansah, *Islamic Talismani Tradition in Nineteenth-century Asante* (1991); M.K.C. Morrison, *Ethnicity and Political Integration: the Case of Ashanti, Ghana* (1982); L.W. Yarak, *Asante and the Dutch* (1990); M.D. McLeod, *The Asante* (1981); P. Sarpong, *Ghana in Retrospect: Some Aspects of Ghanian Culture* (1974).

themselves as the truer believers and, in the early nineteenth century, they conquered the Hausa in a holy war (*jihad*). The Islamic ways have a greater appeal in the diffused nomadic societies than in the kin-structured agricultural societies.

The bush Habe's social structure consists of the households of brothers and their sons under the headship of (i) the eldest son, (ii) the clan, which consists of households claiming common patrilineal descent, and (iii) the village with its farming headman chosen with the approval of the Fulani headman, the latter enjoying the final decision-making power. Allah is formally acknowledged, but it is the spirits which determine health and welfare. These spirits are classified as white (good) and black (evil). The spirit cults survive, since the Muslim men of learning had identified the Habe spirits as pagan jinn and thereby recognized them. However, the clan organization has been affected by Islam to the point of extinction, since it has lost its political and religious functions.

The pastoral Fulani have the nuclear and the extended family as their basic economic unit. The families from a common ancestor, usually limited to three generations, form a lineage group. They travel together with their milking herds and assist each other in difficulties. Marriages are performed within the group or other agnatic relations. The lineage group's leader, or *ardo*, is genealogically closest to the one he succeeds and is selected on the basis of unusual achievements.

The Fulani Way of preferred social virtues is composed of three parts: modesty and reserve, including correct conduct in personal situations, such as respect to elders and cooperation with equals; two, patience and fortitude; and, three, forethought and prudent planning. Parents instruct their children in the Fulani Way. The clan's Guardian of the Fulani Way is selected by descent in the purest line of the clan. In the Fulani Way, shame is felt in the belly, patience and fortitude in the heart, and care and forethought in the head. The importance of the Guardian of the Fulani Way has declined with increasing contacts with the Islamic way of life.

The compounds, or walled units, of the Hausa include two or three groups based on marriage with a compound head. The members of a compound form work units (*gandu*). The *gandu* mesh into communities and the communities into one another. A community has a common chief, a common market, and a common religious authority (*imam*). Achievement of high values, known as *Arziki*, includes birth, prestige, political protection, large family, good farming, money, wealth, and greater than average consumption. Tasks are divided between men and women.

Increased contacts with the Islamic way of life have resulted in disintegration of the lineage group and rise of the nuclear family (man, wives, children). The role of ancestors has diminished. The authority of the head of the extended family is replaced by the authority of the head of the nuclear family. As religious ritual became a personal matter in Islam, the performance of common ritual by family members has disappeared. The Islamic distribution of personal property among children has furthered this disintegration even more.

Disputes are settled by the chief of the village, the *hakimi* or fief-holder, the *Salenke*, and the *Alkali*. The chief decides land disputes and minor offenses. The *hakimi* ensures the observance of the Islamic law and is responsible to the king. The *Salenke* goes with the army to the war and decides all issues there. In times of peace, he decides serious offenses. The *Alkali* decides offenses involving severe punishment and hears appeals from the *Salenke*.[29]

(4) The Yoruba

The Yorubas are an agricultural people who live in southwestern Nigerian and western Benin. They entertain a cosmology wherein the three levels of the sky, the world, and the earth constitute the cosmos. While the sky is the domain of Olorun Oldumare, the supreme God, the world is for the living and is embraced by the sky and the earth. Olorun Oldumare has the *orisa*, or gods, as his subjects who affect relations between the sky and the world, which affect the affairs of the world. The sky-people are spirits of the living and of the souls awaiting rebirth, which dwell in the sky. The

29. M.G. Smith, *The Economy of Hausa Communities of Zaria* (1955); M.G. Smith, "Exchange and Marketing Among the Hausa," in P. Bohannan and G. Dalton, eds., *Markets in Africa*, 299 (1962); M.G. Smith, *Government in Szazzau* (1960); M.G. Smith, "Hausa Inheritance and Succession," in J.D.M. Derrett, *Studies in the Laws of Succession in Nigeria*, 230 (1965); M.G. Smith, "On Segmentary Lineage Systems," 86 *Journal of the Royal Anthropological Institute* 39 (1956); T. Hodgkin, *Nigerian Perspectives: An Historical Anthology* (1960); J.S. Trimingham, *Islam in West Africa* (1959); J. Greenberg, "Islam and Clan Organization Among the Hausa," 3 *Southwestern Journal of Anthropology* 193 (1947); D.J. Stenning, "Transhumance, Migratory Drift, Migration; Patterns of Pastoral Fulani Nomadism," 87 *Journal of the Royal Anthropological Institute* 58 (1957); D.J. Stenning, *Savannah Nomads* (1959); K. Buchanan, 'The Northern Region of Nigeria: The Geographical Background of Its Political Duality," 43 *The Geographical Review* 451 (1953); S.F. Nadel, "The Kedi: A Riverside State in Northern Nigeria," in M. Fortes and E.E. Evans-Pritchard, eds., *African Political Systems*, 177 (1940); V. Azarya, *Aristocrats Facing Change: the Fulbe in Guinea, Nigeria, and Cameroon* (1978); E. Mohammadou, *Peoples et royaumes du Toumbina* (1983); J.O. Gefu, *Pastoralist Perspectives in NIgeria: the Fulbe of Udubo Grazing Reserve* (1992); *Image and Reality in African Interethnic Relations: the Fulbe and Their Neighbors* (Studies in Third World Series, Publication 11; Department of Anthropology, College of William and Mary) (1981).

ancestors and the other dead dwell on earth under the domain of the goddess Onile.

The ancestors provide prosperity, children, and health, as well as punish those who do not behave properly or do not maintain proper relationship with the community. Before his birth, a person's fate is determined by God. After his birth, he remains in the care of the *orisa*. Ifa, the god of divination, reveals the intentions of the gods and enables a person to behave in a manner that would minimize the intervention of the gods. Ashu, the supreme power of evil, reports man's misdeeds to gods which earn the man his punishment. That punishment can be avoided by observing the norms of the community. In addition, there are about four hundred lesser gods. Man is related to the gods through his spirit, which is the divine element in him that controls both his heart-soul and his body.

The Yoruba kingdoms consist of metropolitan towns in which the *oba* (the king) lives, which are surrounded by a three-mile belt of farm land, then small hamlets where the farm workers sleep, and then the subordinate towns. Their towns are composed of compounds inhabited by lineage groups. The descent groups consist of (i) the domestic family, (ii) the larger group of descendants of a common male ancestor, and (iii) the largest group of all, called *idile* or the *ebei*, descending from a founding male ancestor. The *idile* is made up of patrilineal segments at various levels, called *isoko*, which consist of three or four generations. A member of the lineage is connected with it by its name, origin myths, songs, and facial markings. He enjoys the right to live in the lineage compound and use the lineage land. The lineage head (the *bale* or *olori ebi*) has the tasks of leading the performance of ritual, maintaining harmony among the members of the lineage, settling their disputes, judging their offenses, representing them to the community, interceding on their behalf in external disputes, organizing work, allotting land, and making disposition of the use of the land. In all of this, he has the final authority.

The head of an *isoko* or lineage segment holds a similar position within the *isoko*. The king is selected from a royal lineage. The procedure of *kirikiri* is used to remove the king or other power-holders for tyrannical deeds. Under this procedure, a mob parades through the realm, abuses him, pelts his residence with dirt and stones, and, if he does not leave or kill himself within three months, it selects a team to kill him. The *oba* is the paramount ruler who makes decisions in consultation with the council of senior chiefs and is possessed of both the ritual and the temporal authority. The matters of the allocation and use of land among the members of the family, the community, and the kingdoms are decided, respectively, by the head of the lineage, the chief, and the *oba* and his senior chiefs.

The lineage head makes decisions in such lineage affairs as marriages or disposition of land. He settles disputes among its members and adjudges certain offenses. Sanctions are provided by the power of the ancestors to bring misfortune. His decisions can be appealed to the court of the chief of the town, from which an appeal can be taken to the council of state of the *oba* and his chiefs. Custom defines offenses and prescribes the appropriate punishment.[30]

(5) The Ibo

The Ibo live in southwestern Nigeria, mostly in villages. They are composed of many tribes and groups. Together, they are among the most numerous of the peoples of Africa.

A man, for them, is a union of three elements: body, *mmuo* (his soul), which is centered in his heart and is the reincarnation of an ancestor or another being and is subjected to reincarnation again, and *ci* or *chi*, which is a portion of Chuku or Cineke, the Supreme Being. A man is expected to follow the individualistic path of attaining wealth and prestige through his

30. P.C. Lloyd, "The Yoruba Lineage," 25 *Africa* 234 (1955); D. Forde, "The Yoruba-Speaking Peoples of South-Western Nigeria," in D. Forde, ed., *Ethnographic Survey of Africa, Western Africa, Part IV*, 1 (1951, 1969); P. Morton-Williams, "An Outline of the Cosmology and Cult Organization of the Oyo Yoruba," 34 *Africa* 243 (1964); P. Morton-Williams, "The Yoruba Ogboni Cult in Oyo," 30 *Africa* 362 (1960); E.B. Idowu, *Olodumare: God in Yoruba Belief* (1962); J.O. Lucas, *The Religion of the Yorubas* (1948); P.C. Lloyd, *Yoruba Land Law* (1962); P.C. Lloyd, "Agnatic and Cognatic Descent Among the Yoruba," 1 *Journal of the Royal Anthropological Institute* 484 (new series, 1966); W.B. Schwab, "Kinship and Lineage Among the Yoruba," 25 *Africa* 352 (1955); P.C. Lloyd, "Sacred Kingship and Government Among the Yoruba," 30 *Africa* 221 (1960); P.C. Lloyd, "The Traditional Political System of the Yoruba," 10 *Southwestern Journal of Anthropology* 365 (1954); A.K. Ajisafe, *The Laws and Customs of the Yoruba People* (1946); S.O. Biobaku, "An Historical Sketch of Egba Traditional Authorities," 22 *Africa* 35 (1952); G.B.A. Coker, *Family Property Among the Yorubas* (2d ed., 1966); C. Partridge, "Native Law and Custom in Egbaland," 10 *Journal of the African Society* 422 (1911); W. Abimbola, ed., *Yoruba Oral Tradition* (1973); S. Johnson, *The History of the Yorubas: From the Earliest Times to the Beginning of the British Protectorate* (1973); P.F. de Moraes Farias and K. Barber, *Self-Assertion and Brokerage: Early Cultural Nationalism in West Africa* (1990); G.O.Olusanya, ed., *Studies in Yoruba History and Culture: Essays in Honour of Professor S.O. Biobaku* (1983); S.L. Bolaji, *Yoruba Living Heritage* (1984); B.O. Aboyade, *Yoruba Culture and Civilization: An Introductory Bibliography (1845–1976)* (1991); J.O.K. Olupona, *Kingship, Religion, and Rituals in a Nigerian Community* (1991); S. Gbadegesin, *African Philosophy: Traditional Yoruba Philosophy and Contemporary Africa Realities* (1991); H.S. Issah, *Yoruba Customs and Institutions: An Annotated Bibliography* (1988); A. Oquntuyi, *History of Ekiti: From the Beginning to 1939* (1979).

skill, although his family, lineage, and residential grouping provide the necessary support. He even has to decide for himself the particular spirits that he would call upon in difficulties. His social groups assist him in achieving status and influence. There are various groups, such as age grades, secret societies, men's societies, cooperative work groups, and title societies from whom he can obtain assistance for achieving his purposes. Members of a social group are generally considered equal, although there are recognized differences in social rank authority. Personal qualities, and not mere seniority, are the qualifications for a leader.

Chuku or Cineke, the Supreme Being, has sun and moon as his messengers. They inform him of what is happening on earth. The *alosi*, or the spirits created by Chuku, are assigned power over various aspects of human activities. The most important of these spirits is Ale, the god of earth, who governs social life, protects morals, brings fertility, and supervises farming activities. All deeds, such as murder, theft, or adultery, are offenses against Ale. Ale has the power to take life for punishment. The priest of Ale often participates in trials. The soil belongs to the ancestors. They are also the guardians of morality, so that deviation from custom results in their displeasure and punishment through misfortune. Oracles and diviners are consulted. Secret societies play an important role in maintaining order. The members of the secret society Mmo are regarded as ancestral spirits who carry out sanctions in cases of adultery and witchcraft.

Ummuna, which is a patrilineal group living together, is the basic social unit. The tribe or the village group is the largest social and political unit, composed of a number of villages whose members have descended from a common male ancestor. Members of each village have their own male ancestor descending from the tribal ancestor. Each lineage group divides itself into two separate kinship groups headed by a senior male. This dual division of lineage groups enables exogamy as well as cooperation in performing various village activities.

In addition, there are age sets and age grades, which perform social, political, and judicial tasks. Thus, they provide companionship and mutual protection, apprehend offenders, sanction decisions made by the elders, prevent abuse of authority in case of unjust decisions, fix harvest times, control fees, clear paths, guard markets, and defend the village in war.

The council of elders is the governing body for the lineage groups. It makes rules and settles disputes. The elders of the compound settle disputes among members, consult diviners, manage the lineage property, and represent the compound externally. The elders of the patrilineal groups within the compound perform similar tasks for their groups. The elders of the village decide upon the use of the village land, regulate village groupings, decide disputes, represent the village externally, and seek spiritual aid through a diviner in misfortune.

The head of the household (*okpara*) performs ritual, moral, and legal functions, including punishing those who have violated norms.

The lineage group bears a collective responsibility for violations of norms by its members. Adherence to norms is deemed necessary for maintaining the community's harmony with the spirit of the earth, which harmony is needed for good fortune. Violations offend Ale, the earth goddess. Where the perpetrator is unknown, a diviner is consulted. Where the perpetrator is known or suspected, the dispute is settled by a few selected individuals, or by the village elders at a trial, or through invoking the sacred spear of the Yam cult, whereunder its custodial village decides the dispute. A perpetrator caught red-handed is punished on the spot. The rules for land tenure attempt to secure the ultimate control of the land to the community, provide security of tenure for the individual user, and ensure that no member of the community is without land.[31]

---

31. S. Ottenberg, "Ibo Receptivity to Change," in W.R. Bascom and M.J. Herskovits, eds., *Continuity and Change in African Culture*, 130 (1959); S. Ottenberg, "Inheritance and Succession in Afikpo," in J.D.M. Derrett, ed., *Studies in the Laws of Succession in Nigeria*, 33 (1965); M.M. Green, *Ibo Village Affairs* (1947); R.A. Levine, *Dreams and Deeds: Achievement and Motivation in Nigeria* (1966); C.K. Meek, *Law and Authority in a Nigerian Tribe* (1937); W.R.G. Horton, "God, Man, and the Land in a Northern Ibo Village Group," 26 *Africa* 17 (1956); D. Forde and G.I. Jones, "The Ibo and the Ibibio-Speaking Peoples of South-Eastern Nigeria," in D. Forde, ed., *Ethnographic Survey of Africa, Part III*, 25 (1950); G.I. Jones, "Ibo Age Organization, with Special Reference to the Cross-River and North-Eastern Ibo," 42 *Journal of the Royal Anthropological Institute* 191 (1962); R.N. Henderson, "Onitsha Ibo Kinship Terminology: A Formal Analysis and Its Functional Applications," 23 *Southwestern Journal of Anthropology* 15 (1967); D. Forde, "Justice and Judgment Among the Southern Ibo under Colonial Rule," in H. Kuper and L. Kuper, eds., *African Law: Adaptation and Development*, 79 (1965); G.I. Jones, "Ibo Land Tenure," 19 *Africa* 314 (1949); M.M. Green, *Land Tenure in an Ibo Village*, Monographs on Social Anthropology, No. 6 (1941); L.T. Chubb, *Ibo Land Tenure* (1961); S.N.C. Obi, *The Ibo Law of Property* (1963); N.W. Thomas, *Anthropological Report on the Ibo-speaking Peoples of Nigeria* (1913, 1914); P.A. Oquagha, *History and Ethnoarchaeology in Eastern Nigeria: A Study of Igbo-Igala Relations with Special Reference to the Anambra Valley* (1984); S.G. Olisa, *Ossomari: A Kingdom of the Lower Niger Valley (1640–1986): A Comparative Study of the Tradition of Origin, Migration, and Settlement of a Niger Ibo Kingdom* (1990); D. Ohadike and R.N. Shain, *Western Igbo*; M.A. Onwuejeogwu, *An Igbo Civilization* (1981); *Igbo Socio-Political System: Papers Presented at the 1985 Ahiajoku Lecture Colloquium* (1986); L.C. Okere, *The Anthropology of Food in Rural Igboland* (1983); O.A.C. Anigbo, *Commensality and Human Relationship Among the Igbo* (1987); S.I. Bosah, *Groundwork of the History and Culture of Onitsha* (1973).

(6) The Tiv

The Tiv live in northern Nigeria. They are constantly migrating, constantly in conflict within and between groups, and always living in fear of power. They regard magic and witchcraft as instruments for achieving wealth and power and for bringing evil. They believe that heart is the means by which an individual understands the world. *Tsav* is a substance that grows on the heart and determines a person's fortune, whereas his misfortune results from the *tsav* of others. Ancestors are not regarded as a source of fortune and misfortune. Evil supernatural forces are the source that brings about misfortunes. There are people in each community, called *mbatsav*, who possess an exceptional degree of *tsav*, which they use to bring others good fortune or bad. *Swem*, which is a mystical power, has the ability to restrain the *mbatsav*.

The Tiv people are divided into lineage groups, or *tar*, which concept indicates the lineage group's relationship to the land occupied by it. The other concept of lineage, namely *ityo*, indicates a person's status for marriage and performance of ritual. There is no over-all political authority. A man farms the land that belongs to the *tar* of the smallest segment to which he is attached by birth, which usually is his father's lineage. Within this minimal segment, there is no one with authority to assign land. The compound head makes these assignments to his compound members. He coordinates farming, controls the magical forces, and settles disputes among the compound members. Elders and men of wealth and esteem in the lineage group perform ritual, control the invisible forces that are given material form of an *akombo*, or fetish. They exercise *tsav* in the interest of the group, decide offenses, settle disputes, determine widow inheritance, and make peace with other groups. Sometimes, lineage councils of elders perform these functions. Leadership is achieved not by age but by personal abilities and possession of *tsav*.

There is no territorial or kinship structure which controls land other than that held by the compound. Therefore, when demand for land increases, there is no land available for allotment to lineage groups to meet their needs. Consequently, the lineage groups move to other lands. The land selected for migration is the adjoining land of the person who is most distantly related to the person migrating. Other reasons for migration are the need to escape political tyranny and witchcraft. The Tiv consider migration as part of their nature. This migration process results in wars between remote lineages. These wars are regulated by treaties entered with the main object of making travel safe.

The Tiv have a conception of an ideal personality of man versed in their custom and belief who conducts himself accordingly. The bad man commits offenses. Deviant behavior falls in three categories: *dang*, *bo*, and *ifer*. *Dang* are acts which are morally at fault. *Bo* are acts which are more serious and are mystically dangerous. *Ifer* are acts which are so seriously violative of norms as to warrant corrective measures. These measures include self-help, performance of ritual, or resort to a *jir* (court determination). The *jir* instructs the disputing parties to act in the future in accordance with custom. It can impose fines and punishment as well. Issues are viewed mystically, so that disharmony is fraught with the possibility that one might place a curse on the other that would trigger the mystical forces to cause illness or death. The diviner is consulted before a *jir* is convened. *Jir* ordinarily deals with those misfortunes that are caused by witchcraft. Non-witchcraft disputes may be settled by an elder.[32]

(7) The Ganda

The Bantu-speaking Ganda live in Uganda on a plateau between Lake Victoria and Lake Kyoga. They have been a warring people, a predatory society, robbing the surrounding nations. They developed external trade only since the latter half of the nineteenth century. They depend heavily on banana for food, which is easily grown and frees men for war and for maintaining road systems for the movement of armies. War requires complete obedience. This has resulted in a complete control of the king over his subjects' affairs. Largesse is distributed by the king and his chiefs. Support of a chief is voluntary for the followers. Since the chiefs need followers to support them in war, this acts as a restraint upon abuse of authority.

A man is highly authoritarian within the family, demanding and enjoying unquestioning submission from wives and obedience from children. The society is competitive. Men strive for achieving a higher status and its rewards. Advancement is achieved not by heredity but by accomplishments in war and other tasks. The king's supremacy is maintained by a continual dis-

---

32. R.C. Abraham, *The Tiv People* (2d ed., 1940); L.P. Bohannan, "The Tiv of Central Nigeria," in D. Forde, ed., *Ethnographic Survey of Africa, Western Africa, Part VIII* (1953); P. Bohannan, "The Migration and Expansion of the Tiv," 24 *Africa* 11 (1954); L. Bohannan, "Political Aspects of Tiv Social Organization," in J. Middleton and D. Tait, eds., *Tribes Without Rulers: Studies in African Segmentary Systems*, 33 (1958); R.M. East, *Akiga's Story* (1939); R.M. Downes, *The Tiv Tribe* (1933); P. Bohannan, *Tiv Farm and Settlement*, Colonial Research Studies, No. 15 (1954); L. Bohannan, "A Genealogical Charter," 22 *Africa* 301 (1952); M.D. Sahlins, "The Segmentary Lineage: An Organization of Predatory Expansion," 63 *American Anthropologist* 322 (1961); P. Bohannan, *Justice and Judgment Among the Tiv* (1957); R. Anifowose, *Violence and Politics in Nigeria: the Tiv and Yoruba Experience* (1982).

play of power, such as the killing and mutilation of disfavored courtiers, wives, concubines, and servants, or the burning of cowards in war, or the ritual sacrifice of men and women for king's health and his kingdom's prosperity. The king does not ascend to the kingship but is selected on the basis of his ability to lead. The spirits are not clan-connected but localized, so that they are invoked through the local prophet of a particular spirit. Ancestors are consulted through prophets and mediums. The spirits deliver misfortune, not fortune. The prophet performs an important function in war.

The Ganda society is divided into patrilineal clans descending from a single male ancestor and holding common totems. The clan performs special functions for the king. For example, it provides the chief herder, the official for the coronation ceremony, the gate keeper, the keeper of a shrine, or the keeper of the bark clothes. The clan head decides disputes of incest, inheritance, succession, bride wealth, and other kinship questions. His decisions can be appealed to the prime minister and then to the king. Polygamy is favored, though not very common. Families in a homestead are rarely the extended kind. Clientage relationships are pervasive and the act of *kusenga* attaches one to another superior in status. This provides opportunities for advancement.

The king (*kababa*) is the source of legitimate authority, although at an earlier time the clan heads were independent of him. He is selected from the royal family. Upon his death, his successor is named by the chief minister (*katikiro*) and by the custodian of the king's fetishes. There are ten territorial districts (*ssazas*), whose chiefs are appointed by the king. Warfare is a way of life and provides opportunities for personal glory, gain, and rise in importance. The leading *ssaza* chief holds the office of the *sabadu* which hears complaints of abuse of power by officials. The king and his royal council, which is headed by the *katikiro*, hear charges against chiefs.

The land tenure is designed to enable office holders and clan heads carry out their traditional functions and provide a secure sustenance to the peasants and their families. Tilling is not allowed to be postponed for an unduly long period of time.

Disputes are brought to the chief and heard by him in the presence of any persons who happen to be there. Anyone present can participate in the proceedings. Appeal from the decisions of the village headmen and subchiefs is taken to the court of the *ssaza*. Appeal from there goes to the courts of the *katikiro* or *kabaka*. Disputes between members of a clan involving kinship, inheritance, and marriage are decided by the clan head. Disputes where a crime is denied, responsibility disputed, or compensation questioned are decided by the chief. Major offenses include adultery, theft, treason, murder, accidental death, sorcery, and arson. In cases of sorcery, ordeal is employed to determine guilt. Under it, the accused and the accuser are given a highly intoxicating drink and the person more affected by it is found guilty. Punishment includes confinement, mutilation, and death. Self-help takes the form of war between clans and is allowed in cases of murder. The injured party is allowed to kill the guilty party on the spot where the party guilty of murder and adultery is caught while committing these offenses or where the party guilty of theft is caught with the stolen goods in his possession.[33]

(8) The Lugbara

The Lugbara people of Uganda believe that while a man's body rots after death, his soul (*oindi*) goes to God in sky and then returns to the shrines to live under the earth. He also has his guardian spirit (*adro*) and his personality (*tali*). Ancestors are individuals as well as a group. Shrines are built to them in both these capacities. All power and moral order issue from God. Jaki and Dribidu are two mystical heroes from whose sons have descended all the clans. Witches and sorcerers bring harm, pervert relations, and destroy ties. The ancestral spirits of a lineage guard the living and punish them for acts hurtful to the lineage.

The Lugbara dwell in homesteads scattered across the country and live in family clusters which consist of a group of polygynous compound families under the head of the cluster, who is also the lineage head. Within the family cluster, the family head possesses complete authority over his agnatic dependents. A segment consists of three generations, although it can be as small as a single compound family. The segment is identified by descent from a wife of an ancestor three or four generations removed. Clans are divided into sub-clans, which form the agnatic core of tribes. The ances-

33. A. Kagwa, *The Customs of the Baganda*, trans. E.B. Kalibala (1934); M.C. Fallers, "The Eastern Lacustrine Bantu (Ganda, Soga)," in D. Forde, ed., *Ethnographic Survey of Africa, Part XI*, 40 (1960); D.E. Apter, *The Political Kingdom in Uganda* (1961); A.I. Richards, "Traditional Values and Current Political Behavior," in L.A. Fallers, ed., *The King's Men: Leadership and Status in Buganda on the Eve of Independence* (1964); A.I. Richards, "Authority Patterns in Traditional Buganda," *id.*, 256; L.A. Fallers, *et al.*, "Social Stratification in Traditional Buganda," *id.*, 64; M Southwold, "Leadership, Authority, and the Village Community," *id.*, 210; L.P. Mair, *An African People in the Twentieth Century* (1934); J. Roscoe, *The Baganda:An Account of Their Native Customs and Beliefs* (1911); M. Southwold, *Bureaucracy and Chiefship in Buganda*, East African Studies No. 14 (1961); A.B. Mukwaya, *Land Tenure in Buganda: Present Day Tendencies*, East African Studies, No. 1 (1953); E.S. Haydon, *Law and Justice in Buganda* (1961); B.C. Ray, *Myth, Ritual, and Kingship in Buganda* (1991).

tral spirits support the exercise of authority of those legitimately possessed of it.

Harmony disrupted by a deviant conduct is restored through a system wherein, first, an elder recognizes the offensive conduct. Thereupon, the elder invokes ghosts against the offender. Then an ancestor casts visitation of sickness upon the offender as penalty. After recovery from this sickness, a diviner validates that the sickness indeed occurred as a penalty imposed by the ancestor. Finally, a rite of sacrifice is held to purify the offender and restore the relations within the community.[34]

(9) The Kikuyu

The Bantu-speaking, agriculturist Kikuyu live on a high plateau beside the slopes of Mount Kenya. They believe that the individual acquires significance through his relationship with other. Family relationships are marked by respect and obedience to the father's authority. An age-set system reinforces common standards of deportment, reaffirms loyalty and devotion among members of the same age-group, and reassures appropriate behavior. It is essential to maintain harmony with the supreme god Ngai and to have communion with Him at birth, and to have initiation into the age set, marriage, and death. The family group and the elder, not the individual, conduct the sacrificial ceremonies at these occasions, as well as at other important occasions, such as planting or harvesting. Everyone has a soul (*ngoro*) which, after death, becomes his spirit (*ngomo*) and joins the spirits of his father and mother, his clan, and his age-group. Communion with the ancestral spirits is performed regularly to maintain good relations between the two worlds. When a misfortune strikes a person or a family, diviners search out the fault and the appropriate ceremonies are performed to re-establish good relations. The magical powers of medicine-men and sorcerers are employed to attain desired objects.

---

34. E. Ramponi, "Religion and Divination of the Lugbara Tribe of North-Uganda," 32 *Anthropos* 571, 849 (1937); R.E. McConnell, "Notes on the Lugwari Tribe of Central Africa," 55 *Journal of the Royal Anthropological Institute* 439 (1925); P.T.W. Baxter and A. Butt, "The Azanda, and Related Peoples of the Anglo-Egyptian Sudan and Belgian Congo," in D. Forde, ed., *Ethnographic Survey of Africa* 120 (1953); J. Middleton, *Lugbara Religion: Ritual and Authority Among an East African People* (1987); J. Middleton, "Witchcraft and Sorcery in Lugbara," in J. Middleton and E.H. Winter, eds., *Witchcraft and Sorcery in East AFrica*, 257 (1963); J. Middleton, "The Concept of Bewitching in Lugbara," 25 *Africa* 252 (1955); J. Middleton, "Some Social Aspects of Lugbara Myth," 24 *Africa* 189 (1954); J. Middleton, "The Political System of Lugbara of the Nile-Congo Divide," in J. Middleton and D. Tait, eds., *Tribes Without Rulers* 203 (1958); J. Middleton, *The Lugbara of Uganda* (2d ed, 1992); O.J.E. Shiroya, *Essays in the Pre-colonial History of North-western Uganda* (1992).

The polygynous family is headed by the father and, upon his death, by the eldest son. The largest local kinship group is the *mbari*, which is formed by common descent from a single male ancestor and is headed by the senior elder. The *mbari* controls the land. The different *mbari* of a particular district act together in political and ritual situations on the basis of territorial proximity, not common kinship. The clan is the largest kinship group, which is identified by common descent from a remote male ancestor. There are nine such clans, which are divided in sub-clans. They are commonly responsible for a killing committed by a member. The age-sets and generation-sets cut across the society regardless of clan or district. As a consequence of the age-set system, leadership is recognized on the basis of ability, not descent.

A man can acquire land by purchase or by clearing unclaimed land. He controls its allotment to the members of his family. At his death, a family-land unit, or the *mbari*, comes into existence and the land controlled by it is called the *githaka*. The *mbari* remains the same even as grandsons of its founding head are born. The eldest son of the senior wife becomes the *muramati*, who controls the use of the *githaka*. Public lands, such as the grazing lands, salt-licks, sacred groves, public meeting places, public dancing places, and public paths, are controlled by the elders. Disputes concerning land are decided by the elders of the district.

Disputes in the family are decided by the father or, upon his death, by the eldest son of the senior wife. Elders assist in serious disputes. Disputes between different families are decided by a council selected from the heads of the disputant families and related families. Disputes between the members of the same *mbari* are decided by the kinship council of elders, the *kiama kia mbari*. Disputes between persons not related to each other but living in the same district are decided by *kiama kia mwaki*. Ad hoc bodies decide disputes between parties which are neither related nor living in the same district. Improper conduct is determined on the basis of custom, where the objective is to restore peace and harmony disturbed by the deviant behavior.[35]

35. J. Kenyatta, *Facing Mount Kenya: The Tribal Life of the Gikuyu*; with an Introduction by B. Malinowski (1979); J. Kenyatta, "Kikuyu Religion, Ancestor-Worship, and Sacrificial Practices," 10 *Africa* 308 (1937); J. Middleton, "The Central Tribes of the North-Eastern Bantu," in D. Forde, ed., *Ethnographic Survey of Africa, Part V*, 11 (1953); C.W. Hobley, *Bantu Beliefs and Magic* (rev. ed., 1938); W.S. Routledge and K. Routledge, *With a Prehistoric People: The Akikiyu of East Africa* (1910); H.E. Lambert, *Kikuyu, Social and Political Institutions* (1956); A.H.J. Prins, *East African Age-Class Systems* (1953); C. Cagnolo, *The Akikiyu: Their Customs, Traditions, and Folklore* (1933); M. Beech, "Kikuyu Systems of Land Tenure," 17 *Journal of the African Society* 46 (1917–1918); C. Dundas, "The Organization and Law of Some Bantu Tribes of East Africa," 45 *Journal of the Royal Anthropological Institute* 234 (1915); C. Dundas, "Native Laws of Some Bantu Tribes of East Africa," 51 *Journal of the Royal Anthropological Institute* 217 (1921); H.R. Tate, "The

(10) Nandi

These cattle-culture people of Kenya consider themselves a most superior people. Cattle, war, and agriculture have made them self-supporting. They need no substantial commerce with other peoples.

They believe that a person is made up of a body, a shadow-soul, and a soul. The shadow-soul dies with the body. The soul survives the body and, as the body is consumed by the hyena in the usual method of disposing dead bodies, the soul uses the hyena as a means to enter the realm of the spirits, where it becomes the *oiindet*. *Kiet* refers to a world order set up by God which consists of the sky, the heavenly bodies, and the entire nature. A harmony subsists among God, the spirits, and man, which needs be preserved. Its disturbance brings retribution upon the violator. The supreme God Asis regulates the harmony between man and nature. His beneficent influence is invoked by ritual. The ancestral spirits are kind to humans but the failure to express regard for them or the commission of a crime brings their wrath in the form of death, illness, or misfortune. Diviners assist in ascertaining responsibility for offenses.

The Nandi live in scattered homesteads. Their basic political unit is the *koret*, which is a local grouping of twenty to a hundred homesteads, governed by a council of elders, or the *kokwet*. Discussions in the council are led by the elder of the council, or the *poiyot ap kokwet*. The matters of its concern include cattle disputes, offenses, drought, disaster, roads, and the use of salt-licks. Its decisions are accepted because of public disapproval of non-compliance, fear of spirits, and personal acknowledgment of guilt. The *pororiet* is a territorial grouping of warriors, governed by its own council. This council concerns itself with war and other matters affecting all local groups within its area. The *emet* is the largest territorial division, but it has no political significance.

The Nandi are organized in clans, which are patrilineal and totemic, but these clans are not segmented into lineages. A relationship system called the *tiliet* identifies people by blood and marriage, not lineage, and provides the framework for a behavior code. There are also age-sets which perform governing functions on a non-kinship basis.

God Asis is the source of all power and authority. He punishes the incorrigible wrongdoer and forgives the repentant. There is the physical punishment and execution for offenses, but a much stronger sanction is provided by the fear of spirits and Asis.

Native Law of the Southern Gikuyu of East Africa," 9 *Journal of the African Society* 233 (1909–1910); E.N. Mugo, *Kikuyu People: A Brief Outline of Their Customs and Traditions* (1982); G. Muriuki, *A History of the Kikuyu, 1500–1900* (1974).

There are two types of offenses. The first type includes those offenses which affect the tribal group in its relationship with the spiritual realm. These offenses invite physical sanctions. The second type includes those wrongs which affect private interests. These are, for most part, redeemed by compensation. Custom has provided a standard of behavior known as *karuret*.

Land disputes are rare, since the land is plentiful. Cultivated land adjoins the dwelling and each householder has a right to till it. It is inherited as long as it is used. Grazing land consists of (i) the area immediately surrounding a dwelling used for early-morning and late-evening grazing, (ii) the main grazing grounds used in all weather, and (iii) the *kaptic* land used between rainy seasons and composed of land beyond tribal frontiers as well as unsettled land.[36]

(11) The Arusha

The Arusha live in Tanzania on the southwestern slopes of Mt. Meru. They worship Engai, their supreme god, and perform rituals to him conducted by the senior diviner in order to secure general welfare, procure fertility for women, and avert droughts and epidemics. They also believe in ancestral spirits and perform rituals at their shrines to secure their favor.

Their polygynous family is divided into two units of *ilwasheta* (singular, *olwashe*). New wives are assimilated in them. These form the basis for allocation of land to sons, division of the bride wealth, sharing of inheritance, and structuring of the future lineage. A number of families constitute the inner lineages, each divided into *ilwasheta*. A number of inner lineages constitute a maximal lineage. Various maximal lineages constitute sub-clans, which are divided into two *ilwasheta*. A pair of sub-clans constitute a clan-section, a pair of which constitutes each clan. Two clans compose each of the two divisions of the whole Arusha people. Lineage relationships are determined by descent from a common patrilineal ancestor.

Territorially, they are divided into two sub-tribes. The sub-tribes, in turn, are divided into local territorial units, or parishes, composed of family homesteads. The male heads of these homesteads are organized into age groups for purposes of governance, public labor, dispute settlement, war, and other

36. E.E. Evans-Pritchard, "The Political Structure of the Nandi-speaking People of Kenya," 13 *Africa* 250 (1940); G.W.B. Huntingford, "Nandi Witchcraft," in J. Middleton and E.H. Winter, eds., *Witchcraft and Sorcery in East Africa*, 175 (1963); G.W.B. Huntingford, *The Nandi of Kenya: Tribal Control in a Pastoral Land* (1953); G.W.B. Huntingford, *Nandi Work and Culture* (1950); G.W.B. Huntingford, "The Southern Nilo-Hamites," in D. Forde, ed., *Ethnographic Survey of Africa, Part VIII*, 23 (1953); G.S. Snell, *Nandi Customary Law* (1954); M.S. Langley, *The Nandi of Kenya* (1979).

matters. Various age groups have various responsibilities suitable for their particular stage in life. Public matters, such as settlement of disputes or questions concerning roads, are dealt by the parish assembly.

Disputes are settled by a number of conflict-solving bodies in which spokesmen and counsellors assist the parties. Each age group of a parish selects six spokesmen for its members. Lineage counsellors perform similar tasks at lineage meetings. The parish assembly does not decide disputes. It provides a forum wherein the disputants can conduct a procedure for settlement. Preferably, a dispute between lineage members is settled within the lineage. Failing that, counsellors at the higher levels of the sub-clan, or even the whole clan, intervene to induce an agreement. The objective is elimination of the dispute by reaching an agreement for its settlement and performance of that agreement. Thus, the procedures for dispute settlement are not in the nature of third-party decision. The third parties do participate and facilitate the outcome but the resultant agreement is not a binding decision. Compromise is valued not for restoring harmony between the parties but for reducing violence within the community.[37]

(12) The Nyakyusa

The Bantu-speaking Nyakyusa live in Tanzania, at the north end of Lake Nyasa in the Great Rift Valley. They cultivate land and herd cattle. They cherish the enjoyment of good company (*ukwangala*), which means friendliness among adult males. They value *amahala*, which is wisdom acquired from experience as well as companionship and discussion. They value dignity of manners and decency of behavior. They like the display of self or possessions. They like submissiveness in women. It is important for them to be in step with the neighbor.

They believe that two mythical heroes came to their land. One created crops, the other crops and people. Descendants of the people so created became the chiefs of the Nyakyusa.

Rituals are performed by the chiefs to purge rats, wild pigs, and epidemics. Medicines are employed by them to bring rain and fertility of land. Magical medicines invest in the chiefs the spiritual powers and personal qualities needed to govern. The medicines protect the chiefs from dangerous powers of the sacrificial sites and bolster the supernatural powers

37. M. Gluckman, "Reasonableness and Responsibility in the Law of Segmentary Societies," in M. Kuper and L. Kuper, eds., *African Law: Adaptation and Development*, 145 (1965); P.H. Gulliver, *Social Control in an African Society, A Study of the Arusha: Agricultural Masai of Northern Tanganyika* (1963); P.H. Gulliver, "Structural Dichotomies and Jural Processes Among the Arusha of Northern Tanganyika," 31 *Africa* 19 (1961); P.H. Gulliver, *Disputes and Negotiations: A Cross-Cultural Perspective* (1979).

of the chiefs at ceremonies held for achieving various objectives. The ancestral spirits are angered at breaches of kinship obligations. Angry spirits bring misfortune or sickness. A diviner is consulted when a person becomes sick. The diviner determines the true cause for the sickness in failure to discharge a kinship obligation. Witches possess magical powers. Witchcraft is tried before the chief where the suspect is subjected to the ordeal of drinking a potion. Failure to vomit means guilt.

Violations of norms of social behavior and abuse of power by the chief are punished by the 'breath-of-men,' a power which is possessed by the village headmen and is applied in a procedure which consists of six successive steps, namely, the public knowledge of the wrongdoer's failure to meet an obligation, the invocation of punishment by "murmuring" of the wrong conduct by neighbors, the experiencing of the punishment by the wrongdoer, the performance by him of the breached norm, the commensal feast given by the wrongdoer or his father, and the administering to him a medicine by the medicine man which would promote correct conduct by the wrongdoer in the future.

Families are polygynous. Lineage of three generations determines such matters as the ownership and control of cattle, inheritance, and ancestor worship. The chiefdom is not linked to a common descent. Family members cooperate in cultivation. Villages are organized on the basis of age sets. In these age villages, men of closely contemporaneous ages live most of their lives.

The village owns the land and the village headman guards the land rights, makes new allotments, controls unused land, and settles land disputes. A man's land cannot be taken away from him during his life in his age-village. New settlers are given a house site and land for cultivation. Land is inherited through full brothers, failing that through half-brothers, and failing that the eldest son inherits if he is an adult.

Dispute within the village are settled by the decision of a senior relative or a respected neighbor. If this third party cannot make the decision or if the disputants choose not to accept it, the dispute continues and is taken to the village headman. His decision can be appealed to the chief. Violations of certain norms can be vindicated by the individuals resorting to force.[38]

---

38. M. Wilson, *Communal Rituals of the Nyakyusa* (1959); M. Wilson, *Good Company: A Study of Nyakyusa Age-Villages* (1951, 1987); M. Wilson, "Nyakyusa Kinship," in A.R. Radcliffe-Brown and D. Forde, eds., *African Systems of Kinship and Marriage* (1950); M. Wilson, "Divine Kings and the 'Breath of Men'," *Frazer Lecture* (1959); G. Wilson, "The Nyakyusa of South-Western Tanganyika," in E. Colson and M. Glickman, eds., *Seven Tribes of British Central Africa*, 253 (1951); G. Wilson, "An African Morality," 9 *Africa* 75 (1965); G. Wilson, "Introduction to Nyakyusa Law," 10 *Africa* 16 (1937); P.H. Gulliver, *Land Tenure and Social Change Among the Nyakyusa*, East African Studies, No. 11 (1958); R. de Z. Hall,

(13) The Nuer

The Nuer live in the savanna and the swamps of southern Sudan. They believe that God is a creative spirit who dwells in the sky. He is the guardian of norms of human behavior. He punishes the violators with misfortune. There are spirits of air, rain, lightning, rivers, streams, and war. After death, a man's soul continues to exist as a ghost. The ghost of a wronged man can take vengeance (*cien*) on the wrongdoer. Duties are sanctioned by the ability of the wronged person to curse the person who fails to perform them. God is the ultimate arbiter. Sacrifices are made to Him, not to ghosts. The sacrifice is a matter of sincerity of purpose and not a matter of emotion. The leopard-skin priest possesses spiritual powers derived from his relation to the earth. He performs sacrifices, mediates between kin groups, and performs rituals for seeding and crop protection. Diviners are consulted. Witches exist.

The family is the basic unit. The homestead of huts and a cattle byre form the family group of the polygynous family. Lineage relations are determined on the basis of agnatic ties. In absence of such ties, the ties with the dominant lineage of the territory provide the basis for cognation or adoption. All living in the territory are linked to each other with a common ancestor through the male or female lines. The village is an economic and political unit. Several villages with intercommunication constitute a district of the tribe. A tribe is segmented into sections, each segment crystallizing around a lineage of the tribe's dominant clan. There are fifteen tribes. Each territorial unit is associated with a dominant lineage. The age-set system is not that important as among other East African peoples. However, it does define status and indicate certain ritual behavior.

A man and his family enjoy an exclusive right to use the land they cleared, subject to the duty to feed kinsmen in need. Cattle is owned subject to the duty of contributing it to bride wealth and of paying it as compensation for homicide. The eldest son of the decedent inherits his huts and cattle byre, whereas other sons continue to live in the homestead.

Violations of norms of behavior call for reparation of wrongs. Conflicts are resolved by self-help, including blood feud, community pressure, and mediatory procedures. In case of homicide, the leopard-skin priest opens discussion with the 'people of the man (deceased)' and the 'people of compensation' (killer) and acts as an intermediary for reaching a settlement. If necessary, he threatens spiritual sanctions to that end. Wrongs other than

---

"Nyakyusa Law from the Court Records," 2 *African Studies* 153 (1953); O.J.M. Kalinga, *A History of the Ngonde Kingdom of Malawi* (1985); M.H. Wilson, *For Men and Elders: Change in the Relations of Generations and of Men and Women Among the Nyakyusa-Ngonde People, 1875–1971* (1977).

homicide include personal injury, defamation of character, theft of cattle, theft of property, elopement and abduction, adultery, and sexual intercourse with concubines and unmarried girls. In these cases, the leopard-skin priest acts as a mediator between the disputants.[39]

We have examined the above thirteen examples of life-styles in Africa to demonstrate their uniqueness, resulting from their own particular situation.

Until about the beginning of the nineteenth century, Africa remained the Dark Continent for the Europeans. Impingements began about this time. The continent had lagged behind European and Asian civilizations, in spite of the fact that North Africa participated in civilized history from the age of the Pharaohs. Civilized states and empires existed in Ethiopia and the Upper Niger Valley for at least a thousand years prior to the middle of the nineteenth century. Trade with India, the Middle East, Indonesia, and Europe flourished in ports of the African coasts. Many kingdoms existed inland. However, the above mentioned lag was due to the poor soil and poor climate for farming, widespread diseases, especially malaria, yellow fever, and sleeping sickness, and the difficulty of transport and communication. By the same token, though, a much wider variety of human physical types survived here than anywhere else in the world, since this variety was not disrupted by powerful states and far-ranging movement of traders.

However, by about the middle of the nineteenth century, the Muslim elements exerted pressure upon the continent from the north and the west and the Christian Europeans from the west and the south. Vigorous state-building occurred during that century because of certain significant changes in economic factors. Food production had increased substantially, due to introduction of the American crops of maize, peanuts, and sweet potatoes, and that sustained the growth in population and the professional specialists, such as soldiers, that were needed for strong states. Also, while slave trade had earlier accounted for the growth of coastal states, such as Dahomey and Zanzibar, it had drained the population resource and the wealth connected with that resource. Therefore, the suppression of slavery in the nineteenth century strengthened the economic base for state-building. The increase in demand for African products, such as ivory and palm oil, helped further. Introduction of European firearms meant increased slaughter of elephants for the ivory trade. It also gave military advantage to rulers possessing them, which meant destruction of the old military systems, such as

39. E.E. Evans-Pritchard, *The Nuer: A Description of the Modes of Livelihood and Political Institutions of a Nilotic People* (1969); E.E. Evans-Pritchard, *Nuer Religion* (1956); E.E. Evans-Pritchard, *Kinship and Marriage Among the Nuer* (1951, 1990); P.P. Howell, *A Manuel of Nuer Law* (1954); R.C. Kelly, *The Nuer Conquest: The Structure and Development of an Expansionist System* (1985).

the spear-wielding Zulus of Natal or the armored horsemen of Bornu. Moreover, Islam continued to spread throughout this century and, although it did not displace indigenous customs, it assisted the rulers in much of east and west Africa in organizing and expanding their power through its ideas of law, such as, for example, in the Ashanti kingdoms.

Conflict with the Europeans of the superior force often produced strong Islamic movements, such as the dervish brotherhood of Sanusi, founded near Mecca in 1837 by an Algerian, or the movement in Sudan started by a Muslim holy-man, Muhammed Ahmed, who announced in 1881 that he was the Mahdi, the restorer of Islam. Christian missionaries brought schools, hospitals, and knowledge of Western civilization. They steadily educated the Africans in Western ways, thereby alienating them from their traditional patterns of life and weakening the ancestral structures of society. However, the native systems still controlled most of Africa, whether it be a thousand-year old kingdom like Bornu near lake Chad or an upstart like the Zulu military despotism founded in 1817 by Shaka (1787–1828). Exceptions were Algeria in the north and the Boer Republics in the south.

European colonial administrations grew rapidly between 1875 and 1914. The Africans were defeated in all their wars against the colonizing powers, except for Ethiopia, where Emperor Menelik II defeated Italy in 1896. France and Britain were the two major contenders in Africa. France conquered Algeria in 1830, went deep into the Sahara, and linked up with its imperial representatives based in Senegal. The French ambition of building a vast empire across the northern half of the continent clashed with the British scheme for a "Cape to Cairo" railway. The Germans appeared in 1884 and took Tanganyika, Southwest Africa, and the Cameroon. The Italians had moderate successes in the Red Sea region but were defeated in Ethiopia in 1896. The Belgians began exploiting the Congo basin in 1876. The Portuguese laid claim on Angola and Mozambique.

The natives resisted the Europeans. Thus, the Berbers of the Atlas mountains took to arms against the French for decades. The Ashanti kingdom of West Africa fought the British, and it was not until 1901 that it was annexed to the then Gold Coast (now Ghana). The Zulus of South Africa resisted the British until 1879, when their paramount chief was finally subdued in a battle. However, all such efforts failed, except in Ethiopia, as mentioned above.

Except for Algeria and South Africa, where substantial populations of Europeans settled themselves, the European administration remained superficial in most of Africa. The British ruled through controlling native rulers, so that chieftains and kings remained in their position. The French, on the other hand, aimed at cultural assimilation, pursuing the idea of Frenchmen with black skin. However, in the end, they opted to settle for indirect rule.

In any case, the indigenous social structures subsisted even where colonial administration was direct. Kinship groups, community villages, and tribal organization continued.

The superiority of European arms, discipline, and supply systems significantly reduced the level of bloodshed which used to be rampant up to 1900 or so. Socially, former enemies had to co-exist within the colonial administration. Cattle-rustling and slave-raiding had to be abandoned. This resulted in basic changes in social patterns. For example, the Masai lost their traditional occupation of cattle-raising and warriorship. They were outnumbered by their enemies, the agricultural Kikuyu, who increased in population. Rise in rural population precipitated a move into cities built generally on the European pattern. However, up to 1914, the breach from traditional patterns had not been very widespread.

During World War I (1914–1918), the German colonies were easily taken over by the British and the French, without causing much disruption. The inter-war period (1919–1939) witnessed very few rebellions. Three independent states existed, namely, Ethiopia, as above, the Union of South Africa, which was set up in 1908 with full autonomy to the Boer and British whites, and Liberia, which was established in 1847 by American ex-slaves. The British granted independence to Egypt in 1922 and they promised, in a treaty of 1936, to withdraw their troops from the Nile Valley. Italy, on the contrary, attacked and conquered Ethiopia in 1934.

In this period between the two world wars, traditional forms of society were weakened seriously as a result of the exposure of the African people to new experiences. Men serving in European armies would not go back to their villages. Nor would the graduates of the mission schools. They would rather go on to the institutions of secondary and higher education. More importantly, a large number of natives had moved to work in mines and town.

These hundreds of thousands of people moved into a new environment where their old customs, old kinships, and old tribal patterns could not provide a common basis of mutual accommodation among them. The available alternatives were the Islamic and the Western models. While the Islamic model prevailed in those parts of Africa where it had been established for many centuries, the Western model competed strongly with the Islamic model in most of the sub-Saharan regions. The result was that a small but important group of Africans, sharing Western knowledge and attributes, demanded political independence from the colonial powers and they were ready to take over the control from them.[40]

40. R. Hallett, *Africa to 1875* (1970); R. Oliver and G. Matthew, *History of East Africa* (1963); J.D. Fage, *A History of West Africa* (1969); J. Vansina, *Kingdoms of the Savanna* (1966); J.S. Trimingham, *A History of Islam in West Africa* (1962); A.H.M. Jones and E.

Since the end of World War II, the new nations of Africa have displayed a tendency for modernization along European patterns. New legislation has been adopted to change the traditional ways. However, in spite of this modernization, eighty to ninety percent of the population continues to live by traditions, customs, and indigenous structures of social organization outlined above, and not by the Western values of individualism and legalism. They are generally unaffected by reform legislation. In fact, they are largely unaware of the laws and institutions of the cities.

Our point in this Chapter, therefore, has been that civilizations are not merely several, they are diverse as well. With the examples of the Western, Chinese, Indian, and African civilizations, we have attempted to show that they have developed for themselves different principles of life and social organization at the most fundamental level and that such has been the result of their particular historicity. Consequently, it is misleading to proceed as if there exists one single set of universal values at the most fundamental level.

What does this mean for international law? We shall examine that question in the next Chapter.

Munroe, *A History of Ethiopia* (1955); B. Davidson, *Black Mother: The African Slave Trade* (1961); L. Marguard, *The Story of South Africa* (1955); R. Robinson and J. Gallagher, *Africa and the Victorians* (1961); T.O. Ranger, ed., *Aspects of Central African History* (1968); R. Oliver and A. Atmore, *Africa Since 1800* (1967); W.H. McNeill, *A World History* (2d ed., 1971); A. Ajayi and J.D.Y. Peel, eds., *Peoples and Empires in African History* (1992); A.I. Asiwaju, ed., *Partitioned Africans: Ethnic Relations Across Africa's International Boundaries, 1884–1984* (1985); A.A. Boahen, ed., *Africa Under Colonial Domination, 1880–1935* (1985); L. Cockcroft, *Africa's Way: A Journey From the Past* (1990); *Essays in Honour of Judge Taslim Olawale Elias, Vol. 2 (African Law and Comparative Public Law* (1992); R.W. July, *A History of the African People*, (4th ed., 1992); W.J. Mommsen and J.A. de Moor, *European Expansion and Law: The Encounter of European and Indigenous Law in 19th- and 20th- Century Africa and Asia* (1992); R.A. Oliver, *The African Experience* (1991).

Chapter 5

The Consequence of Legal Polycentricity upon International Law

Applying legal polycentricity to international law, we confront the problem of civilizational pluralism of the members of the society of states whose law this international law is.

Contemporary civilizations are plural. They are diverse as well. Our international law, on the other hand, is a very particular system that was invented in Christian Europe of sixteenth and seventeenth centuries. It governed international relations of the European states and sustained their imperial structure right down to the twentieth century. Other civilizations were subjugated to the European states and were of no direct relevance to international law. The practice of states that was consulted for creating the body of international law during its formative period and in the centuries thereafter was the practice of European states. Other civilizations did not contribute in the normative hypostatization of this law.

New states from other civilizations have been added to this system during this century, especially since the end of World War II.[1] They have been admitted on the terms of this law and upon re-constitution of these civilizations into states, in strict compliance with the constitutive rules of this law (*viz.*, territory, population, government, and capacity to enter into international relations). Today, this system embraces all civilizations directly, not merely as an incidental subject-matter of European Empires, as previously. It is the genius of this international law that such a feat has been accomplished without the slightest compromise to its constitutive principles. That genius lies in its concepts of juridical equality and political sov-

1. S.P. Sinha, *New Nations and the Law of Nations* (1967); S.P. Sinha, "Has Self-Determination Become a Principle of Law Today?" 14 *Indian Journal of International Law* 332 (1974); S.P. Sinha, "Is Self-determination Passé?" 12 *Columbia Journal of Transnational Law* 260 (1973); S.P. Sinha, "Self-Determination in International Law and Its Applicability to the Baltic Peoples," in A. Sprudzs an A. Rusis, eds., *Res Baltica*, 256 (1968).

ereignty. Through those concepts as the test for an entity's qualification as the state and, therefore, its eligibility to participate in this system, it has accommodated all differences in cultures, ways of life, and value preferences, apprehending all differences in ideologies, political systems, and social organizations.

However, if our analysis in the previous Chapters is correct, two propositions emerge from that analysis and stare in the face of international law, namely, non-universality of the legal order and axiological diversity among various civilizations. More specifically, three questions arise. One, does the non-universality of the legal order mean that the international legal order is no longer possible? Two, does the non-universality of the legal order invalidate the normative content of this law? Three, does the axiological diversity of the world affect this law?

We shall examine these questions below. Toward that end, we shall first take a stock of international law and attempt a classification of its content. Then we shall apply our questions to those categories.

The content of today's international law includes principles dealing with the sources of this law, the entities that constitute the subjects of this law, the treaties as a means of creating legal obligations, the international responsibility and remedies, the peaceful settlement of disputes, the use of force, the allocation of jurisdiction of states, the jurisdictional immunity of foreign states, state representatives, and international organizations and their agents, the responsibility of states for injury to aliens, the responsibility of states for protecting the human rights of human beings living under their jurisdiction, the international trade, money, and development, the sea, the international waterways, the common areas such as polar regions, moon, celestial bodies, and outer space, the ecological environment, the technical, social, and cultural cooperation, and the regional economic communities.[2] From our point of view, this subject-matter can be classified into three categories. Firstly, there is the inter-state international law. This includes the traditional areas of international law governing the conduct of states, such as territory, jurisdiction, treaty-making, use of force, diplomatic and consular immunities, state responsibility for injuries to aliens, peaceful settlement of disputes, law of the sea, and so on. Secondly, there is the transnational international law, a category imaginatively conceived by the late Judge Jessup,[3] which includes the new fields of international law dealing with economic cooperation, technical, social and cultural coop-

2. Textbooks deal with this content in detail. For example, see L. Henkin, R.C. Pugh, O. Schachter, and H. Smit, *International Law* (3d ed., 1993).

3. P.C. Jessup, *Transnational Law* (1956). Judge Jessup was the founder of the Columbia University Seminar on the Problem of Peace, to which I have had the honor of belonging since 1969 under the successive chairmanships of John Hazard and Oscar Schachter.

eration, environmental protection, and the like. Thirdly, there is what we shall call the intranational international law, which includes those parts of international law which apply directly to the matters of the individual's existence within the state. Its most prominent example is the international law of human rights.

With this content in mind, we shall visit our three questions, put above.

First, does the non-universality of the legal order mean that the international legal order is no longer possible? We have seen in the previous Chapters that the culture of law (*nomos*) originated in Hesiod (8th century B.C.), became law with Aristotle (384–322 B.C.), and eventually came to denote a constituted order of society composed of individual rights and duties, producing the Western ethos. The culture of *li* originated in the Book of History (Shu Ching, about 1122 B.C.) and, developing through the Book of Poetry (1122–600 B.C.), the Spring and Autumn Annals (Tsao Chuan, 770–464 B.C.), Confucius (551–479 B.C.), and the Book of Li (Li Chi, completed in the early part of the Former (206 B.C.–8 A.D.) Han Dynasty), it represents the basis of order in the Chinese society. The culture of *dharma* originated at the very beginning of the Aryan civilization in India (about 2000 B.C.) following the Baluchistan (about 3000 B.C.) and the Harappa Cultures (2500–1000 B.C.). In a remarkable continuity and through developments, refinements, and elaborations, it represents the basis of order for most Indians. Thus, these three different principles, which we have taken as principal examples in our inquiry, represent three essential principles of life.[4]

The differences are significant. They contain concepts that have no counterparts in each other. For example, the *karma* in Hindu *dharma* or the Confucian connection between the *li* and *jen* (humaneness) are non-existent in the Western principle of life, whereas the Western *nomos* containing the potential for man-made law is non-existent in *dharma* or *li*. The *rta* conception of order-that-exists of the Hindus is totally incompatible with the *nomos* idea of the divine agencies creating the universe and the gods issuing commands for governance. *Dharma* produces in man a conviction of duty to comply with the pre-existing order of *rta*. *Li* gives the idea of order wherein ways of conduct regulate man's worldly existence in harmony with nature.

Order in the *nomos* culture of law is granted from outside. In *li* it is granted from within. In *dharma* it is pre-ordained. This has been the result of the

---

4. For an excellent summary of these, see R. May, *Law & Society East and West, Dharma, Li, and Nomos, Their Contribution to Thought and to Life* (1985). S.P. Sinha, "Book Review: Law and Society East and West, by Reinhard May," 75 *Archiv für Rechts- und*Socialphilosophie 423 (1989); S.P. Sinha, "Book Review: Law and Society East and West, Dharma, Li, and Nomos, by Reinhard May," 4 *Pace Yearbook of International Law* 425 (1992).

particular historical developments in these three specific civilizations. Consequently, while *nomos* has laid the groundwork for an idea of law from outside, *li* has become the social obligation directed toward the harmonious state of the world, and *dharma* has produced authoritative texts to teach man his duty to support the *dharmic* state of the world. Accordingly, while *dharma* and *li* produced a general and all-pervasive way of life as an organizational principle of existence, *nomos* proceeded along the basis of specific commands. While the validity of the precepts of *nomos* depended upon the authoritative statement thereof promulgated publicly, the validity of the precepts of *li* never depended upon such a mode. While *nomos* was attributed to a divine law-giver, such an attribution is non-existent in either *li* or *dharma*, although *dharma*, as distinguished from *li*, has sacred literature of eternal validity, namely, the *shruti* literature of Vedas, Brahmanas, Aranyakas, and Upanishads. While *li* is concretized in the five *wu lan* relationships, *nomos* moved on to an abstract way of thinking, producing speculations about laws of nature. Discovery and speculation about the ways of the non-human nature did not interest the Hindu *dharmashastras*, either. The task of the authors and teachers of the *dharmashastras* was to show man his duty and to guide him in close adherence to *shruti*, not the articulation and distribution of individual rights typical of the Western legal ethos. *Li*, too, does not dispense individual rights, since the rights approach, with its antagonistic behavior of claiming those rights, is excluded by the conception of seeking an all-embracing harmony within all human relations.

Where the source of obligation is from outside, as in the Western legal order, a need arises to justify rights and duties, but where that source is from inside, as in *dharma* or *li*, the important task becomes not the justification of laws, and of individual rights and duties thereunder, but the discovery of that obligation and apprehending its hidden sources. The internal coherence of duty-bound ways of life, whether it be pre-ordained as in *dharma* or socially-created as in *li*, is quite incompatible with institutionalization of rights that characterizes the Western legal order.

Thus, while the legal order is the central principle of social organization in the Western civilization, it is too parochial a proposition for the entire world.

Does this mean that the international legal order is no longer possible?

International law primarily governs the external relations of states, as distinguished from their internal social organization. Its concept of sovereignty secures for the state an exclusive competence for the latter. Whether, therefore, a state follows the legal order or the *dharma* order or the *li* order in its internal social life is of no consequence to international law. This law is concerned with states' external relations, such as, for example, how they establish their territorial jurisdiction as to each other, how they treat each other's envoys, how they treat each other's nationals within their territory (although there has been some controversy issuing from the Latin American states and the new states of Asia and Africa whether foreign nationals ought to be treated in accordance with the international standards or the national standards of the host country), how they conduct their activities in the sea, air, outer space, international waterways, and other common areas, how they settle their disputes with each other, how they use force against each other, and so on. These matters are not matters of internal social organization of a society to which the order of law, *li*, or *dharma* pertains. Therefore, the non-universality of legalism does not have the consequence of invalidating the possibility of the international legal order of our present international law.

Does the non-universality of legalism invalidate the normative content of this law? In answering this question, we shall resort to the three categories, developed above, of the content of this law. In the category of interstate international law, this law deals with such matters as determination of statehood, state succession, acquisition of territorial sovereignty, conclusion, applicability, interpretation, modification, termination, and invalidity of treaties, state responsibility, implementation of obligations of reparation, settlement of international disputes, adjudicatory and non-adjudicatory procedures for their resolution, use of force, intervention in civil war in another state, collective use of force, state jurisdiction, conflicts of jurisdiction, extradition, jurisdictional immunities of foreign states and international organizations and of their officials and representatives, responsibility for injury to aliens and assertion of claims, the regime of the seas, international watercourses, polar regions, moon, other celestial bodies, outer space, and so on. These are matters that are not affected by the fact whether the internal social life of states participating in these matters is fashioned on the basis of legalism or not. Similarly, the category of transnational international law is also not affected by the non-universality of legalism. It consists of such matters as the international economic law concerning international trade, monetary management, and economic development, the law for technical, social, and cultural cooperation in education, science, culture, aviation, communication, shipping, labor, agriculture, weather, health, and atomic energy, the law of environmental protection, and so on. In order to engage in these matters, the states need not be possessed of the legal culture. However, it is the third category of intranational international law which is profoundly affected by the non-universality of the legal order.

The most prominent example of this category is human rights. The concern of international law here is how human beings pursue their moral life within the territory of their state and how states are to be held accountable for securing that life. It is misleading for international law to entertain an agenda aimed at transforming non-legal cultures into legal societies. Unfortunately, this is precisely what the present universal system of human rights does. This system is based upon the International Bill of Human Rights, which consists of the Universal Declaration of Human Rights, the International Covenant on Economic, Social, and Cultural Rights, and the International Covenant on Civil and Political Rights (including its Optional Protocol). These instruments prescribe legalism for the entire world. The method of law is chosen as the favored means for resolving conflicts in all societies, and the instruments go on to elaborating the fine principles of a desirable court system.[5]

Thus, the Universal Declaration of Human Rights provides for everyone's recognition everywhere as a person before the law (Art. 6), equal protection of the law (Art. 7), effective remedy by national tribunal (Art. 8), and a fair and public hearing by an independent and impartial tribunal (Art. 10). The International Covenant on Civil and Political Rights provides for due process of law for arrest and detention (Art. 9), proper prosecution of a criminal charge (Art. 14), everyone's recognition everywhere as a person before the law (Art. 16), and protection of the law against interference with privacy, family, home, correspondence, or honor (Art. 17).

And this is fine for Western societies and for the cosmopolitan fringes of non-legal societies which fashion their social ethos along Western modes, although often superficially. However, legalism is too parochial a prescription for the entire world. For example, in China the honorable course is not assertion of rights through recourse to law but conciliation. Law is considered appropriate only for dealing with such elements as the foreigner

5. Articles 6, 7, 8, 10 of the Universal Declaration of Human Rights (UDHR); Articles 9, 14, 16, 17 of the International Covenant on Civil and Political Rights (ICCPR). For the practice of the Human Rights Committee, established under Article 28 of this Covenant, see International Covenant on Civil and Political Rights, Human Rights Committee, *Selected Decisions*, Under the Optional Protocol (Second to Sixteenth Sessions), U.N. Doc. CPR/C/OP/1 (1985), for Article 9 (1): Comm. Nos. 4/1977, 5/1977, 8/1977, 25/1978, 30/1978, 33/1978, 37/1978, 46/1979, 52/1979, 56/1979, 64/1979, 91/1981; for Article 9 (2): Comm. Nos. 33/1978, 44/1979, 46/1979; for Article 9 (3): Comm. Nos. 5/1977, 6/1977, 8/1977, 10/1977, 11/1977, 28/1978, 32/1978, 33/1978, 37/1978,44/1979, 46/1979, 52/1979, 63/1979, 73/1980; for Article 9 (4): 4/1977, 5/1977, 6/1977, 8/1977, 10/1977, 11/1978, 25/1978, 28/1978, 32/1978, 33/1978, 37/1978, 44/1979, 46/1979, 91/1981; for Article 9 (5): Comm. Nos. 9/1977, 91/1981; for Article 14 (1): Comm. Nos. 5/1979, 6/1977, 8/1977, 10/1977, 17/1977, 27/1978, 28/1978, 32/1978, 44/1979, 46/1979, 64/1979, 70/1980, 81/1980; for Article 14 (2): Comm. Nos. 5/1978, 8/1977/ 46/1979; for Article 14 (3): Comm. Nos. 4/1977, 5/1977, 6/1978, 8/1977, 10/1977, 27/1978, 28/1978, 32/1978, 33/1978, 44/1979, 46/1979, 52/1979, 56/1979, 63/1979, 70/1980, 73/1980; for Article 14(5): Comm Nos. 24/1977, 27/1978, 35/1978, 68/1980, 79/1980.

who is alien to the Chinese values, or the morally perverse, or the incorrigible criminal, or the counter-revolutionary. Or, in Japan, conciliation procedures of *jidan* (the parties settling the dispute amicably through mediators), *wakai* (the judge bringing the parties to a settlement), and *chotei* (the parties requesting the court to appoint a panel of conciliators charged with preparing an equitable settlement) are preferred and law is deemed appropriate only for depersonalized matters of business and industry. *Chusai* (arbitration) is avoided in domestic contracts, although accepted in foreign trade contracts. The Western concept of equality is regarded as dehumanizing, since it puts all human beings on the same plane. The African modes of conflict resolution also do not proceed along the lines of Western legalism. Even in India, which possesses a highly complex legal system in its cosmopolitan centers, eighty percent of people live in villages where conflicts are resolved along the traditional modes, instead of the Western-style legalism. Legalism, therefore, is a feature of the Western civilization, which is not shared by other civilizations as their central principle of social life. Consequently, it is improper for international law to attempt to transform all civilizations into Western-style legal cultures.

Thus, while the non-universality of the legal order does not affect the inter-state and transnational categories of international law, it has profound consequences for the intranational category.

Finally, does the axiological diversity of the world affect international law? As we have seen in the previous Chapters, different civilizations possess different value systems as a result of their particular historicity. If the history of the world has shown anything clearly, it is the tenacity with which it has clung to this civilizational pluralism throughout its course. There have always existed three to four civilizations in the world at any given time, each pursuing its own way of life that has been achieved in its own particular history. This continues to be so even in the face of today's global cosmopolitanism. True, there has been an increased interaction among these civilizations in our times. The Western ways of the industrial culture are significantly influencing the non-Western ways. The discovery and perfection of mass production through industrialization is a singularly unique accomplishment of the Western civilization in all history. For the first time in history, this has made the good life possible for the masses. Therefore, peoples of other civilizations have adopted it with great vigor in order to improve their living conditions. However, the converse has not been true. For example, the need to improve standard of living for the masses has resulted in India in a vigorous and sustained industrial culture, but the disenchantment in the West with materialism in recent decades and the quest for spiritual bearings have not resulted in a matching adoption of the Hindu way of life. Even Yoga has settled down in the West to being no more than a means for maintaining one's physical health.

However, this Western influence has not resulted in a replacement of the native ways of life in other civilizations by the Western way, as seen in the previous Chapters. It has no doubt produced certain changes in the native ways, but the non-Western civilizations continue to retain their own particularity. Therefore, it is fallacious to construct a role for international law upon the assumption of a cultural uniformity of the world, or even an expectation thereof. The examples of the major civilizations that we have observed in the preceding Chapters amply illustrate the civilizational pluralism that continues to exist and has given no sign of vanishing. These civilizations differ from each other in fundamental ways, as, for example, in their cosmic imagination that relates human existence to the world of existence, in their modes of social organization that orders private and public life, and in their scheme of values that governs their material and spiritual life.

This lack of axiological homogeneity of the world does not affect the inter-state category of international law, for the variety in value systems has no bearing upon the matters of this category, as shown above. Nor is the category of transnational law affected thereby, since economic, technical, or environmental cooperation among states does not require that their internal societies be axiologically uniform. However, the intranational category (human rights) is profoundly affected by this diversity, since it deals with how people live their daily lives within their habitat. A promising system of human rights must conform to the world's plurality of value systems, rather than crusading for a uniform system of values for the peoples of the entire world.

Unfortunately, the International Bill of Human Rights strives for such uniformity in great part in following a single-catalog approach.[6] Its nor-

6. S.P. Sinha, "The Axiology of the International Bill of Human Rights," 1 *Pace Yearbook of International Law* 21 (1989); S.P. Sinha, "The Missing First Step in the Human Rights Movement," in American Branch, International Law Association, *Proceedings and Committee Reports*, 71 (1985–1986); S.P. Sinha, "Human Rights: A Non-Western Viewpoint," 67 *Archiv für Rechts- und Sozialphilosophie* 76 (1981); S.P. Sinha, "Freeing Human Rights from Natural Rights," 70 *Archiv für Rechts- und Sozialphilosophie* 342 (1984); S.P. Sinha, "Human Rights Philosophically," 18 *Indian Journal of International Law* 139 (1978); S.P. Sinha, "The Anthropocentric Theory of International Law as a Basis for Human Rights," 10 *Case Western Reserve Journal of International Law, Human Rights Issue* 469 (1978). See also, S.P. Sinha, "Why Has It Not Been Possible to Define Law," 75 *Archiv für Rechts- und Sozialphilosophie* 1 (1989); S.P. Sinha, *What Is Law* (1989); S.P. Sinha, *Jurisprudence: Legal Philosophy in a Nutshell* (1993).

mative structure is based predominantly upon the values of individualism and legalism of the Western civilization, although it must be recognized that there are provisions in it which are not so narrowly circumscribed.

The basic axiological document of the International Bill of Human Rights is the Universal Declaration of Human Rights. John P. Humphrey, working at the United Nations at the time, authored the draft that eventually became the Universal Declaration. When, in 1947, the Chinese Vice-Chairman of the Commission on Human Rights, P.C. Chang, requested him to study the Chinese philosophy before writing his draft, Humphrey completely ignored the wise suggestion. He "didn't go to China nor did I study the writing of Confucius!"[7] and he went on to preparing his draft. What a pity![8] The consequence is that this basic axiological document, which was conceived as providing the basis for subsequent documents prescribing human rights for the peoples of all civilizations, ended up substantially ignoring the particular values of the non-Western civilizations. The fallacy is carried through in the two subsequent Covenants, which are based upon this Declaration.

We shall demonstrate this below. However, first we must clearly state that our criticism of the human rights movement in this aspect is not a condemnation of the movement. Quite to the contrary.[9] We quite marvel at the miracle accomplished by this movement in achieving a recognition of the human being's rights in a society of sovereign states and in establishing the state's international legal obligations with respect thereto. The "universal acceptance of the idea of human rights and its general content may be only formal and superficial, in some cases even hypocritical, but no government dissents from the ideology of human rights today or offers an alternative to it."[10] Our own effort here is to strengthen the movement by overcoming its shortcomings, not to condemn it.

The normative provisions of the Universal Declaration of Human Rights (UDHR), the International Covenant on Civil and Political Rights (ICCPR), and the International Covenant on Economic, Social, and Cultural Rights (ICESCR) can be classified into six categories: (1) integrity of the person, (2) personal relationships, (3) social assertion, (4) economic well-being, (5) political assertion, and (6) conflict resolution.

---

7. J.P. Humphrey, *Human Rights and the United Nations: A Great Adventure*, 29 (1984).

8. S.P. Sinha, "Book Review: Human Rights and the United Nations: A Great Adventure," 12 *International Journal of Legal Information* 158 (1984).

9. S.P. Sinha, "Freeing Human Rights," *supra* note 6.

10. L. Henkin, "Introduction," in L. Henkin, ed., *The International Bill of Human Rights*, 1 (1981).

(1) The law governing the integrity of the person[11] provides for: life, liberty, and security of person; freedom of movement and choice of residence; protection from slavery, servitude, forced labor, torture, inhuman or degrading treatment or punishment; and protection from arbitrary arrest, detention, exile, arbitrary interference with home privacy, and attacks upon honor and reputation. These values are common to all value systems of the world, Western and non-Western. However, provisions in other areas are not.

(2) The law of personal relationships[12] deals with family, marriage, and children. It gives eloquent expression of individualism by positing the individual as the fundamental unit of society and the nuclear family as its fundamental group. However, it fails to provide for the hierarchical family of China or Japan, the Hindu joint-family of India, or the lineage and kinship systems of the Tallensi, Ashanti, Hausa-Fulani, Yoruba, Ibo, Tiv, Ganda, Lugbara, Kikuyu, Nandi, Arusha, Nyakyusa, and Nuer peoples of Africa.

(3) The law of social assertion of the human being[13] secures his participation in the cultural life of the community on the basis of equal treatment of all human beings. Its provisions deal with elimination of distinctions based on race, color, sex, language, religion, opinion, national or social origin, property, birth, or status. They provide for participation in the cultural life of the community, enjoyment of the benefit of scientific progress, equal rights to men and women, and freedom of thought, conscience, and religion. Most of these provisions are not limited to the individualistic ideology of the West alone. However, individualism asserts itself in the provisions of equality. This is good for the West, but it leaves out civilizations

11. Articles 3, 4, 5, 9, 12 of UDHR; Articles 6, 7, 8, 9, 10, 11, 12, 13, 17 of ICCPR. For the practice of the Human Rights Committee, see *Selected Decisions*; for Article 6: Comm. Nos. 30/178, 45/197; for Article 7: Comm. Nos. 4/1977, 5/1977, 8/1977, 9/1977, 11/1977, 25/1978, 28/1978, 30/1978, 33/1978, 37/1978, 52/1979, 63/1979, 73/1980; for Articles 9(1), (2), (3), (4), (5), see *supra* note 5; for Article 19 (1): Comm. Nos. 4/1977, 5/1977, 8/1977, 10/1977, 11/1977, 25/1977, 27/1978, 28/1978, 30/1978, 33/1978, 37/1978, 44/1979, 56/1979, 63/1979, 70/1980, 73/1080; for Article 10(2): Comm. No. 27/1978; for Article 11: Comm. No. 91/1981; for Article 12: Comm. Nos. 24/1977, 31/1978, 52/1979, 57/1979, 68/1980; for Article 13333: Comm. Nos. 27/1978, 58/1979; for Article 17, see *supra* note 4.

12. Article 16 of UDHR; Articles 23, 24 of ICCPR; Article 10 of ICESCR. For the practice of the Human Rights Committee, see *Selected Decisions*, for Article 23: Comm. Nos. 24/2977, 35/1978, 68/1980; for Article 24: Comm. No. 24/1977.

13. Articles 1, 2, 27 of UDHR; Articles 2, 3, 18 of the ICCPR; Article 15 of ICESCR. For the practice of the Human Rights Committee, see *Selected Decisions*, for Article 2: Comm. Nos. 9/1977, 19/1977, 24/1978, 25/1978, 28/1978, 35/1978, 50/1979, 52/1979, 56/1979, 57/1979, 79/1979, 81/1980; for Article 3: Comm. Nos. 24/1977, 35/1978; for Article 18: Comm. No. 40/1978.

that seek human emancipation on the basis of hierarchical, not equal, relationships, as in China or Japan or, even, India to a great extent.

(4) The law of economic well-being[14] contains provisions for right to work, fair wages, choice of employment, safe and healthy working conditions, job promotions, rest, leisure, reasonable working hours, holidays, trade unions, social security, adequate standard of living, physical and mental health, and education. These provisions secure salutary protection to the workers in the industrial societies. However, they make no provision for other economic styles, such as the rural India or the non-industrial Africa.

(5) The law of political assertion[15] provides for fine principles of political democracy, but since our focus is on value systems, we shall not discuss these here.

(6) Finally, the law concerning conflict resolution[16] provides only for the legalism of the West and neglects the fundamental principles of social organization practiced in other civilizations, as pointed above.

At least six major shortcomings result from this approach of the International Bill of Human Rights wherein it, being inadequately informed of the civilizational diversity of the world, prescribes but one single catalog for how all peoples of the world should live.

Firstly, seeking universals in this diversity results in the minimality of a common denominator. This weakens human rights by reducing them to a minimalist level and it ignores the deeper dynamics that exist in the inner folds of various civilizations where real problems of human rights arise and should become the concern of the human rights movement.

Secondly, the universality claimed under this approach is often a fake. For example, inhumane treatment, dealt in the Bill as a universal proposition, does not have the same meaning in all cultures. Even life has a differ-

---

14. Articles 17, 22, 23, 24, 25, 26 of UDHR. Articles 6, 7, 8, 9, 11, 12, 13, 14 of ICESCR.

15. Articles 12, 13, 14, 15, 18, 19, 20, 21 of UDHR; Articles 19, 20, 21, 22, 25, 26, 27 of ICCPR. For the practice of the Human Rights Committee, see *Selected Decisions*, for Article 19: Comm. Nos. 8/1977, 11/1978, 28/1978, 31/1978, 33/1978, 44/1979, 52/1979, 61/1979; for Article 22(1): Comm. No. 52/1979; for Article 25: Comm. Nos. 5/1978, 10/1977, 19/1977, 28/1978,34/1978, 35/1978, 44/1979; for Article 26: Comm. Nos. 17/1977, 24/1977, 28/1978, 35/1978, 68/1980; for Article 27: Comm. No. 24/1977.

16. Articles 6, 7, 10 of UDHR; Articles 9, 14, 16, 17 of ICCPR. For the practice of the Human Rights Committee, see *Selected Decisions*, for Article 9: *supra* note 20; for Article 14 (1): Comm. Nos. 5/1977, 6/1977, 8/1977, 10/1977, 17/1978, 27/1978, 28/1978, 32/1978, 44/1979, 46/1979, 64/1979, 70/1980, 81/1980; for Article 14(2): Comm. Nos. 4/1977, 5/1977, 6/1977, 8/1977, 10/1977, 27/1978, 28/1978, 32/1978, 33/1978, 44/1979, 46/1979, 46/1979, 52/1979, 56/1979, 63/1979, 70/1980, 73/1980; for Article 14(5): Comm. Nos. 24/1977, 27/1978, 35/1978, 68/1980, 79/1980.

ent meaning in cultures which see it in the foetus from those which see it only after delivery.

Thirdly, this single-catalog approach dismisses other approaches to human emancipation, worked out by different peoples of the world in their own civilizational contexts, than the Western-style individualism and legalism.

Fourthly, the Bill adopts as universal certain institutions which have no meaning for many cultures, such as consensual marriage for village India.

Fifthly, the Bill excludes some very serious problems of human existence which have been gnawing at human well-being in the non-Western cultures, such as the pernicious dowry system of India.

Finally, the single-catalog approach prevents, of its logical necessity, the accommodation of fundamentally different institutions adopted by different peoples for pursuing their own lives. For example, the right to own property either had to be included for all (as in the Universal Declaration) or, upon objections from Communist states, it had to be dropped for all (as in the Covenants). Both alternatives are inconsistent with the pluralistic reality.

It is sometimes argued that the concerns raised by our approach of legal polycentricity to international law might be met by the actual practice of the Human Rights Committee, which is the functional organ of the International Covenant for Civil and Political Rights.

This argument is defective in two respects.

Firstly, the Committee has to work within its constitutive instrument. It cannot cure the defects of its conceptual scheme. Secondly, the evidence of the actual practice of the Committee[17] shows that it neither has been involved with non-Western civilizations in any significant way, nor has it been seized of the axiological issues raised by legal polycentricity.

It has also been argued that our point about the axiological deficiency has been met by the regional systems of human rights. Thus, the American Branch of the Committee on Human Rights of the International Law Association,[18] in adopting my study,[19] noted that some of its members felt that "the impressive development of regional protection of human rights evi-

---

17. *Selected Decisions*. T. Meron, "Book Review: International Covenant on Civil and Political Rights, Human Rights Committee; Selected Decisions Under the Optional Protocol (Second to Sixteenth Sessions), U.N. DOC. CCPR/C/OP/1 (1985)," 80 *American Journal of International Law* 267 (1986).

18. The Committee was then composed of James A.R. Nafziger (Chairman), Robert L. Bard, Thomas Buergenthal, Lung-Chu Chen, Anthony D'Amato, Thomas H. Franck, Malvina Halberstam, Hurst Hannum, Joan F. Hartman, Louis Henkin, Farrokh Jhabvala, Sidney Liskofsky, Bert B. Lockwood, David A. Martin, Jordan J. Paust, W. Michael Reisman, Charles D. Siegal, Surya Prakash Sinha, Louis Sohn, and Amy Young. American Branch, International Law Association, *Proceedings and Committee Reports*, 72 (1985–1986).

19. S.P. Sinha, "The Missing First Step in the Human Rights Movement," *id.*, 73.

dences growing concurrence in the scope and the content of human rights notwithstanding cultural and other divergences."[20]

This argument probably makes two points.

In the first place, it is probably looking toward a civilizational uniformity which would guarantee human rights in this world through a concurrence, notwithstanding cultural divergences. However, this is not isomorphic to the reality of our world. We have pointed out in the preceding Chapters the tenacity with which civilizational pluralism has existed throughout civilized history and continues to do so in our times. While there are certain aspects of human existence in which cultural concurrence does exist, such as, for example, protection of the person from physical violence, there are major areas of personal and social relationships where different civilizations practice their own historically developed particular value systems. Moreover, even in matters where an apparent concurrence might exist on the surface, its uselessness is exposed when we consider the specifics of the value involved, which is practiced variously in different cultures. For example, as pointed out above, one might argue a cultural concurrence on a right to life, but this is of no assistance when we are faced with the problem of abortion in a culture which considers that life begins with the foetus or a culture which sees the human being only after birth. Or, one might argue a cultural concurrence against inhumane treatment, but the meaning of inhumane treatment is very different in different cultures. It is an illusion to hope for a civilizational uniformity in the world. Nor is that uniformity necessary for securing human existence on earth.

Secondly, the regional argument is probably pointing to the fact of regional treaties as filling the axiological gap that exists in the International Bill. However, two of the three regional treaties in operation are within the folds of the Western civilization, representing two variations of that civilization, namely, the European Convention on Human Rights and Fundamental Freedoms and the American Convention on Human Rights. The third, the African [Banjul] Charter on Human and Peoples' Rights, in spite of its vagueness and inadequacies, does make a conscious reference in its Preamble to the historical traditions and values of the African civilization and it mandates the African Commission on Human and Peoples' Rights to undertake research on African problems in this field (Article 45(1)(a)) and to apply African customs and practices (Article 61). However, civilizations other than the Western and the African cannot be said to have been accounted for by the regional systems. In any case, if the objective of the International Bill is to provide protection to the human being on a worldwide scale, it is incongruous for it to pass the buck to non-existent regional systems.

---

20. *Id.*, 71.

While our position calls for a reconstruction of the human rights movement to respond to the civilizational diversity of the world, it most certainly cannot be used for reducing the existing human-rights obligations of non-Western states. It is sometimes argued by the developing countries, as at the 1993 International Conference on Human Rights in Vienna, that their human-rights obligations should be reduced, postponed, or suspended in face of their more urgent problem of economic development. This kind of an argument is unsustainable for two reasons.

One, it perverts the human rights movement by making it impossible, because there is no way in the foreseeable future that these countries will equal the developed countries in economic development. They will always remain developing, for the very concept of 'developing' is relative to the 'developed.' Therefore, the argument amounts to a permanent exemption of these countries from the obligations of human rights, which is a perversion indeed.

Two, it is strange to argue that repression of human rights is necessary in order to achieve economic development. Even if, for the sake of argument, one concedes to it, then the very basic question arises that what good economic development is to me if I am deprived of the protection of my material and spiritual existence which the human rights movement provides. In any case, it is unconvincing that people have to be deprived in order to prosper.

Thus, the conclusion to which our analysis of legal polycentricity as applied to international law leads is that the non-universality of legalism and the non-homogeneity of the world's value systems do not affect the validity of the system of international law. Nor do they have any significance for the inter-state and the transnational categories of this law. However, they have profound consequences for the intranational category.

What, then, is the proper role of international law in our multi-civilizational context?

A system of imperatives has two aspects, namely, the normative and the performative. Law being such a system, in its normative aspect it is possessed of norms for its subjects and, in its performative aspect, it provides for the accountability of these subjects for their behavior in accordance with those norms.[21]

The performative or the accountability aspect of international law is not affected by civilizational pluralism. A state, which is a creature of international law, cannot claim that it is not accountable to that law just because

21. As to the nature of law, see S.P. Sinha, *What Is Law?* (1989); S.P. Sinha, *Jurisprudence: Legal Philosophy in a Nutshell* (1993).

it belongs to one civilization or another.[22] Therefore, the fact of civilizational pluralism itself does not call for any change in the performative aspect of the existing system of international law.

As to the normative aspect, while inter-state and transnational aspects of international law remain unaffected by this pluralism, the intranational aspect is significantly affected by it. International law needs to redefine its role in this aspect in order to do its part in maximizing the realization of values for all humanity. It certainly must not abandon this category. However, it cannot fully succeed here by following a single-catalog approach of imposing one normative scheme upon all civilizations. International law can accommodate civilizational pluralism without releasing a state from its performative accountability. It can do so by making the states responsible for implementing the value ideals of their own respective civilizations and by obliging them to assist human beings living within their jurisdictions to realize values which are not alien but, rather, pertinent to them.

This is not an argument for extreme relativism run amok, wherein a state becomes its own normative arbiter. A state is not a civilization. Nor is it the spokesman for the values of that civilization. The norms of a particular civilization are determined objectively. The proper role of international law is to ensure that in culture-specific matters, such as human rights, the state adheres to the norms of the civilization to which it belongs and is made accountable therefor.

Therefore, the focus of legal polycentricity upon international law, i.e., the fact of the present diversity of civilizations among the members of the society of states, does not argue for either the invalidity of international law or the denial by a state of its performative aspect. What it argues for is that the normative content of this law be informed of a distinction between that which is universal and that which is culture-specific.

22. Nor, generally speaking, have the new states of Asia and Africa claimed so. See, S.P. Sinha, *New Nations and the Law of Nations* (1967).

Bibliography

Chapter 1

Abel, R.L., *The Politics of Informal Justice*, 2 vols., New York, 1982

Ackerman, B., "Why Dialogue?" 86 *Journal of Philosophy* 5 (1989)

Adewoye, O., "Legal Practice in Abadan, 1904–1960," 24 *Journal of Legal Pluralism* 57 (1986)

Arthurs, H.W., *Without the Law: Administrative Justice and Legal Pluralism in Mid 19th-Century England*, Toronto, 1985

Auerback, J.S., *Justice Without Law?*, New York, 1983

A.N. Allot and G.R. Woodman, eds., *People's Law and State Law: The Bellagio Papers*, Dordrecht, 1985

Aristotle, Nichomachean Ethics, in R. Mckeon, ed., *Basic Works of Aristotle*, New York, 1941

Asch, S., *Social Psychology*, Englewood Cliffs, 1952

Bartlett, K.T., "Feminist Legal Methods," 103 *Harvard Law Review* 829 (1990)

Bender, L., "Feminist (Re)torts: Thoughts on the Liability Crisis, Mass Torts, Power, and Responsibilities," 1990 *Duke Law Journal* 848 (1990)

Bender, L., "From Gender Difference to Feminist Solidarity: Using Carol Gilligan and an Ethic of Care in Law," 15 *Vermont Law Review* 1 (1990)

Benedict, R., *Patterns of Culture*, Boston, 1934

Bentsi-Enchill, "The Colonial Heritage of Legal Pluralism," 1 *Zambia Law Journal* 1 (1969)

Berlin, I., *Concepts and Categories*, New York, 1979

Berlin, I., *Four Essays on Liberty*, London, 1969

Berlin, I., *Against the Current*, London, 1979

Black, A., *Guilds and Civil Society in European Political Thought from the Twelfth Century to the Present*, London, 1984

Boas, F., *The Mind of Primitive Man*, rev. ed., London, 1938

Brandt, R., *Hopi Ethics*, Chicago, 1954

Brigham, J., "Right, Rage, and Remedy: Forms of Law in Political Discourse," in *Studies in American Political Development*, 1987

Buckle, L. and Thomas-Buckle, S.R., "Doing Unto Others: Dispute and Dispute-Processing in an Urban American Neighborhood," in R. Tomasic and M. Feeley, eds., *Neighborhood Justice*, New York, 1982

Burke and Reber, "State Action, Congressional Power, and Creditors' Rights: An Essay on the Fourteenth Amendment," 46 *Southern California Law Review* 1003 (1973)

Chanock, M., *Law, Custom, and Social Order: The Colonial Experience in Malawi and Zambia*, Cambridge, 1985

Chiba, M., ed., *Asian Indigenous Law—In Interaction with Received Law,* London, *1986*

Chiba, M., *Legal Pluralism: Toward a General Theory through Japanese Legal Culture*, Tokyo, 1989

Comaroff, J., *Body of Power, Spirit of Resistance: Culture and History of a South African People,* Chicago, (1985)

Comaroff, J. and Comaroff, J.L., "Christianity and Colonialism in South Africa," 13 *American Ethnologist* 1 (1986)

Cook, "Beyond Critical Legal Studies: The Reconstruction Theology of Dr. Martin Luther King, Jr.," 103 *Harvard Law Review* 985 (1990)

Crenshaw, K., "A Black Feminist Critique of Antidiscriination Law and Politics," in D. Kairys, ed., *The Politics of Law*, 195, 2d ed., New York, 1990

Crenshaw, K., "Race, Reform, and Retrenchment: Transformation and Legitimation in Antidiscrimination Law," 101 *Harvard Law Review* 1331 (1988)

Dahl, R.A., *After Revolution*, New Haven, 1970

Delgado, R., "The Imperial Scholar: Reflections on a Review of Civil Rights Literature," 132 *University of Pennsylvania Law Review* 561 (1984)

Duclos, N., "Lesson of Difference: Feminist Theory on Cultural Diversity," 38 *Buffalo Law Review* 325 (1990)

Edel, A., *Ethical Judgment*, Glencoe, Ill., 1955

Editorial, "The Subsidiarity Principle," 27 *Common Market Law Review* 181 (1990)

Engel, D.M., "Legal Pluralism in an American Community: Perspectives on a Civil Trial Court," 3 *American Bar Foundation Research Journal* 425 (1980)

Engel, D.M., "The Oven Bird's Song: Insiders, Outsiders, and Personal Injuries in an American Community," 18 *Law and Society Review* 549 (1984)

Engel, D.M., "Law, Time, and Community," 21 *Law and Society Review* 605 (1987)

Erjin, C., *China, Crossroads to Socialism*, 1984

Figgis, J.N., *Churches in Modern State*, London, 1913

Findlay, *Kant and Transcendental Object*, Oxford, 1981

Fish, S., "Interpretation and the Pluralist Vision," 60 *Texas Law Review* 495 (1982)

Fitzpatrick, P., "Law and Societies," 22 *Osgoode Hall Law Journal* 115 (1984)

Fletcher, G.P., "The Right and the Reasonable," 98 *Harvard Law Review* 949 (1985)

Forer, N., "The Imposed Wardship of American Indian Tribes: A Case Study of the Prairie Band Potawatomi," in Burman and Harrell-Bond, *Imposition*, New York, 89

Freedman, "Sex, Equality, Sex Differences, and the Supreme Court," 92 *Yale Law Journal* 913 (1982)

Frenkel-Brunswik, "Social Research and the Problem of Values: A Reply," 49 *Journal of Abnormal and Social Psychology* 466 (1954)

Galanter, M., "Justice in Many Rooms: Courts, Private Ordering, and Indigenous Law," 19 *Journal of Legal Pluralism and Unofficial Law* 1 (1981)

Galston, W.A., "Pluralism and Social Unity," 99 *Ethics* 711 (1989)

Geertz, C., *Local Knowledge: Further Essays in Interpretive Anthropology*, New York, 1983

Giddens, A., *Central Problems in Social Theory: Action, Structure, and Contradiction in Social Analysis*, London, 1979

Gillisen, J., *La pluralisme juridique*, Bruxelles, 1972

Green, T.J., "Subsidiarity During the Code Revision Process: Some Initial Reflections," 48 *The Jurist* 771 (1988)

Greenhouse, C., "Nature is to Culture as Praying is to Suing: Legal Pluralism in an American Suburb," 20 *Journal of Legal Pluralism* 17 (1982)

Griffiths, J. "What is Legal Pluralism?" 24 *Journal of Legal Pluralism* 1 (1986)

Hamilton and Cairns, eds., *The Collected Dialogues of Plato*, Princeton, 1963

Harrington, C., *Shadow Justice: The Ideology and Institutionalization of Alternatives to Court*, Westport, 1985

Harrington C., and Merry, S.E., "Ideological Production: The Making of Community Mediation," 22 *Law and Society Review* 709 (1988)

Harris, A.P., "Race and Essentialism in Feminist Legal Theory," 42 *Stanford Law Review* 581 (1990)

Henry, S., *Private Justice*, London, 1983

Henry, S., "Community Justice, Capitalist Society, and Human Agency: The Dialectics of Collective Law in the Cooperative," 19 *Law and Society Review* 303 (1985)

Henry, S., "The Construction and Deconstruction of Social Control: Thoughts on the Discursive Production of State Law and Private Justice," in J. Lowman, R. Menzies, and T. Palys, eds., *Transcarceration*, Aldershot, 1987

Honoré, "The Right to Rebel," 8 *Oxford Journal of Legal Studies* 34 (1988)

Hooker, M.B., *Legal Pluralism: An Introduction to Colonial and Neo-Colonial Laws*, Oxford, 1975

International Legal Center, *Law and Development: The Future of Development Research*, New York, 1974

James, W., *The Will to Believe and Other Essays in Popular Philosophy*, New York, 1956

James, W., "Hegel and His Method and Monistic Idealism," in J. McDermett, ed., *The Writings of William James: A Comprehensive Edition*, Chicago, 1977

Kaufman, F., "The Principle of Subsidiarity Viewed by the Sociology of Organizations (The Nature and Future of Episcopal Conferences)," 48 *The Jurist* 275 (1988)

Kay, "Models of Equality," 1985 *University of Illinois Law Review* 39

Kidder, R.L., "Formal Litigation and Professional Insecurity: Legal Entrepreneurship in South India," 9 *Law and Society Review* 11 (1974)

Kidder, R.L., "Toward an Integrated Theory of Imposed Law," in Burman and Harrell-Bond, *Imposition*, 289

Kluckhohn, C., "Universal Categories of Culture," in *Anthropology Today*, 1953

Kolb, "A Social-Psychological Conception of Human Freedom," 63 *Ethics* 180 (1953)

Komonchak, J.A., "Subsidiarity in the Church: The State of the Question (The Nature and Future of Episcopal Conferences)," 48 *The Jurist* 298 (1988)

Kroeber, A.I., "The Concept of Culture in Science," 35 *Journal of General Education* 188 (1949)

Kronman, "Practical Wisdom and Professional Character," 4 *Social Philosophy and Policy* 203 (1986)

Law, "Rethinking Sex and Constitution," 132 *University of Pennsylvania Law Review* 955 (1984)

Levi, *Philosophy and the Modern World*, Chicago, 1977

Lindblom, C.E., *Politics and Markets*, New York, 1977

Linna, J.E., "Subsidiarity, Collegiality, Catholic Diversity and Their Relevance to Apostolic Visitations," 49 *The Jurist* 399 (1988)

Linton, R. "Universal Ethical Principles: An Anthropological View," in R. Ashen, ed., *Moral Principles of Action*, 646 (1952)

Linton, R., "The Problem of Universal Values," in R.R. Spencer, ed., *Method and Perspective in Anthropology*, 150 (1954)

Littleton, "Reconstructing Sexual Equality," 75 *California Law Review* 1279 (1987)

Macaulay, S., "Images of Law in Everyday Life: The Lessons of School, Entertainment, and Spectator Sport," 21 *Law and Society Review* 185 (1987)

Macaulay, S., "Private Government," in L. Lipson and S. Wheeler, eds., *Law and Social Sciences*, New York, 1986

Macedo, "The Politics of Justification," 18 *Political Theory* 280 (1990)

Maitland, F.W., Introduction to Otto von Gierke, in *Political Theory of the Middle Age*, Cambridge, 1900

Malinowski, B., *Crime and Custom in a Savage Society*, New York, 1926

Marshall, "Diluting Constitutional Rights: Rethinking 'Rethinking State Action'," 80 *Northwestern University Law Review* 558 (1985)

Maslow, A., "Psychological Progress in Understanding Human Nature and a Scientific Ethics," 10 *Main Currents* 75 (1954)

Matsuda, M., "Affirmative Action and Legal Knowledge: Planting Seeds in Plowed-up Ground," 11 *Harvard Women's Law Journal* 1 (1988)

McKinnon, C., *Toward a Feminist Theory of the State*, Cambridge, 1989

McKinnon, C., "Feminism, Marxism, Method, and the State: Toward Feminist Jurisprudence," 8 *Signs* 635 (1985)

Merry, S.E., "Everyday Understandings of the Law in Working-class America," 13 *American Ethnologist* 253 (1986)

Merry, S.E., "Going to Court: Strategies of Dispute Management in an American Urban Neighborhood," 13 *Law and Society Review* 891 (1979)

Merry, S.E., "Legal Pluralism," 22 *Law and Society Review* 869 (1988)

Minow, M., "Pluralisms," 21 *Connecticut Law Review* 965 (1989)

Minow, M., "The Supreme Court, 1986 Term—Foreword: Justice Engendered," 101 *Harvard Law Review* 10 (1987)

Moore, S.F., "Law and Social Change: The Semi-Autonomous Social Field as an Appropriate Subject of Study," 7 *Law and Society Review* 719 (1973)

Moore, S.F., "Legal Systems of the World: An Introductory Guide to Classification, Typological Interpretetations, and Bibliographical Resources," in Lipson and Wheeler, *Law and Social Sciences.*

Moore, S.F., *Social Facts and Fabrications: Customary Law on Kilimanjaro, 1880–1980* (1986)

Moore, S.F., "The Semantics of Judging," 54 *Southern California Law Review* 151 (1981)

Moore, S.F., "Moral Reality," 1982 *Wisconsin Law Review* 1061

Murdock, G., "The Common Denominators of Cultures," in R. Linton, ed., *The Science of Man in the World Crisis*, New York, 1945

Nader, L., "Introduction," in L. Nader, ed., *Law in Culture and Society*, 4 (1969)

Nader, L., ed., *Law in Culture and Society*, Chicago, 1969

Nader, L., *No Access to Law*, New York, 1980

Nader, L., "The Recurrent Dialectic Between Legality and Its Alternatives," 132 *University of Pennsylvania Law Review* 621 (1984)

Nelken, D., "Legislation and Its Constraints: A Case Study of the 1965 British Rent Act," in A. Podgorecki, C.J. Whelan, and D. Khosla, eds., *Legal Systems and Social Systems*, London, 1985

Nelken, D., "Review Essay: Beyond the Study of 'Law and Society'?

Henry's *Private Justice* and O'Hagen's *The End of the Law?*" 1986 *American Bar Foundation Research Journal* 323

Nicholls, D., *The Pluralistic State*, London, 1975

Okoth-Ogendo, H.W.O., "The Imposition of Property Law in Kenya," in S.B. Burman and B.E. Harrell-Bond, eds., *The Imposition of Law*, 147, New York, (1979)

Olson, M., *The Rise and Decline of Nations*, 1982

Olson, "Statutory Rape: A Feminist Critique of Rights," 63 *Texas Law Review* 387 (1984)

Parsons, T. and Shils, E., *Toward a General Theory of Action*, Cambridge, 1951

Peller, G., "Race Consciousness," 1990 *Duke Law Journal* 758

Petersen, H., *Informel Ret*, in Danish, summary in English, 1991

Pospisil, *The Anthropology of Law: A Comparative Theory of Law*, New York, 1971

Ranger, T., "The Invention of Tradition in Colonial Africa," in E. Hobsbawm and T. Ranger, eds., *The Invention of Tradition*, Cambridge, 1983

Rawls, J., *A Theory of Justice*, Cambridge, 1971

Rawls, J., "The Idea of Overlapping Consensus," 7 *Oxford Journal of Legal Studies* 4 (1987)

Roheim, G., *Psychoanalysis and Anthropology*, New York, 1950

Sack, P.G. and Minchin, E., eds., *Legal Pluralism: Proceedings of the Canberra Law Workshop VII*, Canberra, 1986

Sandel, M., "The Procedural Republic and the Unencumbered Self," 12 *Political Theory* 90 (1984)

Sarat, A., and Felstiner, W., "Law and Strategy in the Divorce Lawyer's Office," 20 *Law and Society Review* 93 (1986)

Scales, "The Emergence of Feminist Jurisprudence: An Essay," 95 *Yale Law Journal* 1273 (1986)

Schneider, "The Dialectics of Right and Politics: Perspectives from the Women's Movement," 61 *New York University Law Review* 589 (1986)

Schwarzchild, M., "Value Pluralism and the Constitution: In Defense of the State Action Doctrine," 5 *The Supreme Court Review* 129 (1988)

Sherwin, R.K., "Rhetorical Pluralism and the Discourse Ideal: Countering *Division of Employment v. Smith*, a Parable of Pagans, Politics, and Majoritarian Rule," 85 *Northwestern University Law Review* 388 (1991)

Scheingold, S.A., *The Politics of Rights: Lawyers, Public Policy, and Political Change*, New Haven, 1974

Silbey, S.S. and Bittner, E., "The Availability of Law," 4 *Law and Policy* 399 (1982)

Sinha, S.P. "The Axiology of the International Bill of Human Rights," 1 *Pace Yearbook of International Law* 21 (1981)

Sinha, S. P., "The Missing First Step in the Human Rights Movement," in American Branch, International Law Association, *Proceedings and Committee Reports*, 71 (1985–86

Sinha, S.P., "Human Rights: A Non-Western Viewpoint," 67 *Archiv für Rechts- und Sozialphilosophie* 76 (1981)

Sinha, S.P., "Freeing Human Rights from Natural Rights," 70 *Archiv für Rechts- und Sozialphilosophie* 342 (1984)

Sinha, S.P., "Human Rights Philosophically," 18 *Indian Journal of International Law* 139 (1978)

Sinha, S.P., "The Anthropocentric Theory of International Law as a Basis for Human Rights," 10 *Case Western Reserve Journal of International Law, Human Rights Issue* 469 (1978)

Sinha, S.P., "Non-universality of Law," *Archiv für Rechts- und Sozialphilosophie,* forthcoming, (1995)

Sinha, S.P., "Why Has It Not Been Possible to Define Law," 75 *Archiv für Rechts- und Sozialphilosophie* 1 (1989)

Sinha, S.P., *Asylum and International Law*, The Hague, 1971

Sinha, S.P., *New Nations and the Law of Nations*, Leyden, 1967

Sinha, S.P., *What Is Law?*, New York, (1989)

Sinha, S.P., *Jurisprudence: Legal Philosophy in a Nutshell*, St. Paul, 1993.

Starr, J., and Collier, J.F., *History and Power in the Study of Law: New Directions in Legal Anthropology*, 1989

Starr, S., and Collier, J.F., "Historical Studies of Legal Change," 28 *Current Anthropology* 367 (1987)

Strijbosch, F., "The Concept of Pela and Its Social Significance in the Community of Moluccan Immigrants in the Netherlands," 23 *Journal of Legal Pluralism* 177 (1985)

Sugarman, D., "Law, Economy, and the State in England, 1750–1914: Some Major Issues," in D. Sugarman, ed., *Legality, Ideology, and the State*, 213, London, (1983)

Taub and Schneider, "Perspectives on Women's Subordination and the Role of Law," in D. Kairys, ed., *The Politics of Law: A Progressive Critique*, 117, New York, (1982)

Torres, G., "Critical Race Theory: The Decline of the Universalist Ideal and the Hope of Plural Justice—Some Observations and Questions of an Emerging Phenomenon," 75 *Minnesota Law Review* 993 (1991)

Torres, G., "Local Knowledge, Local Color: Critical Legal Studies and the Law of Race Relations," 25 *San Diego Law Review 1043 (1988)*

Torres, G. and Milun, "Translating Yonnondio by Precedent and Evidence: The Mastpee Indian Case," 1990 *Duke Law Journal* 625

Tucker, *The Marxian Revolutionary Idea*, New York, 1969

von Benda-Beckmann, K., "Anthropology and Comparative Law," in von Benda-Beckmann, K. and Strijbosch, F., eds, *Anthropology or Law in the Netherlands*, 1986

von Benda-Beckmann, K., "Why Law Does Not Behave: Critical and Constructive Reflections on the Social Scientific Perception of the Social Significance of Law," in H. Finkler, ed., *Proceedings of the Symposium of Folk Law and Legal Pluralism*, Ottawa, 1983

Waldron, "Theoretical Foundations of Liberalism," 37 *Philosophical Quarterly* 127 (1987)

West, R., "Jurisprudence and Gender," 55 *University of Chicago Law Review* 1 (1988)

White, I., "Energy and the Evolution of Culture," 45 *American Anthropologist* 335 (1943)

Wiggins, D., "Deliberation and Practical Reason," in A. Rorty, ed., *Essays on Aristotle's Ethics*, Berkeley, 1980

Wissler, C., *Man and Culture*, London, 1923

Woodman, G.R., "What Is the Commission About?" 14 *Newsletter of the Commission on Folk Law and Legal Pluralism* 3 (1987–88)

Yngvesson, B., "Private Nuisance of Public Crime: The Clerk, The Court, and the Constructive Order in a New England Town," 22 *Law and Society Review* 409 (1988)

Chapter 2

Abel, A. "'Daral-Harb' and Daral-Islam,'" 2 *Encyclopedia of Islam* 1960.

Abusulayman, A., *The Islamic Theory of International Relations*, Herndon, VA, 1987.

Ago, R., "The First International Communities in the Mediterranean World, " 53 *British Yearbook of International Law*, 213, 1982.

Ago, R., "Pluralism and Origins of the International Community," 3 *Italian Yearbook of International Law* 3 (1977).

Alexandrowicz, C. H., *An Introduction to the History of the Law of Nations in the East Indies (16th, 17th, and 18th Centuries)*, Oxford, 1967.

Alexandrowicz, C. H. "The Afro-Asian World and the Law of Nations (Historical Aspects," *Recueil des cours*, 1968, Vol. 1.

Amman, E. and A. Dumas, *L'Éqlise au porvoir des laiques 888–1057*, Books I, II, III (1948).

Anand, R. P., ed., *Asian States and the Development of Universal International Law*, Delhi, 1972.

Armour, W. S. "Customs of Warfare in Ancient India," 8 *Transactions of the Grotius Society* 71 (1923).

Bandyopadhyay, P., *International Law and Custom in Ancient India*, New Delhi, 1982.

Barraclough, G. *The Origins of Modern Germany*, New York, 1949.

Basham, A. L., *The Wonder That Was India*, New York, 1954.

Bentwich, N., *The Religious Foundation of Internationalism*, London, 1933.

Bernard, M., *Lectures on Diplomacy*, Vol. II, London, 1868.

Bhatia, H. S. ed., *International Law and Practice in Ancient India*, New Delhi, 1977.

Bodin, J., *Six Books of a Commonweal*, (1606), trans. by Knolles, Cambridge, 1962.

Bos, M. and I. Brownlie, Eds., *Liber Amicorum for the R. Hon. Lord Wilberforce*, New York 1987.

Bloche, J., *Les Inscriptions d'Asoka*, Paris, 1950.

Bury, J. B., *History of Greece*, New York, 1975.

Cantor, N., *Church, Kingship, and Lay Investiture in England*, New York, 1958.

Cazelles, R., *La Société Politique et la Crise de la royaute sous Philippe de Vojois*, Paris, 1958.

Davids, T.W.R., *Buddhist India*, New York, 1911.

Delisle, L., "Des revenues publics en Normandie au XIIe et XIIIe siècles," *Bibliotheque de 1'écoles des chartes*, (1848–1949), 1852.

Depping, G., *Histoire du Commerce Entre le Levant et 1"Europe*, Vol. II., New York,, 1830.

Deutsch, K. and Foltz, W.J., eds., *Nation-Building*, New York 1963.

Fairbank, J.K., Reischauer, E. O., and Craig, A.M., *East Asia the Modern Transformation*, Boston, 1965.

Fliche, A., *La réforme qrégorienne*, Paris, 1946.

Ganshof, F.L., *Frankish Institutions Under Charlemagne*, Providence, 1968.

Gardot, A., "Jean Bodin, sa place parmi les fondateurs du droit international," 50 *Recueil des cours* 549 (1934).

Gong, G. W., *The Standard of "Civilization" in International Society*, Oxford, 1984.

Gross, L., "The Peace of Westphalia," 42 *American Journal of International Law*, 20 (1948).

Hamidullah, M., *Muslin Conduct of State*, 5th ed., Lahore, 1968.

Haskins, C.H., *Renaissance of the Twelfth Century*, Cambridge, 1927.

Havell, E. B., *A Short History of India*, London, 1924.

Hershey, A.S., *The Essentials of International Public Law*, New York, 1921.

Hobbes, T., *De Cive* (1642) and *Leviathan* (1651), Latin and English texts by van Vollenhoven, 6 *Bibliotheia Visseriana* 67 (*De Cive*), 74 (*De Cive*), 74 (*De Corpore Politico and Leviathan*) (1926).

Jolliffe, J.E.A., *Constitutional History of Medieval England*, New York, 1937.

Jolowicz, H.F., *Historical Introduction to the Study of Roman Law*, 2d ed., Ann Arbor, 1952.

Kane, P.V., *History of Dharmasastra*, Vol. III, Poona, 1930.

Kantorowicz, E.H., *King's Two Bodies*, Princeton, 1981.

Khadduri, M., "Islam and the Modern law of nations," 50 *American Journal of International Law* 358 (1956).

Khadduri, M., *The Islamic Law of Nations*, Baltimore, 1966.

Khadduri, M., *War and Peace in the Law of Islam*, New York, 1962.

Knowler, D., *The Evolution of Medieval Thought*, New York, 1962.

Lot, F. and Fawtier R., *Histoire des institutions françaises au Moyen Age*, Vol. II, Paris, 1958.

Lot, F., *Le Premier Budget de la Monarchie Française: Le compte general de 1202–1203*, Paris, 1932.

Lyon B. and Verhulst A.E., *Medieval Finance*, Ann Arbor, 1967.

MacKinney, L.C., "The People and Public Opinion in the Eleventh Century Peace Movement," 5 *Speculum* 181 (1930).

Mallet, D., "Les Premiers établissements de Grècs en Egypte," 12 *Memoires publie par les membres de la Missiones archéoloqique française au Caire*, 58 (1987).

Mahaffy, J.P., *Social Life of the Greeks*, Darby, 1883.

Molinie, G., *L'organization Judiciare, Militaire et Finacière des Associations de la Pait*, Toulouse, 1912.

Moore, J.B., *History of Arbitration*, Vol. 5, Washington, DC, 1898.

Nardin, T. and Mapel, D.R., *Traditions of International Ethics*, Cambridge/New York, 1992.

Nussbaum, A., *A Concise History of Nations*, New York, revised ed., 1954.

Nys, E., "Le droit des gens dans les rapports des Arabes et des Byzantins," 26 *Revue de droit international et de législation Comparée*, (1894).

Oechsli, W., *History of Switzerland, 1499–1914*, New York, 1922.

Oppenheim, L., *International Law*, 8th ed., London, 1955.

Pare, G., Brunet A., & Tremblay P., *La renaissance du XIIe Siècle*, Paris, 1933.

Phillipson, C., *The International Law and Custom of Ancient Greece and Rome*, Vols. I & II, Salem, 1911.

Pierenne, Jr., *Les Grands Courants de l'histoire universelle*, Vol. I, New York, 1959.

Pirenne, J., "L'organisation de la paix dans le Proche-Orient aux 3e et 2e millénaires," 14 *Recueil de la Société Jean Bodin*, 200 (1962).

Pollock, E. & Maitland F.W., *History of English Law*, New York, 1923.

Post, G., *Studies in Medieval Legal Thought*, Princeton, 1964.

Pramathanath, B., *International Law and Custom in Ancient India*, London, 1920.

Prasad, B., *The State in Ancient India*, London, 1904.

Prentout, H., "La treve de Dieu en Normandie," 6 *Memoires de L'Académie de Caen*, 1 (1931).

Pufendorf, S., *De Jure Naturae et Gentium Libri Octo*, trans. in *Classics of International Law.*

Reader, A., *L'arbitrage International Chez les Hellenes*, New York, 1912.

Ralston, J., *International Arbitration from Athens to Locarno*, New York, 1929.

Rapisardi-Mirabelli, A., "Le Congrès de Westphalie Entre les puissances de l'Europe, etc." 8 *Bibliotheca Visseriana*, 5 (1929).

Renouvin, P., ed., *Histoire des Rélations Internationales*, Vol. I, Paris, 1958.

Rey, F., "Rélationes internationales de L'Egypte Ancienne du 15 em Siecle avant Jesus-Christ," 48 *Revue générale de droit international public*, 35 (1941–1945).

Rostovtseff, M., "International Relations in the Ancient World," in E. Walsh, ed., *History and Nature of International Relations*, 31 (1922).

Sanborn, F.R., *Origins of the Early English Maritime and Commercial Law*, New York, 1930.

Sandquist, T.A., and Rowicke M.R., *Essays in Medieval History Presented to Bertie Wilkinson*, Toronto, 1969.

Schultz, F., *History of Roman Legal Science*, Oxford, 1946.

Singh, N., *India and International Law*, New Delhi, 1973.

Sinha, S.P., *Asylum and International Law*, The Hague, 1971.

Sinha, S.P., "Identifying a Principle of International Law Today" 1973 *Canadian Yearbook of International Law*, 106.

Sinha, S.P., *New Nations and the Law of Nations*, Leyden, 1967.

Smith, V., *Asoka the Buddhist Emperor of India*, New York, 1920.

Smith, V., *Early History of India, including Alexander's Campaigns*, New York, 1924.

Southern, R.W., *The Makiong of the Middle Ages*, New Haven, 1987.

Stenton, F.M., *Anglo-Saxon England*, New York, 1943.

Strayer, J.R., *On the Medieval Origins of the Modern State*, Princeton, 1970.

Stubbs, W., *Select Charters*, Littleton, CO., 1921.

Susa, N., *The Capitulary Regime in Turkey*, New York, 1933.

Taube, Le Baron Michel de., "Les Origines de l'arbitrage International: Antiquité et Moyen Age," 42 *Recueil des Cours*, 5 (1932).

Tellenbach, G., *Church, State, and Christian Society at the Time of the Investiture Conflict*, New York, 1940.

Thompson, J.W., *Feudal Germany*, New York, 1928.

Tod, M.N., *Interantional Arbitration Among the Greeks*, Oxford, 1913.

Ullmann, W., *The Growth of Papal Government in the Middle Ages*, New York, 1955.

Umozurike, V.O., *International Law and Colonialism in Africa*, Enugu, Nigeria, 1979.

United Nations Institute for Training and Research, *African International Legal History*, New York, 1975.

Viswanatha, S.V., *International Law in Ancient India*, Bombay, 1925.

Von Heyd, W., *Histoire du Commerce du Levant au Moyen Age*, tr. F. Raynaud, Vol. I, Philadelphia, 1923.

Walsh, E., ed., *History and Nature of International Relations*, Salem, 1922.

Watson, A., *International Law in Archaic Rome: War and Religion*, Baltimore, 1993.

Woodbine, G.E., ed., *De Legibus et Consuetudines Regni Angliae (1187)*, Cambridge, 1932.

Yuer, J., "L'interdiction de la guerre privée en Normandie," 1927 *Travaux de la semaine d'histoire de droit normand*, 307 (1928).

Chapter 3

Abegglen, J.C., *The Japanese Factory: Aspects of Its Social Organization*, Glencoe, Ill., 1958.

Albrektson, B., *History and the Gods: An Essay on the Idea of Historical Events as Divine Manifestations in the Ancienty Near East and in Israel*, 1967.

Albright, W.F., *The Archaeology of Palestine*, rev. ed., 1960.

Alexiou, S., N. Platon & H. Guanella, *Ancient Crete*, London, 1968.

Allchin, B., and Allchin, F.R., *The Birth of Indian Civilization: India and Pakistan Before 500 B.C.*, Baltimore, 1968.

Antonius, G., *The Arab Awakening*, London, 1938.

Arberry, A.J., *Sufism: An Account of the Mystic of Islam*, London, 1950.

Ardrey, R., *African Genesis*, New York, 1961.

Arnold, T.W., *The Preaching of Islam*, Westminister, 2d ed., 1913.

Arnold, T.W., *The Caliphate*, Oxford, 1924.

Avery, P., *Modern Iran*, New York, 1965.

Barraclough, G., *The Medieval Papacy*, London, 1968.

Barraclough, G., *The Origins of Modern Germany*, London, 1947.

Basham, A.L., *The Wonder That Was India*, New York, 2d ed., 1954.

Baynes, N.H. and Moss, H. St. L.B., eds., *Byzantium*, Oxford, 1961.

Beckman, G.M., *The Modernization of China and Japan*, New York, 1962.

Bellah, R.N., *Tokugawa Religion*, Scottsdale, 1957.

Billington, J.H., *The Icon and the Axe, an Interpretative History of Russian Culture*, New York, 1966.

Blakemore, H., *Latin America*, London, 1966.

Bloch, M., *Feudal Society*, Chicago, 1961.

Block, R., *Origins of Rome*, New York, 1960.

Bongard-Levin, G.M., *Ancient Indian Civilization,* New Delhi, 1985.

Borton H., *Japan's Modern Century*, New York, 1955.

Boxer, C.R., *The Christian Century in Japan, 1549–1650*, Berkeley, CA., 1951.

Boxer, R., *Four Centuries of Portuguese Expansion, 1415–1825*, 1961.

Branigan, K., *The Foundations of Palatial Crete: A Survey of Crete in the Early Bronze Age*, London, 1970.

Burn, A.R., *Persia and the Greeks: The Defense of the West*, London, 1962.

Bury, J.B., *History of Greece to the Death of Alexander the Great*, London, 3rd ed., 1951.

Cady, J.F., *Southeast Asia: Its Historical Development*, New York, 1964.

Cambridge Modern History, 12 vols., 1956.

Cary M., *History of Rome Down to the Reign of Constantine the Great*, London, 2d ed., 1954.

Cassirer, E., *et al.*, eds., *The Renaissance Philosophy of Man*, Chicago, 1948.

Chang, C., *The Chinese Gentry: Studies in Their Role in Nineteenth-Century Chinese Society*, Seattle, 1955.

Chaney, E. and Mack P., eds., *England and the Continental Renaissance: Essays in Honor of J.B. Trapp*, Woodbridge (England)/Rochester (NY), 1990.

Chi, L., *The Beginnings of Chinese Civilization*, Seattle, 1957.

Childe, V.G., *The Dawn of European Civilization*, New York, 6th ed., 1958.

Childe, V.G., *The Aryans: A Study of Indo-European Origins*, New York, 1926.

Childe, V.G., *What Happened in History*, New York, 1943.

Christensen, A., *L'Iran sous les Sassanides*, Copenhague, 2d ed., 1944.

Clapham, J.H., *The Economic Development of France and Germany*, Cambridge, 4th ed., 1936.

Clark, G., *Space, Time, and Man: A Prehistorian's View*, Cambridge/New York, 1992.

Clark, J.G.D., *Prehistoric Europe: the Economic Basis*, London, 1952.

Clark, J.G.D., *World Prehistory: A New Outline*, 2d ed., London, 1969.

Clark, W.E. Le Gros, *The Antecedents of Man*, New York, 1963.

Clark, G., *Aspects of Prehistory*, Berkeley, 1970.

Clark, G., *World Prehistory in New Perspective*, Cambridge/New York, 1977.

Coleman, J., *Ancient and Medieval Memories: Studies in the Reconstruction of the Past*, Cambridge, 1992.

Coles, J.M. and Higgs, E.S., *The Archaelogy of Early Man*, New York, 1969.

Coone, C.S., *The Origin of Races*, New York, 1962.

Creel, H.G., *The Birth of China*, London, 1936.

Creel, H.G., *Confucius, the Man and the Myth*, London, 1949.

Creel, H.G., *The Origins of Statecraft in China*, Chicago, 1970.

Daniel, G.E., *The First Civilizations: The Archaeology of Their Origins*, 1968.

Daniel, G.E., *The Idea of Prehistory*, 2d ed., Edinburgh, 1988.

Davidson, B., *African History: Themes and Outlines*, rev. ed., London, 1992.

Davidson, B., *Black Mother: The African Slave Trade*, Boston, 1961.

Dawson, C., *The Making of Europe*, London, 1932.

Deane, P., *The First Industrial Revolution*, Cambridge, 1965.

deBary, W.T., ed., *Sources of Chinese Tradition*, New York, 1966.

Debevoise, N.C., *A Political History of Parthia*, Chicago, 1938.

Dellapiccola, A.L., ed., *Vijayanagara: City and Empire*, Wiesbaden, 1985.

DiCesare, ed., *Reconsidering the Renaissance*, Binghamton, New York, 1992.

Diringer, D., *The Alphabet: A Key to the History of Mankind*, 3rd ed., 1968.

Dodds, E.R., *The Greeks and the Irrational*, Magnolia, MA, 1957.

Driver, H.E., ed., *The Americas on the Eve of Discovery*, Englewood Cliffs, NJ, 1964.

Eberhard, W., *Conquerors and Rulers: Social Forces in Medieval China*, Leiden, 1952.

Evans, J.D., *Malta*, London, 1959.

Fage, J.D., *A History of West Africa*, London, 1969.

Fagg, J.E., *Latin America: A General History*, Madrid, 2d ed., 1969.

Fairbank, J.K., *The United States and China*, Cambridge, 1958.

Fairbank, J.K., ed., *Chinese Thought and Institutions*, Chicago, 1957.

Fairbank, J.K., *The Chinese World Order: Traditional Chinese Foreign Relations*, Cambridge, 1968.

Fasi, M.E., *Africa From the Seventh to the Eleventh Century*, London/Berkeley/Paris, 1988.

Fieldhouse, D.K., *The Colonial Empires*, New York, 1966.

Finegan, J., *Light from the Ancient Past: The Archaelogical Background of Judaism and Christianity*, Princeton, 2d ed., 1959.

Finley, M.I., *The World of Odysseus*, New York, 1954.

Forbes, R.J., *Metallurgy in Antiquity*, Leiden, 1950.

Forrest, W.G.G., *The Emergency of Greek Democracy*, London, 1966.

Frank, T., *et al., An Economic Survey of Ancient Rome*, 5 vols., 1933–40.

Frankfort, H., *The Birth of Civilization in the Near East*, Bloomington, 1951.

Frye, R.N., *Heritage of Persia*, London, 1963.

Gabel, C., *Analysis of Prehistoric Economic Patterns*, 1967.

Gay, P., *The Enlightenment, an Interpretation*, New York, 1966.

Gelb, I.J., *A Study of Writing*, Chicago, rev. ed., 1964.

Gernet, J., *Ancient China from the Beginnings to the Empire*, London, 1968

Ghirshman, R., *Iran from the Earliest Times to the Islamic Conquest*, New York, 1961.

Gibb, H.A.R. and Bowen, H., *Islamic Society and the West, I: Islamic Society in the Eighteenth Century*, 2 parts, London/New York, 1950, 1957.

Gibb, H.A.R., *Modern Trends In Islam*, Chicago, 1947.

Gibb, H.A.R., *Mohammedanism: An Historical Survey*, London, 2d ed., 1953.

Goodrich, L.C., *A Short History of the Chinese People*, New York, 3rd ed., 1959.

Gopal, R., *How India Struggled for Freedom: A Political History*, Bombay, 1967.

Griffith, G.T., ed., *Alexander the Great: The Main Problems*, New York, 1966.

Grousset, R., *The Empire of the Steppes*, New Brunswick, N.J., 1970.

Hall, D.G.E., *A History of Southeast Asia*, New York, 1955.

Hallett, R., *Africa to 1875*, Ann Arbor, 1970.

Harden, D., *The Phoenicians*, Milano, 1968.

Haring, C.H., *The Spanish Empire in America*, Magnolia, MA, 1947.

Haskins, C.H., *The Normans in European History*, Boston/New York, 1915.

Haskins, C.H., *The Renaissance of the Twelfth Century*, Cambridge, 1927.

Hawkes, C.F.C., *The Prehistoric Foundations of Europe to the Mycenean Age*, 1940.

Haynes, M.S., *The Italian Renaissance and Its Influence on Western Civilization*, Lanham, 1991.

Heichelheim, F.M., *Ancient Economic History*, 3 vols., London, 1958.

Herring, H.C. and Herring, H.B., *A History of Latin America: From the Beginning to the Present*, New York, 3rd ed., 1968.

Ho, P. and Tsou, T., eds., *China in Crisis I: China's Heritage and the Communist Political System*, Chicago, 1968.

Ho, P., *The Ladder of Success in Imperial China: Aspects of Social Mobility, 1368–1911*, The Hague, 1962.

Hobsbawm, E.J., *The Age of Revolution, 1789–1848*, New York, 1963.

Hood, S., *The Home of the Heroes: The Aegean Before the Greeks*, New York, 1967.

Hsu, I.C.Y., *The Rise of Modern China*, New York, 1970.

Hudson, G.F., *Europe and China*, London, 1931.

Huizinga, J., *The Waning of the Middle Ages*, London, 1924.

Humphreys, R.A., *Tradition and Revolt in Latin America*, New York, 1969.

Hutchinson, R.W., *Prehistoric Crete*, Baltimore, 1962.

Jones, A.H.M., *The Greek City: From Alexander to Justinian*, Oxford, 1940.

Jones, T.B., *From the Tigris to the Taber: An Introduction to Ancient History*, 4th Ed., Chicago, 1989.

Kirk, G., *The Middle East, 1945–1950*, London, 1954.

Knowles, D., *The Evolution of Medieval Thought*, Baltimore, 1962.

Kohn, H., *The Age of Nationalism: The First Era of Global History*, Westport, 1962.

Kondakov, N.P., *The Russian Icon*, Oxford, 1927.

Kramer, S.N., *The Sumerians: Their History, Culture, and Character*, Chicago, 1963.

Kristeller, P.O., *Renaissance Thought: The Classic, Scholastic, and Humanistic Strains*, 2 vols., New York, rev. ed., 1961.

Lach, D.F., *Asia in the Making of Europe I: The Century of Discovery*, Chicago, 1965.

Langer, W.L., ed., *Western Civilization*, 2d ed., New York, 1975.

Lewis, B., *The Arabs in History*, London/New York, 1950, 1966.

Lopez, R.S., *The Birth of Europe*, New York, 1967.

Majumder, R.C. and Pusalkar, A.D., eds., *History and Culture of the Indian People, I: The Vedic Age*, London, 1951.

Marguard, L., *The Story of South Africa*, London, 1955.

McGovern, W.M., *The Early Empires of Central Asia*, Chapel Hill, 1939.

McIlwain, C.H., *The Growth of Political Thought in the West*, New York, 1932.

McNeill, W.H., *A World History*, New York/London/Toronto, 2d ed., 1971.

McNeill, W.H., *The Rise of the West: A History of the Human Community*, Chicago, 1990.

Melko, M., *Peace in the Ancient World*, Jefferson, N.C., 1981.

Mommsen, W.J., and de Moor, J.A., *European Expansion and Law: The Encounter of European and Indigenous Law in 19th- and 20th-Century Africa and Asia*, Oxford/New York, 1992.

Monroe, E., *Britain's Moment in the Middle East*, London, 1963.

Moreland, W.H., *From Akbar to Auranqzeb: A Study in Indian Economic History*, London, 1923.

Moreland, W.H., *India at the Death of Akbar: An Economic Study*, London, 1920.

Morrison, E.S. and Commager, H.S., *The Growth of the American Republic*, New York, 6th Ed., 1969.

Moscate, S., *The World of Phoenicians*, London, 1968.

Mosse, G., *The Culture of Western Europe: The Nineteenth and Twentieth Centuries, and Introduction*, New York, 1961.

Narain, A.K., *The Indo-Greeks*, Oxford, 1957.

Naravane, V.S., *A cultural History of Modern India: Nineteenth Century*, New Delhi, 1991.

Neugebauer, O., *The Antiquity*, Hanover, N.H., 2d ed., 1957.

Oakley, K.P., *Man the Tool-Maker*, 4th ed., Chicago, 1958.

Oga, B.A., ed., *Africa from the Sixteenth to the Eighteenth Century*, London/Berkeley/Paris, 1992.

Oliver, R. and Atmore, A., *Africa Since 1800*, London, 1967.

Oliver, R. and Mathew, G., *History of East Africa*, Oxford, 1963.

Olmstead, A.T., *A History of Assyria*, Ann Arbor, 1923.

Olmstead, A.T., *A History of the Persian Empire*, Chicago, 1948.

Oppenheim, A.L., *Ancient Mesopotamia, Portrait of a Civilization*, Chicago, 3rd ed., 1968.

Ozment, S., ed., *Religion and Culture in the Renaissance and Reformation*, Kirksville, Mo., 1989.

Palmer, R.R., *The Age of the Democratic Revolution: A Political History of Europe and America, 1760–1800*, 2 vols., Princeton, 1959, 1964.

Palmer, R.R. and Coulton, J., *A History of the Modern World*, New York, 3rd ed., 1965.

Panikkar, K.M., *A Survey of Indian History*, Bombay, 3rd ed., 1956.

Panikkar, K.M., *The Foundations of New India*, London, 1963.

Parry, J.H., *Europe and a Wider World, 1415–1715*, New York, 1949.

Pirenne, P.H., *The Age of Vikings*, 1962.

Polk, W.R. and Chambers, R.L., eds., *Beginnings of Modernization in the Middle East: The Nineteenth Century*, Chicago, 1968.

Powell, T.G.E., *The Celts*, London, 1958.

Ranger, T.O., ed., *Aspects of Central African History*, London, 1968.

Reischauer, E. O., Fairbank, J.K., and Craig, A.M., *A History of East Asian Civilization, II: East Asia: A Modern Transformation*, Boston, 1965.

Rice, T.T., *The Scythians*, London, 1957.

Robinson, R. and Gallaghar, J., *Africa and the Victorians*, Atlantic Highlands, 1961.

Rostovtzeff, M., *Iranians and Greeks in South Russia*, Oxford, 1922.

Rothermund, D. and Saha, S.K., eds., *Regional Disparities in India: Rural and Industrial Dimensions*, New Delhi, 1991.

Rowley, H.H., ed., *The Old Testament and Modern Study*, Oxford, 1951.

Runciman, S., *Byzantine Civilization*, London, 1959.

Runciman, S., *A History of the Crusades*, 3 vols., Cambridge, 1951–54.

Sanson, G.B., *Japan: A Short Cultural History*, New York, rev. ed., 1962.

Sastri, K.A.N., *A History of South India From Prehistoric Times to The Fall of Vijayanagar*, Madrid, 3rd ed., 1966.

Sawyer, P.H., *The Age of the Vikings*, London, 1962.

Schirokauer, C., *A Brief History of Chinese and Japanese Civilization*, 2d ed., San Diego, 1989.

Shryock, J.K., *Origin and Development of the State Cult of Confucius*, New York/London, 1932.

Singer, C.,*et. al.*, eds., *A History of Technology, I: From Early Times to Fall of Ancient Empires*, Oxford, 1954.

Singh, V.B., ed., *Economic History of India 1857–1956*, Bombay, 1965.

Sinha, S.P., *Asylum and International Law,* The Hague, 1971.

Sinha, S.P., *New Nations and the Law of Nations*, Leyden, 1967.

Sinha, S.P., *What is Law?*, New York, 1989.

Sinha, S.P., *Jurisprudence: Legal Philosophy in a Nutshell*, St. Paul, 1993.

Sinha, S.P., "The Anthropocentric Theory of International Law as a Basis for Human Rights," 10 *Case Western Reserve Journal of International Law*, 139 (1978).

Sinha, S.P., "Human Rights Philosophically," 18 *Indian Journal of International Law*, 139 (1978).

Sinha, S.P., "Human Rights: A Non-Western Viewpoint," *Archive fur Rechts-und Sozialphilosophie*, (1981).

Sinha, S.P., "The Axiology of the International Bill of Human Rights," *Pace Yearbook of International Law*, 21 (1989).

Sitwell, N.H.H., *The World the Romans Knew*, London, 1984.

Smith, V.A., *The Oxford History of India*, (rev. ed., by P. Spear), Oxford, 3rd ed., 1958.

Smith, W.C., *Islam in Modern History*, Princeton, 1957.

Smith, W.C., *Modern Islam in India: A Social Analysis*, Columbia, rev. ed., 1947.

Smith, W.C. *Interconnections in the Ancient Near East: A Study of the Relationships Between the Arts of Egypt, the Aegean, and Western Asia*, 1965.

Spear, P., *India: A Modern History*, Ann Arbor, 1961.

Starr, C.G., *Origins of Greek Civilization 110–650 B.C.*, New York, 1961.

Starr, C.G., *A History of the Ancient World*, 4th Ed., New York, 1991.

Steindorf, G and Steele, K.C., *When Egypt Ruled the East*, Chicago, rev. ed., 1957.

Stephenson, C., *Medieval Feudalism*, Ithaca, 1942.

Tarn, W.W., *The Greeks in Bactria and India*, Chicago, 2d ed., 1951.

Tarn, W.W. and Griffith, G.T., *Hellenistic Civilization*, London, 3d ed., 1952.

Tax, S., ed., *Evolution After Darwin*, 3 vols., Chicago, 1960.

Teng, Ssu-yu and Fairbank, J., *et al.*, *China's response to the West: A Documentary Survey, 1839–1923*, Cambridge, 1954.

Tinker, H., *Experiment with Freedom: India and Pakistan, 1947*, Oxford, 1967.

Trevor-Roper, H., *The Rise of Christian Europe*, London, 1965.

Tse-tsung, C., *The May Fourth Movement: Intellectual Revolution in Modern China*, Cambridge, 1960.

von Grunebaum, G.E., *Medieval Islam: A Study in Cultural Orientation*, Chicago, 2d ed., 1955.

von Grunebaum, G.E., ed., *Unity and Variety in Muslim Civilization*, Chicago, 1955.

Wales, H.G.Q., *The Making of Greater India: A Study in Southeast Asian Culture Change*, London, 1950.

Warmington, E.H., *Carthage*, New York, 1960.

Warmington, E.H., *Commerce Between the Roman Empire and India*, New York, 1928.

Watson, W., *China: Before the Han Dynasty*, New York, 1961.

Wheeler, R.E.M., *Early India and Pakistan, to Ashoka*, London, 1959.

Wheeler, R.E.M., *The Indus Civilization, the Cambridge History of India*, Supp. vol., Cambridge, 3rd ed., 1968.

Willcox, W.B., *Star of Empire: A Study of Britain as a World Power 1485–1945*, New York, 1950.

Williams, E., *Capitalism and Slavery*, North Pomfret, VT., 1944.

Wilson, J.A., *The Burden of Egypt: An Interpretation of Ancient Egyptian Culture*, Chicago, 1951.

Wilson, N.G., *From Byzantium to Italy: Greek Studies in the Italian Renaissance*, Baltimore, 1992.

Wright, F., *Buddhism in Chinese History*, Stanford, 1959.

Yuge, T. and Doi, M., eds., *Forms of Control and Subordination in Antiquity*, Tokyo/Leiden/New York, 1988.

Zaehner, R.C., *The Dawn and Twilight of Zoroastrianism*, London, 1961.

Zeine, Z.N., *The Emergency of Arab Nationalism*, Sherman Oaks, 1966.

Zeine, Z.N., *The Struggle for Arab Independence*, Sherman Oaks, 1960.

Zimmern, A.E., *The Greek Commonwealth*, Oxford, 5th ed., 1931.

Chapter 4

1. The Western Way of Life

Abbott, F.F., *The Common People of Ancient Rome*, Lanham, 1931.

Abbott, F.F., *A History and Description of Roman Political Institutions*, New York, 1963.

Adock, F. E., *Roman Political Ideas and Practice*, Ann Arbor, 1959.

Anderson, M.S., *Europe in the Eighteenth Century, 1713–1783*, White Plains, NY, 2d ed., 1977.

Andrews, A., *The Greeks-The History of Human Society*, New York, 1967.

Badian, E., *Roman Imperialism in the Late Republic*, Ithaca, New York, 1968.

Baker, E., *From Alexander to Constantine: Passages and Documents Illustrating the History of Social and Political Ideas*, Lanham, 1956

Barnes, H.E., *The History of the Western Civilization*, Vol. 2, New York, 1935.

Birnie, A., *Economic History of Europe*, London, 1930.

Bloch, R., *The Origins of Rome*, New York, 1960.

Boak, A.E.R. and Sinnegan, W.G., *A History of Rome to A.D. 565*, London, 1969.

Boissonade, P., *Life and Work in Medieval Europe*, Westport, 1927.

Bonner, R.J. and Smith G., *The Administration of Justice from Homer to Aristotle*, 2 vols., Chicago, 1930.

Botsford, G.W., *Hellenic History*, New York, 1926.

Bouwsma, W.J., *The Interpretation of Renaissance Humanism*, Washington, 1959.

Burckhardt, J. and Hilty, F.P., *History of Greek Culture*, New York, 1963.

Burckhardt, J., *The Civilization of the Renaissance in Italy*, Topsfield, MA, 1958.

Burn, A.R., *The Lyric Age of Greece*, New York, 1960.

Bury, J.B. and Meiggs, R., *A History of Greece*, New York, 4th ed., 1975.

Bury, J.B., *The Idea of Progress: An Inquiry into its Origin and Growth*, New York, 1921.

Bury, J.B., *History of the later Roman Empire*, 2 vols., Chicago, 1957.

Carcopino, J., *Daily Life in Ancient Rome*, New Haven, 1940.

Cassirer, E., Kristeller, P.O., and Randell, Jr., J.H., eds., *The Renaissance Philosophy of Man*, New York, 1953.

Cassirer, E., *The Individual and Cosmos in Renaissance Philosphy*, Philadelphia, 1927, trans. 1964.

Cary, M. and Litt, D., *A History of Rome Down to the Reign of Constantine*, 2d ed., London, 1957

Cary, M. and Haarhoff, T.J., *Life and Thought in the Greek and Roman World*, Westport, CT, 1940.

Chadwick, O., *The Reformation*, New York, 1963.

Chambers, M., *et al.*, *The Western Experience*, 5th ed., New York, 1991.

Chaney, E. and Mack, P., eds., *England and the Continental Renaissance: Essays in Honor of J.B. Trapp*,Woodbridge/England/Rochester (NY), 1990.

Chase, S., *Men and Machines*, New York, 1929.

Cipolla, C.M., *Before the Industrial Revolution: European Society and Economy 100–1700*, New York, 1976.

Cochrane, E. and Kirshner, J., eds., *The Renaissance*, Chicago, 1986.

Cronin V., *The Florentine Renaissance*, New York, 1967.

Crook, J., *Law of Rome*, Ithaca, 1967.

Davies, J.K., *Democracy and Classical Greece*, Stanford, CA., 1983.

Davis, R., *The Rise of the Atlantic Economies*, Ithaca, NY, 1973.

Desborough, V.R., d'A., *The Greek Dark Ages*, New York, 1968.

DiCesare, ed., *Reconsidering the Renaissance*, Binghamton, New York, 1992.

Dickens, A.G., *Reformation and Society in Sixteenth Century Europe*, San Diego, 1960.

Dietz, F.C., *The Industrial Revolution*, Westport, 1927.

Dill, S., *Roman Society from Nero to Marcus Aurelius*, New York, 1956.

Doyle, W., *The Old European Order, 1660–1800*, New York, 1978.

Dudley, D. R., *The Romans, 850 B.C.–A.D. 337*, New York, 1970.

Dunning, W.A., *History of Political Theories from Rousseau to Spencer*, New York, 1920.

Dunning, W.A., *History of Political Theories from Luther to Montesquieu*, New York, 1905.

Ehrenberg, V., *The Greek City States*, New York, 1976.

Ehrenberg, V., *The Greek State*, New York, 2d ed., 1969.

Ehrenberg, V., *Aspects of the Ancient World*, Oxford, 1946.

Ehrenberg, V., *From Solon to Socrates*, London, 1968.

Elton, G.R., *Reformation Europe, 1517–1559*, New York, 1963.

Ergang, R., *The Renaissance*, Princeton, 1967.

Ferguson, Jr., *Moral Values in the Ancient World*, London, 1958.

Finley, M.I., *Early Greece*, New York, 1981.

Fisher, H.A.L., *A History of Europe*, London, 1936.

Fisher, N.R.E., *Hybris: A Study in the Values of Honour and Shame in Ancient Greece*, Warminster, 1992.

Fowler, W.W., *Social Life at Rome in the Age of Cicero*, London, 1908.

Frank, T., *A History of Rome*, New York, 1923.

Friedlander, L., *Roman Life and Manners Under the Early Empire*, trans. by L.A. Magnus, London, no date.

Fussell, P., *The Great World War and Modern Memory*, New York, 1975.

Garin, E., *Italian Humanism: Philosophy and Civic Life in the Renaissance*, Westport, 1941, trans. 1965.

Garnsey, P., *Social Status and Legal Privilege in the Roman Empire*, Oxford, 1970.

Gillespie, J.E., *History of Europe, 1500–1815*, New York, 1928.

Gilmore, M.P., *The World of Humanism, 1453–1517*, New York, 1952.

Goodenough, S., *Citizen Rome*, New York, 1979.

Grant, M., *The World of Rome*, New York, 1960.

Green, W.C., *The Achievement of Rome*, Cambridge, 1933.

Grenridge, A.M.J., *Roman Public Life*, London, 1922.

Guthrie, W.K.C., *A History of Greek Philosophy*, vol. I., Cambridge, 1962.

Hadas, Mr., *Hellenistic Culture*, New York, 1959.

Hadas, M., *A History of Rome*, Magnolia, 1956.

Hammond, N.G.L., *A History of Greece to 322 B.C.*, New York, 1959.

Haney, L.H., *History of Economic Thought*, New York, 1911.

Hay, D., *The Italian Renaissance in Its Historical Background*, New York, rev. ed., 1977.

Hayes, C.J.H., *A Generation of Materialism, 1871–1900*, Westport, 1941.

Haynes, M.S., *The Italian Renaissance and Its Influence on Western Civilization, Lanham, 1991.*

Hertzler, J.O., *History of Utopian Thought*, London, 1923.

Heurgon, J., *The Rise of Rome*, trans. James Willis, Berkeley, 1973.

Hill, H., *TheRoman Middle Class*, Westport, 1952.

Hobson, J.A., *Evolution of Modern Capitalism*, New York, 1926.

John, J.A., *Manners and Customs of Ancient Greece*, Vol. III, Port Washington, 1971.

Johnston, H.W., *The Private Life of the Romans*, Salem, 1903.

Jones, J.W., *The Law and Legal Theory of the Greeks*, Oxford, 1956.

Katz, S., *The Decline of Rome and the Rise of Medieval Europe*, Ithaca, 1955.

Kristeller, P. O., *The Classic and Renaissance Thought*, Cambridge, 1955.

Kristeller, P., *Renaissance Thought: The Classic, Scholastic, and Humanistic Strains*, Magnolia, 1961.

Langer, W. L., *Political and Social Upheaval 1832–1852*, New York, 1969.

Lecky, W., *The Rise and Influence of Rationalism in Europe*, London, 1865.

Lewis, N. and Reinhold, M., *Roman Civilization*, 2 vols., New York, 1951–55.

Lot, F., *The End of the Ancient World and the Beginning of the Middle Ages*, London, 1931.

Lucki, E., *History of Renaissance, Vol. I: Economy and Society*, Salt Lake City, 1964.

Mantoux, P., *The Industrial Revolution in the Eighteenth Century*, Chicago, 1961.

Marshall, L. C., *Readings in Industrial Society: A Study in the Structure and Functioning of Modern Economic Organization*, Norwood, PA, rev. ed., 1929.

Mattingly, H., *Roman Imperial Civilization*, London, 1959.

May, R., *Law and Society East and West: Dharma, Li, and Nomos*, Wiesbaden, 1985.

Mayo, E., *The Human Problems of an Industrial Civilization*, Salem, N.H., 1977.

Mazzeo, J.A., *Renaissance and Revolution: The Remakiong of European Thought*, London, 1969.

MacDowell, D.M., *The Law in Classical Athens*, London, 1978.

McLure, G. W., *Sorrow and Consideration in Italian Humanism*, Princeton, 1991.

McNeill, W.H., *A World History*, New York, 2d ed., 1971.

Meakin, W., *The New Industrial Revolution*, Salem, 1928.

Mommsen, T., *The History of Rome*, New York 1959.

Mosse, G.L., *The Culture of Western Europe: The Nineteenth and Twentieth Centuries*, London, 61.

Mowat, R.B., *The Age of Reason*, Boston, 1934.

Monholland, J.K., *Origins of Contemporarty Europe 1890–1914*, 1970.

Nussbaum, F.L., *History of Economic Institutions of Modern Europe*, New York, 1935.

Ogg, D., *Europe in the Seventeenth Century*, London, 1925, 1961.

Ogg, F. A. and Sharp, *Economic Development of Modern Europe*, St. Clair Shores, MI, 1968.

Ostwald, M., *Nomos and the Beginnings of the Athenian Democracy*, Oxford, 1969.

Ozment, S., ed., *Religion and Culture in the Renaissance and Reformation*, Kirksville, MO,, 1989.

Palmer, R.R. and Colton, Jr., *A History of the Modern World*, New York, 6th ed., 1984.

Pirenne, H., *The Stages in the History of Capitalism*, Stanford, CA., 1953.

Pope, M., *The Ancient Greeks*, Springs, PA., 1976.

Postan, N.M., *An Economic History of Western Europe*, New York, 1967.

Potterm, G.R., ed., *The New Cambridge Modern History*, vol. I., Cambridge, 1967.

Poulsen, F., *Glimpses of Roman Culture*, Kobenhaven, 1950.

Quennell, M. and Quennell, C.H.B., *The Rise of Industrialism, 1733–1851*, London, 1932.

Renard, G. and Weulersse, G., *The Life and Work in Modern Europe, (Fifteenth and Eighteenth Centuries)*, London, 1926.

Rich, N., *The Age of Nationalism and Reform, 1850–1890*, New York, 1970.

Robertson, P.S., *Revolutions of 1848: A Social History*, Princeton, 1952.

Robinson, C.E., *Everyday Life in Ancient Greece*, Oxford, 1947.

Robinson, J.H. and Beard, C.A., eds., *The Development of Modern Europe*, 2 vols, Boston, rev. ed., 1929–30.

Rostovtzeff, M., *Rome*, Trans. by J.D. Duff, New York, 1960.

Rostovtzeff, M., *The Social and Economic History of the Hellenistic World*, Vol. II, Oxford, 1941.

Rostovtzeff, M., *Social and Economic History of the Roman Empire*, New York, 2d ed., 1957.

Salmon, E.T., *A History of the Roman World from 30 B.C. to A.D. 138*, Westport, 3d ed., 1957.

Scott, J.F. and Baltzly, A., eds., *Readings in European History Since 1814*, New York, 1930.

Scullard, H.H., *A History of the Roman World from 753 to 146 B.C.*, London, 1969.

Searly, R., *A History of the Greek City States*, Berkeley, 1976.

See, H.E., *Modern Capitalism: Its Origins and Development*, New York, 1928.

Segal, D., ed., *Crossings Cultures: Essays in Displacement of Western Civilization*, Tucson, 1992.

Showerman, G., *Rome and the Romans*, New York, 1931.

Sidgwick, H., *The Development of European Polity*, Millwood, 1903.

Snodgrass, A.M., *The Dark Age of Greece*, Edinburgh, 1971.

Sombart, W., *The Quintessence of Capitalism*, New York, 1915.

Starr, C.G.Jr., *The Emergency of Rome as Ruler of the Western World*, Ithaca, 2d ed., 1953.

Starr, C.G., *The Origins of Greek Civilization 100–650 B.C.*, New York, 1961.

Stephens, J.N., *The Italian Renaissance: The Origins of Intellectual and Artistic Change Before the Reformation*, London/New York, 1990.

Stobart, J.C., *The Glory That Was Greece*, London, 1911, 1978.

Stromberg, R.N., *European Intellectual History Since 1789*, Englewood Cliffs, 3d ed., 1981.

Talmon, J.R., *Romanticism and Revolt: Europe 1815–48*, New York, 1968.

Thomas, H., *A History of the World*, New York, 1979.

Thompson, J.W., *Economic and Social History of Later Middle Ages*, New York, 1931.

Thomson, P., *Europe Since Napoleon*, New York, 2d ed., 1962.

von Martin, A., *Sociology of the Renaissance*, New York, 1963.

Walbank, F.W., *Decline of the Roman Empire in the West*, Atlantic Highlands, NJ, 1947.

Weiss, R., *The Dawn of Humanism in Italy*, Brooklyn, NY, 1947.

Whyte, R.J., *Europe in the Eighteenth Century*, New York, 1965.

Wilson, C., *The Transformation of Europe, 1958–1648*, Berkeley, 1976.

Wilson, N.G., *From Byzantium to Italy: Greek Studies in the Italian Renaissance*, Baltimore, 1992.

Zimmen, A., *The Greek Commonwealth*, Oxford, 1924.

2. *The Chinese Way of Life*

Anderson, J.G., *Children of the Yellow Earth; Studies in Prehistoric China*, Cambridge, 1934.

Banno, M., *China and the West 1858–1861: The Origins of the Tsungli Yamen*, Cambridge, 1964.

Beckman, G.M., *The Modernization of China and Japan*, Chicago, 1962.

Bingham, W., *The Founding of the T'ang Dynasty: The Rise of T'ang*, Baltimore, 1941.

Bodde, D., *Chinese Thought, Society, and Science: The Intellectual and Social Background of Science and Technology in Pre-Modern China*, Honolulu, 1991.

Bodde, D., *China's First Unifier: A Study of the Ch'in Dynasty as Seen in the Life of LiSsu*, Leiden, 1938.

Bodde, D., "Dominant Ideas in the Formation of Chinese Culture," in D. Bodde, ed., *Essays on Chinese Civilization*, 132, Princeton, 1981.

Bodde, D., "Harmony and Conflict in Chinese Philosophy," in A. F. Wright, ed., *Studies on Chinese Thought*, Chicago, London, 1953–1967.

Chan, S., *Buddhism in Late Ch'in Political Thought*, Hong Kong/Boulder, 1985.

Chan, W., *A Source Book in Chinese Philosophy*, Princeton, 1963, 1969, 1973.

Chang, C.L., *The Chinese Gentry: Studies on Their Role in Nineteenth-Century Chinese Society*, Seattle, 1955.

Chang, K., *The Archaeology of Ancient China*, New Haven, 2d ed., 1971.

Chi, L., *The Beginnings of Chinese Civilization*, Seattle, 1957.

Chiang, S., *The Nien Rebellian*, Seattle, 1954.

Childe, V.G., *New Light on the Most Ancient East*, London, 1952.

Chu, T.T., *Han Social Structure*, ed., J.L.Dull, Seattle, 1972.

Chu, T.T., *Law and Society in Traditional China*, Paris, 1961.

Clubbo, O.E., *20th Century China*, New York, 1964.

Clyde, P.H., *The Far East: A History of the Impact of the West on Eastern Asia*, Englewood Cliffs, 3rd ed., 1958.

Cohen, P. A. *China and Christianity: The Missionary Movement and the*

Growth of Chinese Antiforeignism 1860–1870, Cambridge, 1963.

Creel, H.G., *The Birth of China: A Study of the Formative Period of Chinese Civilization*, London, 1937, 1954.

Creel, H.G., *Confucius: The Man and the Myth*, London, 1949.

Creel, H.G., *Chinese Thought from Confucius to Mae Tse-tung*, Chicago, 1955.

Creel, H.G., *The Origins of Statecraft in China*, Chicago, 1970.

deBary, W.T., ed al., *Self and Society in Ming Thought*, New York, 1970.

deBary, Jr., W.T., Chan, W. and Watson, B., *Sources of Chinese Tradition*, New York, 1960.

DeBary, Jr., W.T., *Sources of Chinese Traditiona*, Vol. I, New York, London, 1966.

DArdess, J.W., *Conquerors and Confucians: Aspects of Political Change in Late Yuan China*, New York, 1973.

Dawson, R., *The Chinese Experience*, London, 1978.

Dubs, H.H., trans., *History of the Former Han Dynasty [From Pan Ku's Han-su]*, 3 vols., London, 1938–55.

Eberhard, W., *Conquerors and Rulers: Social Forces in Medieval China*, Leiden, 1952.

Eichhorn, W., *Chinese Civilization, and Introduction*, trans. by J. Seligman, London, 1969.

Fairbank, J.K., Reischauer, E.O., and Craig, A.M., *A History of East Asian Civilization: Volume Two: East Asia, The Modern Transformation*, Boston, 1965.

Fairbank, J.K., ed., *Chinese Thought and Institutions*, Chicago, 1957.

Fairbank, J.K., *Trade and Diplomacy on the China Coast: The Opening of the Treaty Posts, 1842–1854*, Cambridge, 1953.

Fehl, N.E., *Li: Rites and Prpriety in Literature and Life*, Hong Kong, 1971.

Fitzgerald, C.P., *China: A Short Cultural History*, London, 1935–1950.

Fung, Y., *A History of Chinese Philosophy*, Princeton, 1952.

Fung, Y.L., *A Short History of Chinese Philosophy*, ed., D. Bodde, New York, 1948, 1960.

Hao, Y., *The Compradore in Nineteenth Century China: Bridge Between East and West*, Cambridge, 1970.

Hsiao, K.C., *Rural China: Imperial Control in the Nineteenth Century*, Seattle, 1960.

Hsu, C.Y., *Ancient China in Transition: An Analysis of Social Mobility, 722–222 B.C.*, Stanford, 1965.

Hsu, I.C.Y., *The Rise of Modern China*, Oxford, 2d ed., 1975.

Hucker, C.O., *China's Imperial Past: An Introduction to Chinese History and Culture*, Stanford, CA, 1975.

Hucker, C.O., *Imperial Past*, Stanford, CA, 1975.

Hucker, C.O., *The Traditional Chinese State in Ming Times, 1368–1644*, Tuscon, 1961.

Hughes, E.R., *The Invasion of China by the Western World*, London, 1938.

Hughes, E.R., *Chinese Philosophy in Classical Times*, London, 1942, 1971.

Gernet, J., *Ancient China: From the Beginnings to the Empire*, trans. by R. Rudorff, Berkeley, 1968.

Gernet, Jr., *Daily Life in China on the Eve of the Mongol Invasion, 1250–1276*, trans. by H.M. Wright, New York, 1962.

Goodrich, L.C., *A Short History of the Chinese People*, 3rd ed., 1959.

Lee, T.H.C., ed., *China and Europe: Images and Influences in Sixteenth to Eighteenth Centuries*, Hong Kong, 1991.

Levenson, J.R., *Confucian China and its Modern Fate*, 2 vols., London, 1958, 1964.

Lin, Y., *The Wisdom of China and India*, Shanghai, 1942.

Lin, K., ed., *Orthodoxy in Late Imperial China*, Berkeley, 1990.

Lie, J.T.C. and Golas, P.J., eds., *Change in Sung China: Innovation or Renovation?*, Lexington, 1969.

Loewe, M., *The Pride that was China*, London/New York, 1990.

Loewe, M., *Everyday Life in Early Imperial China*, Cambridge, 1968.

Malraux, A., *The Temptation of the West*, tr. by R. Hollander, new preface by J.D. Spence, Chicago, 1992.

May, R., *Law and Society East and West: Dharma, Li, and Nomos*, Wiesbaden, 1985.

Mei, Y.P., "The Basis of Social, Ethical, and Spiritual Values in Chinese Philosphy," inC.A. Moore, ed., *The Chinese Mind*, 149, Honolulu, 1967, 1977.

Meskill, J.T., ed., *The Patterns of Chinese History: Cycles, Development, or Stagnation?*, Boston, 1965.

Michael, F., *The Origin of Manchu Rule in China: Frontiers and Bureaucracy as Interacting Forces in the Chinese Empire*, Baltimore, 1942, 1965.

Moore, C.E., ed., *The Chinese Mind: Essentials of Chinese Philosophy and Culture*, Hawaii, 1967.

Munro, D.J., *The Concept of Man in Early China*, Stamford, 1969.

Needham, J. and Ling, W., *Science and Civilization in China*, Cambridge, 1956.

Nivison, N. and Wright, A.F., eds., *Confucianism in Action*, Stanford, 1959.

Phillips, E.D., *The Mongols*, New York, 1969.

Prawdin, M., *The Mongol Empire: Its Rise and Legacy*, trans. by E. and C. Paul, London, 1940.

Purcell, V., *The Boxer Uprising, A Background Study*, Cambridge, 1963.

Reischauer, E.O. and Fairbank, J.K., *The History of East Asian Civilization: Volume One: East Asia, The Great Tradition*, Boston, 1958, 1960.

Ropp, P.S., ed., *Heritage of China: Contemporary Perspectives on Chinese Civilization*, Berkeley, 1990.

Spence, J.D., *Chinese Roundabout: Essays in History and Culture*, New York, 1992.

T'ang Chun-i., "Cosmologies in Ancient Chinese Philosophy," 5 *Chinese Studies in Philosophy* 4 1973.

Teng, S. and Fairbanks, J.K., *China's Response to West*, Cambridge, 1954.

Tse-tung, C., *The May Fourth Movement: Intellectual Revolution in Modern China*, Cambridge, 1960.

van de Spenkel, S., *Legal Institutions in Manchu China, A Sociological Analysis*, London, 1962.

Vinacke, H.M., *A History of the Far East in Modern Times*, New York, 6th ed., 1961.

Waley, A., *Three Ways of Thought in Ancient Civilization*, Garden City, 1957.

Waley, A., *Analects of Confucius*, London, 1938, 1971.

Wang, G., *The Chineseness of China: Selected Essays*, Hong Kong/New York, 1991.

Watson, W., *China Before the Han Dynasty*, London, 1961.

Watson, W., *Cultural Frontiers in Ancient East Asia*, Edinburgh, 1971.

Welch, H., *The Parting of the Way; Lao Tzu and the Taoist Movement*, London, 1957.

Wittfogel, K.A. and Feng, C., *History of Chinese Society, Liao (907–1125)*, New York, 1949.

Wright, A.F., *Buddhism in Chinese History*, Stanford, 1959.

Wright, A.F., ed., *The Confucian Persuasion*, Stanford, 1960.

Wright, A.F. and Twitchett, D., eds., *Perspectives on the T'ang*, Stanford, 1973.

Wright, M.C., *The Last Stand of Chinese Conservatism, the T'ung- chih Restoration, 1862–1874*, Stanford, 1957.

Yu-wei Hsieh., "Filial Piety and Chinese Society," in C.A. Moore, ed., *The Chinese Mind*, 167 (1967, 1977).

Yu-lan, F., *A History of Chinese Philosophy*, trans. by D. Bodde, 2 vols., 1937–, 1952.

3. The Indian Way of Life

Aiyangar, K.V.R., *Some Aspects of the Hindu View of Life According to Dharmashastra*, Baroda, 1952.

Allchin, B. and F.R., *The Birth of Indian Civilization: India And Pakistan Before 500 B.C.*, New York, 1968.

Basham, A.L.,*The Wonder That Was India*, New York, 1954.

Basham, A.L., *The Origins and Development of Classical Hinduism*, Boston, 1989.

Basham, A.L., "Medieval Hindu India," in A.L. Basham ed., *A Cultural History of India*, Oxford, 1975.

Bongard-Levin, G.M., *Ancient Indian Civilization*, New Delhi, 1985.

Burrow, T., "The Early Aryans," in A.L. Basham, ed., *A Cultural History of India*, Oxford, 1975.

Childe, V.G., *New Light on the Most Ancient East*, London, 4th ed., 1952.

Childe, V.G., *The Aryans: A Study of Indo-European Origins*, London, 1926.

Conze, E., *Buddhist Thought in India*, London, 1962.

Dasgupta, S., *A History of Indian Philosophy*, 5 vols. Cambridge, 1932–55.

Dasgupta, S.N., "Philosophy," in A.L. Basham, ed., *A Cultural History of India*, Oxford, 1975.

DeBary, W. Th., ed., *Sources of Indian Tradition*, New York, 1958.

Derrett, J.D.M., *Essays in Classical and Modern Hindu Law*, Leiden,1977.

Derrett, J.D.M., "Social and Political Thought and Institutions," in A.L. Basham, ed., *A Cultural History of India*, Oxford, 1975.

Derrett, J.D.M., "The Concept of Duty in Ancient Indian Jurisprudence," in W.D. O'Flaherty and J.D.M. Derrett, eds., *The Concept of Duty in South Asia*, New Delhi, 1978.

Derrett, J.D.M., *Dharmashastra and Juridical Literature*, Weisbaden, 1973.

Edgerton, F., *The Beginnings of Indian Philosophy*, Cambridge, 1965.

Farquhar, J.N., *Modern Religious Movements in India*, London, 1924.

Gupta, R. C., *Hindu Society and Influence of the Great Epics*, Delhi, 1991.

Heimsath, C.H., *Indian Nationalism and Hindu Social Reform*, Princeton, 1964.

Hutton, J.H., *Caste in India: Its Nature, Functions, and Origins*, Cambridge, 1946.

Jaini, J.L., *Outlines of Jainism*, Oxford, 1916, rev. ed., 1940.

Jettmar, K., *The Religions of the Hindukush*, tr. by A. Nayyar, Warminster, 1986.

Jha, G., *Hindu Law in Its Sources*, vol. I., Allahabad, 1930.

Jordens, J.T.F., "Hindu Religions and Social Reform in British India," in A.L. Basham, ed., *A Cultural History of India*, Oxford, 1975.

Jordens, J.T.F., "Medieval Hindu Devotionalism," in A.L. Basham, ed., *A Cultural History of India*, Oxford, 1975.

Kane, P.V., *History of Dharmashastra*, vols. 1–5., Poona, 1930–62, 2d ed., 1968.

Kunst, A., "Use and Misuse of Dharma," in W.D. O'Flaherty and J.D.M. Derrett, eds., *The Concept of Duty in South Asia*, New Delhi, 1978.

Kosambi, D.D., *The Culture and Civilization of Ancient India*, London, 1965.

Heimann, B., *Facets of Indian Thought*, London, 1964.

Lal, B.B., "The Indus Civilization," in A. L. Basham, ed., *A Cultural History of India*, Oxford, 1975.

Lingat, R., *The Classical Law of India*, trans., J.D.M. Derrett, Berkeley, 1973.

McLeod, H., "Sikhism," in A.L. Basham, ed., *A Cultural History of India*, Oxford, 1975.

McNeill, W.H., *A World History*, New York, 2d ed., 1971.

Mahadevan, T.M.P., *Outlines of Hinduism*, Bombay, 2d ed., 1960.

Majumdar, R.C. and Pusalkeer, A.D., eds., *History and Culture of the Indian People, I: The Vedic Age*, London, 1951.

Majumdar, D.N., *Races and Cultures of India*, Bombay, 4th ed., 1961.

Marr, J.P., "The Early Dravidians," in A.L. Basham, ed., *A Cultural History of India*, Oxford, 1975.

May, R., *Law and Society East and West, Dharma, Li, and Nomos*, Wiesbaden, 1985.

Moreland, W.H., *From Akbar to Aurangzeb*, London, 1923.

Naravane, V.S., *A Cultural History of Modern India: Nineteenth Century*, New Delhi, 1991.

Natarajan, S.A., *A Century of Social Reform*, Bombay, 1959.

Owen, H., "The Nationalist Movement," in A.L. Basham, ed., *A Cultural History of India*, Oxford, 1975.

Panikkar, K.M., *A Survey of Indian History*, Bombay, 3d ed., 1956.

Panikkar, K.M., *The Foundations of New India*, London, 1963.

Radhakrishnan, S., "Hinduism," in A. L. Basham, ed., *A Cultural History of India*, Oxford, 1975.

Radhakrishnan, S., *The Hindu View of Life*, New York, 1968.

Raju, P.T., " The Concept of Man in Indian Thought," in S. Radhakrishnan and P. T. Raju, eds., *The Concept of Man: A Study in Comparative Philosophy*, London, 2d ed., 1966.

Renou, L., *Religions of Ancient India*, London, 1953.

Rizvi, S.A.A., "Islam in Medieval India," in A. L. Basham, ed., *A Cultural History of India*, Oxford, 1975.

Rizvi, S.A.A., "The Muslim Ruling Dynasties," in A.L. Basham, ed., *A Cultural History of India*, Oxford, 1975.

Rothermund, D. and Saha, S.K., eds., *Regional Disparities in India: Rural and Industrial Dimension*, New Delhi, 1991.

Rudolph, L.I. and S.H., *The Modernity of Tradition: Political Development of India*, Chicago, 1967.

Sangharakshita, B., "Buddhism," in A. L. Basham, ed., *A Cultural History of India*, Oxford, 1975.

Sastri, K.A. Nilakanta, *A History of South India from Prehistoric Times to the Fall of Vijayanagar*, Madras, 3d ed., 1966.

Sen-gupta, N.C., *Evolution of Ancient Indian law*, London, 1953.

Singh, V.B., ed., *Economic History of India: 1857–1956*, Bombay, 1965.

Smith, V.A., *Early History of India*, Oxford, 4th ed., 1924.

Smith, V.A., *The Oxford History of India*, Oxford, 3d ed., 1958.

Sontheimer, G, and Aithal, P.K., eds., *Indology and Law: Studies in Honour of Professor J. Duncan, M. Derrett*, Wiesbaden, 1982.

Spear, P., *India: A Modern History*, Ann Arbor, 1961.

Spear, P., "The Mughals and the British," in A. L. Basham, ed., *A Cultural History of India*, Oxfrod, 1975.

Thapar, R., *A History of India*, Hammondworth, 1966.

Tinker, H., *Experiment with Freedom: India and Pakistan, 1947*, London, 1967.

Upadhyaye, A.N., "Jainism," in A.L. Basham, ed., *A Cultural History of India*, Oxford, 1975.

Wheeler, R.E.M., *The Indus Civilization*, The Cambridge History of India, Supplementary Volume, Cambridge, 3d ed., 1968.

Wheeler, R.E.M., *Early India and Pakistan, to Ashoka*, Londoen, 1959.

4. The African Way of Life

Abimbola, W., ed., *Yoruba Oral Tradition*, Ife, 1975.

Aboyade, B.O., *Yoruba Culture and Civilization: An Introductory Bibliography (1846–1976)*, Ibadan (Nigeria), 1991.

Abraham, P., *The Mind of Africa*, Chicago, 1952.

Abraham, R.C., *The Tiv People*, London, 2d ed., 1940.

Ajayi, A. and Peel, J.D.Y., eds., *People and Empires in African History*, London, 1992.

Ajisafe, A.K., *The Laws and Customs of the Yoruba People*, Logos, 1946.

Anigbo, O.A.C., *Commensality and Social Relationship Among the Igbo*, Nsukka (Nigeria), 1987.

Anifowose, R., *Violence and Politics in Nigeria: The Tiv and Yoruba Experience*, New York, 1982.

Asiwaju, A.I., ed., *Partitioned Africans: Ethnic Relations Across Africa's Internatinal Bounderies, 1884–1984*, New York, 1985.

Apter, D.E., *The Political Kindom in Uganda*, Princeton, 1961.

Asante, S.K.B., "Interests in Land in the Customary Law of Ghana—A New Appraisal," 74 *Yale Law Journal*, 848 (1965).

Azarya, V., *Aristocrats Facing Change: The Fulbe in Guinea, Nigeria, and Cameroon*, Chicago, 1978.

Baxter, P.T.W., and Butt, A., "The Azanda, and Related Peoples of the Anglo-Egyptian Sudan and Belgian Congo," in D. Forde, ed., *Ethnographic Survey of Africa*, London, 1953.

Beech, M., "Kikuyu System of Land Tenure," 17 *Journal of the African Society* 46 (1917–1918).

Bentsi-Enchill, K., *Ghana Land Law: An Exposition, Analysis, and Critique*, London, 1964.

Biobaku, S.O., "An Historical Sketch of Egba Traditional Authorities," 22 *Africa*, 35 (1952).

Boahen, A.A., ed., *Africa Under Colonical Domination, 1805–1935*, London/Berkeley, 1985.

Bohannan, L., "A Genealogical Charter," 22 *Africa* 301, 1952.

Bohannan, L., "Political Aspects of Tiv Social Organization," in Middleton, J. and Tait, D., eds., *Tribes Without Rulers: Studies in African Segmentary Systems*, London, 1958.

Bohannan, L. and P., "The Tiv of Central Nigeria," in Forde, D., ed., *Ethnographic Survey of Africa, Western Africa, Part VIII*, London, 1953.

Bohannan, P., "The Migration and Expansion of the Tiv," 24 *Africa*, 11, 1954.

Bohannan, P., *Tiv Farm and Settlement*, Colonial Research Studies, No. 15, London, 1954.

Bohannan, P., *Justice and Judgment Among the Tiv*, London, 1957.

Bolaji, S.L., *Yoruba Living Heritage*, Ibadan (Nigeria), 1984.

Buchanan, K., "The Northern Region of Nigeria: The Geographical Background of its Political Duality," 43 *The Geographical*, Review 451, 1953.

Busia, K.A., "The Ashanti," in Forde, D., ed., *African Worlds*, London, 1954.

Busia, K.A., *The Position of the Chief in the Modern Political System of the Ashanti*, London, 1951.

Bosah, S.I., *Groundwork of the History and Culture of Onitsha*, Nigeria, 1973.

Cagnolo, C., *The Akikiya: Their Customs, Traditions and Folklore*, Nyeri, Kenya, 1933.

Chubb, L.T., *Ibo Land Tenure*, Ibadan, 1961.

Cockcroft, L., *Africa's Way: A Journey from the Past*, London, 1990.

Coker, G.B.A., *Family Property Among the Yorubas*, London, 2d ed., 1966.

Danajuah, J.B., *Akan Laws and Customs*, London, 1928.

Davidson, B., *Black Mother: The African Slave Trade*, Boston, 1961.

deMoraes Farias, P.F. and Barber, K., *Self-Assertion and Brokerage: Early Cultural Nationalism in West Africa*, Birmingham, 1990.

Downes, R.M., *The Tiv Tride*, Kaduna, Nigeria, 1933.

Dundas, C., "Native Laws of Some Bantu Tribes of East Africa," 51 *Journal of Royal Anthropological Institute*, 217 (1921).

Dundas, C., "The Organization and Laws of Some Bantu Tribes of East Africa," 45 *Journal of the Royal Anthropological Institute* 234 (1915).

East, R.M., *Akiga's Story*, London, 1939.

Essays in Honour of Judge Taslim Olawale Elias, Vol. 2 (African Law and Comparative Public Law) Dordrecht/Boston/Norwell (MA), 1992.

Evans-Pritchard, E.E., *Kinship and Marriage Among the Nuer*, Oxford, 1951, 1990.

Evans-Pritchard, E.E., *The Nuer: A Description of the Modes of Livelihood and Political Institutions of a Nilotic People*, New York, 1969.

Evans-Pritchard, E.E., *Nuer Religion*, Oxford, 1956.

Evans-Pritchard, E.E., "The Political Structure of the Nandi- Speaking People of Kenya," 13 *Africa* 250, 1940.

Fage, J.D., *A History of West Africa*, Cambridge, 1969.

Fallers, L.A., et al., "Social Stratification in Traditional Buganda," in L.A. Fallers, ed., *The King's Men: Leadership and Status in Buganda on the Eve of Independence*, London, 1964.

Fallers, M.C., "The Eastern Lacustrine Banta (Ganda, Soga)," in D. Forde, ed., *Enthnographic Survey of Africa, Part XI*, London, 1960.

Forde, D., "Justice and Judgment Among the Southern Ibo Under Colonial Rule," in H. Kuper and L. Kuper, eds., *African Law: Adaptation and Developement*, Berkeley, 1965.

Forde, D., "The Yoruba-Speaking Peoples of South-Western Nigeria," in D. Forde, Ed., *Ethnographic Survey of Africa, Western Africa, Part IV*, London, 1951, 1969.

Forde, D. and Jones G.I., "The Ibo and the Ibidio-Speakiong Peoples of South-Eastern Nigeria," in D. Forde, Ed., *Ethnographic Survey of Africa, part III*, London, 1950.

Fortes, M., *Religion, Morality, and the Person: Essays on Tallensi Religion*, Cambridge/New York, 1987.

Fortes, M., *Oedipus and Job in West African Religion*, Cambridge, 1983.

Fortes, M., "Ritual and Office in Tribal Society," in M. Gluckman, ed., *Essays on the Ritual of Social Relations*, Manchester, 1962.

Fortes, M., *The Dynamics of Clanship Among the Tallensi*, London, 1967.

Fortes, M., "The 'Submerged Descent Line' in Ashanti," in I. Schapera, ed., *Studies in Kinship and Marriage*, Royal Anthropological Institute Occasional Paper No. 16, London, 1963.

Fortes, M., *The Web of Kinship Among the Tallensi*, London, 1949, 1969.

Fortes, M., "Time and Social Structure: An Ashanti Case Study," in M. Fortes, Ed., *Social Structure*: Studies Presented to A.R. Radcliffe-Brown, New York, 1963.

Gefu, J.O., *Pastoralist Perspectives in Nigeria: The Fulbe of Udubo Grazing Reserve*, Uppsala, 1993.

Gluckman, M., "Reasonableness and Responsibility in the Law of Segmentary Societies," in H. Kuper and L. Kuper, eds., *African Law: Adaptation and Development*, Berkeley, 1965.

Green, M.M., *Ibo Village Affairs*, London, 1947.

Green, M.A., *Land Tenure in an Ibo Village*, Monographs on Social Anthropology, No. 6, London, 1941.

Greenberg, J., "Islam and Clan Organization Among the Hausa," 3 *Southwestern Journal of Anthropology* 193, 1947.

Gulliver, P.H., *Land Tenure and Social Change Among the Nyakyusa*, East African Studies, No. 11, Kampala, Uganda, 1958.

Gbadegesin, S., *African Philosophy: Traditional Yoruba Philosophy and Contemporary African Realities*, New York, 1991.

Gulliver, P.H., *Disputes and Negotiations: A Cross-Cultural Perspective*, New York, 1979.

Gulliver, P.H., *Social Control in an African Society, A Study of The Arusha: Agricultural Masai of Northern Tanganyika*, Boston, 1963.

Gulliver, P.H., "Structural Dichotomies and Jural Processes Among the Arusha of Northern Tanganyika," 31 *Africa* 19, 1961.

Hall, R. de Z., "Nyakyusa Law from the Court Records," 2 *African Studies* 153, 1943.

Hallett, R., *Africa to 1875*, Ann Arbor, 1970.

Haydon, E.S., *Law and Justice in Buganda*, London, 1960.

Henderson, R.N., "Onitsha Ibo Kinship Terminology: A Formal Analysis and Its Functional Applications," 23 *Southwestern Journal of Anthropology* 15 (1967).

Hobley, C.W., *Bantu Beliefs and Magic*, London, Rev. ed., 1938.

Hodgkin, T., *Nigerian Perspectives: An Historical Anthology*, London, 1960.

Horton,W.R.G., "God, Man, and the Land in a Northern Ibo Village Group," 26 *Africa* 17, 1956.

Howell, P.P., *A Manuel of Nuer Law*, London, 1954.

Huntingford, G.W.B., *The Nandi of Kenya: Tribal Control in a Pastoral Land*, London, 1953.

Huntingford, G.W.B., "Nandi Witchcraft," in J. Middleton and E.H. Winter, Eds., *Witchcraft and Sorcerty in East Africa*, New York, 1963.

Huntingford, G.W.B., *Nandi Work and Culture*, London, 1950.

Huntingford, G.W.B., "The Southern Nilo-Hamites," in D. Forde, ed., *Ethnographic Survey of Africa, Part VIII*, London, 1953.

Idowu, E.D., *Oludumare: God in Yoruba Belief*, London, 1962.

Igbo Socio-political System: Papers Presented at the 1985 Abiajoku Lecure Colloquium, Owerri, 1986.

Image and Reality in African Interethnic Relations, The Fulbe and Their Neighbors, (Studies in Third World Societies: Publication No. 11), Williamsburg (VA.), 1981.

Issah, H.S., *Yoruba Customs and Institutions: An Annotated Bibliography*, Lagos, 1988.

Johnson, S., *The History of the Yorubas: From the Earliest Times to the Beginning of the British Protectorate*, London, 1973.

Jones, A.H.M. and Munroe, E., *A History of Ethiopia*, Oxford, 1955.

Jones, G.I., "Ibo Age Organization, With Special Reference to the Cross-River and North-Estern Ibo," 42 *Journal of the Royal Anthropological Institute* 191 (1962).

Jones, G.I., "Ibo Land Tenure," 19 *Africa*, 314 (1949).

July, R.W., *A History of the African People*. 4th ed., Propsect Heights (Ill.), 1992.

Kagwa, A., *The Customs of the Baganda*, in M.M. Edel, Ed., trans. E.B. Kalibala, New York, 1934.

Kalinga, O.J.M., *A History of the Ngonde Kingdom of Malawi*, Berlin/New York, 1985.

Kellly, R.C., *The Nuer Conquest: The Structure and Development of an Expansionist System*, Ann Arbor, 1985.

Kenyatta, J., *Facing Mount Kenya: The Tribal Life of the Gikuyu*, New York, 1978.

Kenyatta, J., "Kikuyu Religion, Ancestor-Worship, and Sacrifical Practices," 10 *Africa* 308 (1937).

Kyermaten, A.A.Y., *Kingship and Ceremony in Ashanti*, Kumasi, 1970.

Lambert, H.E., *Kikuyu, Social and Polticial Institutions*, London, 1956.

Langley, M.S., *The Nandi of Kenya: Life Crisis Rituals in a Period*, London, 1979.

Levine, R.A., *Dreams and Deeds: Achievement and Motivation in Nigeria*, Chicago, 1966.

Lewin, T.J., *Asante Before the British: The Prempean Years, 1875–1900*, Lawrence (Kansas), 1978.

Lloyd, P.C., "Agnatic and Cognatic Descent Among the Yoruba," 1 *Journal of the Royal Anthropological Institute*, 484 (New Series, 1966).

Lloyd, P.C., "Sacred Kingship and Government Among the Yoruba," 30 *Africa* 221 (1960).

Lloyd, P.C., "The Traditional Political System of the Yoruba," 10 *Southwestern Journal of Anthropology*, 365 (1954).

Lloyd, P.C., *Yoruba Land Law* London, 1962.

Lloyd, P.C., "The Yoruba Lineage," 25 *Africa* 234 (1955).

Lucas, J.O., *The Religion of the Yorubas*, Lagos, 1948.

McConnell, R.E., "Notes on the Lugwari Tribe of Central Africa," 55 *Journal of the Royal Anthropological Institute*, 439 (1925).

McLeod, M.D., *The Asante*, London, 1981.

McNeill, W.H., *A World History*, New York, 2d ed., 1971.

Mair, L.P., *An African People in the Twentieth Century*, London, 1934.

Manoukian, M., "Akan and Ga-Adangme Peoples of the Gold Coast," in D. Forde, ed., *Ethrographic Survey of Africa, Western Africa, Part I.*, London, 1950.

Marguard, L., *The Story of South Africa*, London, 1955.

Meek, C.K., *Law and Authority in a Nigerian Tribe*, London, 1937.

Meyerowitz, E.L.R., *The Sacred State of the Akan*, London, 1951.

Michel-Jones, F., *Retour aux Dogon: Figure du Double et Ambivalence*, Paris, 1978.

Middleton, J., "The Central Tribes fo the North-Eastern Bantu," in D. Forde, ed., *Ethnographic Survey of Africa, Part V*, London, 1953.

Middleton, J., "The Concept of Bewitching in Lugbara," 25 *Africa* 252 (1955).

Middleton, J., *The Lugbara of Uganda*, 2d ed., Fort Worth, 1992.

Middleton, J., *Lugbara Religion: Ritual and Authority Among an East African People*, Washington, 1987.

Middleton, J., "The Political System of the Lugbara of the Nile- Congo Divide," in J. Middleton and D. Tait, Eds., *Tribes without Rulers*, 203 (1958).

Middleton, J., "Some Social Aspects of Lugbara Myth,' 24 *Africa* 189 (1954).

Middleton, J., "Witchcraft and Sorcery in Lugbara," in J. Middleton and E. H. Winter, eds., *Witchcraft and Sorcesy in East Africa*, New York, 1963.

Middleton, J. and Taits, D., "Introduction," *Tribes Without Rulers: Studies in African Segmentary Systems*, London, 1958.

Mohammadou, E., *Peuples et Royaumes du Toumbina*, Tokyo, 1983.

Mommsen, W.J., and de Moore, J.A., *European Expansion and Law: The Encounter of European and Indigenous Law in 19th and 20th Century Africa and Asia*, Oxford/New York, 1992.

Morrison, M.K.C., *Ethnicity and Political Integration: The Case of Ashanti, Ghana*, Syracuse, 1982.

Morton-Williams, P., "An Outline of the Cosmology and Cult Organization of the Oyo Yoruba," 34 *Africa* 243 (1964).

Morton-Williams, P., "The Yoruba Ogboni Cult in Oyo," 30 *Africa* 362 (1960).

Mugo, E.N., *Kikuyu People: A Brief Outline of Their Customs and Traditions*, Nairobi, 1982.

Mukwaya, A.B., *Land Tenure in Buganda: Present Day Tendencies*, East African Studies, No. 1., Kampala, Uganda, 1953.

Muriuki, G., *A History of The Kikuyu, 1500–1900*, Nairobi, 1974.

Nadel, S.F., "The Kede: A Riverain State in Northern Nigeria," in M. Fortes and E.E. Evans-Pritchard, eds., *African Political Systems*, London, 1940.

Obeng, E.E., *Ancient Ashanti Chieftaincy*, Tema (Ghana), 1988.

Obi, S.N.C., *The Ibo Law of Property*, London, 1963.

Oliver, R.A., *The African Experience*, London, 1991.

Oliver, R. and Atmore, A., *Africa Since 1850*, London, 1967.

Oliver, R. and Mathew, G., *History of East Africa*, Cambridge, 1963.

Ollenu, N.A., *Principles of Custormay Law In Ghana*, London, 1962.

Onwuejeogw, M.A., *An Igbo Civilization: Nri Kingdom and Hegemony*, London/Benin City/Ethiope, 1981.

Ohadike, D. and Shain, R.N., eds., *Western Igbo*.

Okere, L.C., *The Anthroplogy of Food in Rural Igboland, Nigeria: Socioeconomic and Cultural Aspects of Food and Food Habit in Rural Igboland*, Lanham (MD), 1983.

Olisa, C.G., *Ossomari: A Kingdom of the Lower Niger Valley (1640–1986)*, Onitsha (Nigeria), 1990.

Olomola, I., *A Thousand Years of Ado History and Culture*, Ado- Ekiti (Nigeria), 1984.

Olupona, J.O.K., *Kingship, Religion, and Rituals in a Nigerian Community: A Phenomenological Study of Ondo Yoruba Festivals*, Stockholm, 1991.

Olusanya, G.O., ed., *Studies in Yoruba History and Culture: Essays in Honor of Professor S.O. Bibaku*, Ibadan (Nigeria), 1983.

Oquagha, P.A., *History and Ethnoarchaeology in Estern Nigeria*, Oxford, 1984

Oquntuyi, A., *History of Ekiti: From the Beginning to 1939*, Ibadan, 1979.

Ottenberg, S., "Ibo Receptivity to Change," in W.R. Bascom and M.J. Herskovits, eds., *Continuity and Change in African Culture*, Chicago, 1959.

Ottenberg, S., "Inheritance and Succession in Afrikpo," in J.D.M. Jerrett, ed., *Studies in the Laws of Succession in Nigeria*, London, 1965.

Owusu-Ansha, D., *Islamic Talismanic Tradition in Nineteenth- Century Asante*, Lewiston, (N.Y.), 1991.

Partridge, C., "Native Law and Custom in Egbaland," 10 *Journal of the African Society* 422 (1911).

Prins, A.H.J., *East African Age-Class Systems*, Groningen, Diakanta, 1953.

Ramponi, E., "Religion and Divination of the Logbara Tribe of North-Uganda," 32 *Anthropos*, 571 (1937).

Ranger, T.O., ed., *Aspects of Central African History*, London, 1968.

Rattray, R.S., *Ashanti*, London, 1923, 1955.

Rattray, R.S., *Ashanti Law and Constitution*, London, 1929, 1956.

Rattray, R.S., *Religion and Art in Ashanti*, London, 1927, 1954.

Ray, B.C., *Myth, Ritual, and Kingship in Buganda*, New York, 1991.

Richards, A.I., "Authority Patterns in Traditional Buganda," in L. A. Fallers, ed., *The King's Men: Leadership and Status in Buganda on the Eve of Independence*, London, 1964.

Richard, A.I., "Traditional Values and Current Political Behavior," in L.A. Fallers, ed., *The King's Men: Leadership and Status in Buganda on the Eve of Independence*, London, 1964.

Robinson, R. and Gallager, J., *Africa and the Victorians*, London, 1961.

Roscoe, J., *The Baganda: An Account of Their Native Customs and Beliefs*, London, 1911.

Routledge, W.S. and Routledge, K., *With A Prehistoric People: The Akikiyu of East Africa*, London, 1910.

Sahlins, M.D., "the Segmentary Lineage: An Organization of Predatory Expansion," 63 *American Anthropologist* 322 (1961).

Sargong, P., *Ghana in Retrospect: Some Aspects of Ghanian Culture*, Tema (Ghana), 1974.

Schwab, W.B., "Kinship and Lineage Among the Yoruba," 25 *Africa* 352 (1955).

Shiroya, O.J.E., *Essays on the Pre-colonial History of North- western Uganda*, Nairobi, 1992.

Smith,M.G., *The Economy of Hausa Communities of Zaria*, London, 1955.

Smith, M.G., "Exchange and Marketing Among the Hausa," in P. Bohannan and G. Dalton, eds., *Markets in Africa*, Chicago, 1962.

Smith, M.G., *Government in Zazzau*, London, 1960.

Smith, M.G., "Hausa Inheritance and Succession," in J.D.M. Jerrett, *Studies in the Laws of Succession in Nigeria*, London, 1965.

Smith, M.G., "On Segmentary Lineage Systems," 86 *Journal of the Royal Anthropological Institute* 39 (1956).

Snell, G.S., *Nandi Customary Law*, London, 1954.

Southwold, M., *Bureaucracy and Chiefship in Buganda*, East African Studies, No. 14, London, 1961.

Southwold, M., "Leadership, Authority, and the Village Community," in L.A. Fallers, ed., *The King's Men: Leadership and Status in Buganda on the Eve of Independence*, London, 1964.

Stenning, D.J., *Savannah Nomads*, London, 1959.

Stenning, D.J., "Transhumance, Migratory Drift, Migration: Patterns of Pastoral Fulani Nomadism,: 87 *Journal of the Royal Anthropological Institute* 58 (1957).

Tate, H.R., "The Native Law of the Southern Gikuyu of East Africa," 9 *Journal of African Society* 233 (1909–1910).

Thomas, N.W., *Anthropological Report on the Ibo-Speaking Peoples of Nigeria*, London, 1913–1914.

Trimingham, J.S., *A History of Islam in West Africa*, London, 1962.

Trimingham, J.S., *Islam in West Africa*, Oxford, 1959.

Ugwu, D.C., *This is Obukpa: A History of Typical Ancient Igbo State*, Enugu (Nigeria), 1987.

Vansina, J., *Kingdoms of the Savanna*, Machson, 1966.

Wilks, I., *Asante in the Nineteenth Century: The Structure and Evolution of a Political Order*, London/New York, 1975.

Wilks, I., *Forests of Gold: Essays on the Akan and the Kingdom of Asante*, Athens (Ohio) 1993.

Wilson, G., "An African Morality," 9 *Africa* 75 (1965).

Wilson, G., "Introduction to Nyakyusa Law," 10 *Africa* 16 (1937).

Wilson, G., "The Nyakyusa of South-Western Tanganyika," in E. Colson and M. Gluckman, eds., *Seven Tribes of British Central Africa*, London, 1951.

Wilson, M., *For Men and Elders: Change in the Relations of Generations and of Men and Women Among the Nyakyusa- Ngondo People, 1875–1971*, New York, 1977.

Wilson, M., *Communal Rituals of the Nyakyusa*, London, 1959.

Wilson, M., "Divine Kings and the 'Breath of Men'," *Frazer Lecture*, Cambridge, 1959.

Wilson, M., *Good Company: A Study of Nyakyusa Age-Villages*, Prospect Heights (Ill.), 1987.

Wilson, M., "Nyakyusa Kinship," in A.R. Radcliffe-Brown and D. Forde, eds., *African Systems of Kinship and Marriage*, London, 1950.

Worsley, P.M., "The Kinship System of the Tallensi: A Revaluation," 86 *Journal of the Royal Anthropological Institute* 37 (1956).

Yarak, L.W., *Asante and The Dutch, 1744–1873*, Oxford/New York, 1990.

Index[1]

1. Index prepared by Madeleine J. Wilken.